TALES FROM THE
CANADIAN
ROCKIES

TALES FROM THE
CANADIAN
ROCKIES

edited by

BRIAN PATTON

M&S

Canadian Cataloguing in Publication Data

Main entry under title:

Tales from the Canadian Rockies

ISBN 0-7710-6948-0

1. Rocky Mountains, Canadian (B.C. and Alta.).*
2. Rocky Mountains, Canadian (B.C. and Alta.) – History.*
I. Patton, Brian, 1943-   .

FC219.T34 1993   971.1   C92-095354-9
F1090.T34 1993

Printed and bound in Canada by Webcom Limited

McClelland & Stewart Inc.
The Canadian Publishers
481 University Avenue
Toronto, Ontario
M5G 2E9

Contents

The Railway Years: The Tourists and Settlers, 1885–1918/113

Legends from a New Era: The Rockies, Post–1918/207

Epilogue/287

Preface

The first book on the Canadian Rockies I ever read was R. M. Patterson's *The Buffalo Head*. It was a book filled with wonderful stories of Patterson's trips into the Rockies from his ranch in the southern Alberta foothills. Most of these journeys were made in the 1930s, but the feel of the frontier was still strong in them. There was a magic in Patterson's writing that matched the romantic names of the places he visited — Highwood, Kananaskis, Nyahé-ya-'nibi, Misty Mountain. I was a long way from these mountains at the time, but *The Buffalo Head* reinforced a desire to come here to live. I was convinced that this was a place where a person could wander away a lifetime without losing the spirit of adventure and discovery.

When I finally did emigrate to the Canadian Rockies, I soon discovered that R. M. Patterson was just the tip of an extensive body of regional literature which extended back over some two hundred years. Most of this literature is composed of travel and adventure writing, as one might expect, but thanks to a landscape that surpasses most in ruggedness and beauty and thanks to a diverse cast of literate travellers and settlers, the stories that have emerged from the Canadian Rockies are the equal of the best produced by any region of North America.

The first-hand accounts by explorers, travellers, and settlers have long served as important records of the exploration and historical development of the region. They reflect the way in which man has perceived these mountains from the days of the early fur trade to the present, perceptions that have influenced the way we utilize the mountain landscape today. Additionally, time is beginning to enlarge upon these tales, and a mythology of the mountains is emerging, continually being refined and developed by contemporary writers of poetry and prose.

In *Tales from the Canadian Rockies* I have endeavoured to select the best from the past two centuries of writing in this region. Only a few of the writers are from the Canadian Rockies; the majority reflect the spectrum of pilgrims who have passed this way. The selections have not always been made on their literary merit, but rather by what they tell us about the landscape and the people who travelled and lived here. Many of the diary and journal entries, often reproduced in their original, unedited form, are quite homely and fragmented, but they project a sense of landscape and time that gives them the quality of found poems. Whether they were chosen for their literary or historical significance, all of the pieces in this book were selected to entertain.

The selections in this book are presented in an order that is basically chronological. Because of the historical nature of most of the writing, it seems a logical arrangement, and approached in this manner the anthology serves as something of a documentary history of the Rockies. Where a contemporary writer has utilized a particular historical period or event in poetry or prose, the piece is placed within its historical *milieu*.

Many of the items are presented without introduction as they seem to be self-explanatory as to time, place, and event, with notes on the contributing writers at the end of the book providing additional insight. Other stories are given a brief introduction where it seems to be necessary. Most of the selections have been published before, though usually some time ago, and many are considered regional classics. A number of items, both historical and contemporary, appear in print for the first time, and a couple of these historical items have been transcribed and edited by me.

The collecting of selections for this volume inadvertently began ten years ago when, assisted by an Explorations grant from the Canada Council, I travelled across Canada to gather material relating to the exploration of the Rocky Mountains. When this book was suggested by Mel Hurtig in 1982, many of the writings collected during my early research seemed appropriate for inclusion. I thank the Public Archives of Canada, the McGill University Archives, the Provincial Archives of British Columbia, the Provincial Archives of Alberta, the Glenbow Archives, and the University of Calgary Library for past assistance, and I recognize that important original support by the Canada Council.

In addition to the above institutions, I would like to offer special thanks to Director E. J. Hart and the staff of the Archives of the Canadian Rockies who have put up with me throughout the compiling of this book. The ACR has been my "home" research facility for many years, and without the generous support of its staff this book would not have been possible.

A special tribute is due to Jon Whyte. Over the years we have shared discoveries in the area of Rocky Mountain lore, and this free trade of information has expanded my own view of the region. As in the past, Jon pointed out a number of unturned stones for this book, and for that I am deeply grateful.

And as always, I thank my wife, Louise, who typed all of these writings into manuscript form and added her own comments as to the strengths and weaknesses of the selections.

Acknowledgements

The editor wishes to extend grateful acknowledgement to copyright-holders for permission to include material in this anthology. Every effort has been made to contact copyright owners. If there have been any errors or omissions, the publisher would be grateful for information enabling suitable acknowledgement to be made in future editions.

"These Mountains Are Our Sacred Places" by Chief John Snow, from *These Mountains Are Our Sacred Places* (Toronto: Samuel-Stevens, Publishers, 1977). Reprinted by permission of the author.

"The Thunderbird" by Chief Brings-down-the-Sun, from *The Old North Trail* by Walter McClintock (London: Macmillan & Co., 1910).

"Spirit Legends" by George McLean, "The Great Lizard," and "The First White Men" from *Indian Days on the Western Prairie* by Marius Barbeau (Ottawa: Queen's Printer, 1965).

"Whitewater" by Alexander Mackenzie, from *Voyages from Montreal . . . to the Frozen and Pacific Oceans in the Years 1789 and 1793 . . .* (London: T. Cadell, 1801).

"Journey to the Bow River and Rocky Mountains" by David Thompson, from *Journals*, vol. 6 (microfilm, Glenbow Archives, Calgary).

Acknowledgements

"The Discovery of Athabasca Pass" by David Thompson, from *David Thompson's Narrative of His Explorations in Western America, 1784–1812* edited by J.B. Tyrrell. Publications of The Champlain Society, vol. 12 (Toronto: The Champlain Society, 1916).

" 'I'll take my oath . . .' " by Ross Cox, from *The Columbia River* (Norman: University of Oklahoma Press, 1957).

"The Committee's Punch Bowl" by George Simpson, from *Fur Trade and Empire — George Simpson's Journal* edited by Frederick Merk (Cambridge: Harvard University Press, 1931).

"The Botanist and the Bear" by Thomas Drummond, from "Sketch of a Journey to the Rocky Mountains and to the Columbia River in North America" in *Botanical Miscellany*, vol. 1, edited by Sir William J. Hooker (London: John Murray, 1830).

"The Ascent of Mount Brown" by David Douglas, from *Journal, 1823–1827* (London: William Wesley & Son, 1914).

"Simpson's Pass" by George Simpson, from *Narrative of a Journey Round the World during the years 1841 and 1842* (London: Henry Colburn, 1874).

"Rundle's Climb" by Robert Rundle, from *The Rundle Journals, 1840–1848* edited by Hugh A. Dempsey (Calgary: Glenbow-Alberta Institute, 1977). Reprinted by permission of the publisher.

"The Mountain Man" and "With the Stoney Indians" by Father Pierre De Smet, from *Oregon Missions and Travels over the Rocky Mountains in 1845–46* (New York: Edward Dunigan, 1847).

"The Last of the Snake Indians" by Henry John Moberly, from *When Fur Was King* (New York: E.P. Dutton & Co., 1929).

"An Artist on the Athabasca Trail" by Paul Kane, from *Wanderings of an Artist . . .* (London: Longman, Brown, Green, Longmans, and Roberts, 1859).

"A Hard Crossing" by Henry James Warre, from *Journal of an Overland Journey from Montreal in Canada to the Columbia River and Pacific Ocean* (manuscript collection, Public Archives of Canada, Ottawa).

"The Emigrants" by James Sinclair, from *Correspondence* (manuscript collection, Provincial Archives of British Columbia, Victoria). Reprinted by permission of the Provincial Archives of British Columbia.

"The Discovery of the Kicking Horse Pass" by James Hector, from *The Journals, Detailed Reports, and Observations Relative to the Exploration by Captain John Palliser . . . During the Years 1857, 1858, 1859, and 1860* by John Palliser (London: Eyre and Spottiswoode, 1863).

Acknowledgements

"Memories of Dr. Hector and the Kicking Horse" by Peter Erasmus, from *Buffalo Days and Nights* (Calgary: Glenbow-Alberta Institute, 1976). Reprinted by permission of the publisher.

"A Sportsman in the Rocky Mountains" by the Earl of Southesk, from *Saskatchewan and the Rocky Mountains* (Edinburgh: Edmonston and Douglas, 1875).

"The Last Monument" by Charles Wilson, from *Journal, Vol. 2, June 12th, 1860–July 17th, 1862 by Charles Wilson* (manuscript collection, Provincial Archives of British Columbia, Victoria). Add. MSS. 368, reprinted by permission of the Provincial Archives of British Columbia.

"The Rock Whistler" by John Keast Lord, from *A Naturalist in British Columbia* (London: 1866).

"Across the Rockies with Mr. O'B." by Viscount Milton and W.B. Cheadle, from *The North-West Passage by Land* (London: Cassell, Petter, and Galpin, 1865).

"The Death of the Moose" by William Francis Butler, from *The Wild North Land* (London: Sampson, Low, Marston, Searle, & Rivington, 1878).

"Ordeal in the Mountains" by Pierre Berton, from *The National Dream: The Great Railway 1871–1881*, used by permission of The Canadian Publishers, McClelland and Stewart Limited, Toronto.

"Winter Journey" by Jon Whyte (unpublished poem). Reprinted by permission of the author.

"The Major's Bath" by Tom Wilson, from *Trail Blazer of the Canadian Rockies* (Calgary: Glenbow-Alberta Institute, 1972). Reprinted by permission of the publisher.

"Mr. Holt's Horse" by Samuel B. Steele, from *Forty Years in Canada*, used by permission of The Canadian Publishers, McClelland and Stewart Limited, Toronto.

"End of Track" by A. P. Coleman, from *The Canadian Rockies: New and Old Trails* (London: T. Fisher Unwin, 1911).

"By Car and by Cowcatcher" by Susan Agnes Macdonald, from *Murray's Magazine*, vol. 1, January–June, 1887 (London: John Murray, 1887).

"Harassment at the Hot Springs" by Edward Roper, from *By Track and Trail: A Journey Through Canada* (London: W.H. Allen & Co., 1891).

"B.C., 1887" by J. A. Lees and W. J. Clutterbuck, from *B.C. 1887: A Ramble in British Columbia* (London: Longmans, Green, & Co., 1892).

Acknowledgements

"An Outing to Lake Louise" by William Spotswood Green, from *Among the Selkirk Glaciers* (London: Macmillan & Co., 1890).

"How We Climbed Cascade" by Ralph Connor, from *Canadian Alpine Journal*, vol. I, no. 1 (Alpine Club of Canada, 1907).

"Some Memories of the Mountains" by Elizabeth Parker, from *Canadian Alpine Journal*, vol. XVII, 1929 (Alpine Club of Canada, 1929).

"Changes at Banff" by Alice Huntington, from "The Cozy Corner," *Calgary Weekly Herald*, August 19, 1897.

"The First Ascent of Mount Temple" by Walter D. Wilcox, from *Camping in the Canadian Rockies* (New York: G.P. Putnam's Sons, 1897).

"Death on Mount Lefroy" by Charles E. Fay, from "The Casualty on Mount Lefroy" in *Appalachia*, vol. VIII, 1896–1898. The Journal of the Appalachian Mountain Club. (New York: The Riverside Press, 1898).

"Misadventures on the Glacier" by Hugh E.M. Stutfield and J. Norman Collie, from *Climbs and Explorations in the Canadian Rockies* (London: Longmans, Green & Co., 1903).

"Bill Peyto" by Walter D. Wilcox, from *The Rockies of Canada* (New York: G.P. Putnam's Sons, 1900).

"Bill Peyto Alone" by Gordon Burles, from *Storm Warning II* edited by Al Purdy, used by permission of The Canadian Publishers, McClelland and Stewart Limited, Toronto.

"Edward Whymper" by Robert E. Campbell, from *I Would Do It Again* (Toronto: The Ryerson Press, 1959).

"My Grizzly-Bear Day" by William T. Hornaday, from *Camp-Fires in the Canadian Rockies* (New York: Charles Scribner's Sons, 1907).

"The Exploration of Maligne Lake" by Mary Schäffer, from *Old Indian Trails of the Canadian Rockies* (New York: The Knickerbocker Press, 1911).

"Camping in the Rockies" by Mary Vaux, from *Canadian Alpine Journal*, vol. I, no. 1 (Alpine Club of Canada, 1907).

"Hip-Hip-Hurrah!" by Conrad Kain, from *Where the Clouds Can Go* (Boston: Charles T. Branford Co., 1954, reprint).

"To the Top of Mount Robson" by George Kinney, from *Canadian Alpine Journal*, vol. II, no. 2 (Alpine Club of Canada, 1910).

"Mount Robson Reprise" by Conrad Kain, translated by P. A. W. Wallace, from *Canadian Alpine Journal*, vol. VI (Alpine Club of Canada, 1915).

"Christmas Dinner" by A. O. Wheeler and Tom Wilson, from "An Act of Heroism" by A. O. Wheeler in *Canadian Alpine Journal*, vol. II, no. 1 (Alpine Club of Canada, 1909).

"Swift, the Frontiersman" by F. A. Talbot, from *The New Garden of Canada* (London: Cassell and Co., 1911).

"Along the New Transcontinental" by J. Burgon Bickersteth, from *The Land of Open Doors* (London: Wells Gardner, Darton & Co., 1914).

"Tay John" by Howard O'Hagan, from *Tay John*, used by permission of The Canadian Publishers, McClelland and Stewart Limited, Toronto.

"The Rockies" by Rupert Brooke, from *Letters from America* (New York: Charles Scribner's Sons, 1916).

"A Wonderful Delusion" by Morley Roberts, from *On the Old Trail* (London: Eveleigh Nash & Grayson, 1927).

"The Birth of an Iceberg" by Cora Johnstone Best, from "Horse Thief Creek and the Lake of the Hanging Glaciers" in *Canadian Alpine Journal*, vol. XIII (Alpine Club of Canada, 1923).

"Hollywood at Lake Louise" by Walter D. Wilcox, from "Early Days in the Canadian Rockies" in *American Alpine Journal*, vol. IV, no. 2 (New York: The American Alpine Club, 1941).

"The Grizzly" by James Oliver Curwood, from *The Grizzly King* (New York: Doubleday, Doran & Co., 1928).

"David" by Earle Birney, from *Selected Poems 1940–1966*, used by permission of The Canadian Publishers, McClelland and Stewart Limited, Toronto.

"Memories of a Mountain Guide" by Edward Feuz, Jr. (as told to Imbert Orchard), from "In the Western Mountains: Early Mountaineering in British Columbia" edited by Susan Leslie, in *Sound Heritage*, vol. VIII, no. 4 (Victoria: Provincial Archives of British Columbia, 1980). Reprinted by permission of the publisher.

"Spring Skiing in Assiniboine Park" by Avis E. Newhall, from *Bulletin*, Appalachian Mountain Club, vol. XXII, no. 4, December, 1928. Reprinted by permission of the Appalachian Mountain Club.

"The Bridegroom's Ski Tour" by Erling Strom, from *Pioneers on Skis* (Banff: Summerthought, 1979). Reprinted by permission of the publisher.

"To the Heart of the Mountains" by R. M. Patterson, from *The Buffalo Head* (New York: William Sloane Associates, 1961). Reprinted by permission of the author.

Acknowledgements

"Shoot-out" by Dan McCowan, from *Hill-Top Tales* (Toronto: Macmillan of Canada, 1950). Reprinted by permission of Mary Helen Boyer.

"Mona's Fire Dress" by Sid Marty, from *Men for the Mountains,* used by permission of The Canadian Publishers, McClelland and Stewart Limited, Toronto.

"It's a Woman's World" by Nello Vernon-Wood, from *National Sportsman,* October 1938. Reprinted by permission of William Vernon-Wood.

"Companions of the Bath" by Dan McCowan, from *Tidewater to Timberline* (Toronto: Macmillan of Canada, 1951). Reprinted by permission of Mary Helen Boyer.

"Grizzly Country" by Andy Russell, from *Grizzly Country,* copyright © 1967 by Andy Russell. Reprinted by permission of Alfred A. Knopf, Inc.

"Too Hot to Sleep" by Sid Marty, from *Headwaters,* used by permission of The Canadian Publishers, McClelland and Stewart Limited, Toronto.

"Paradise Lost?" by Valerius Geist, from *Mountain Sheep and Man in the Northern Wilds,* copyright © 1975 by Cornell University. Used by permission of the publisher, Cornell University Press.

"When I Joined the Outfit" by Sid Marty, from *Nobody Danced with Miss Rodeo,* used by permission of The Canadian Publishers, McClelland and Stewart Limited, Toronto.

"Death of a Warden" and "Floe Lake" by Dale Zieroth, from *Mid-River* (Toronto: House of Anansi Press, 1981). Reprinted by permission of the publisher.

"The Rescue" by Andrew Jones, from "Guardians of the High Wilderness" in *Reader's Digest,* vol. 108, no. 649, May 1976. © 1976 by The Reader's Digest Association (Canada) Ltd. Reprinted by permission.

"Beyond Here" by Jim Green, from *Beyond Here* (Saskatoon: Thistledown Press, 1983). Reprinted by permission of the publisher.

"The Woman at Banff" by William Stafford, from *Stories That Could Be True: New and Collected Poems.* Copyright © 1959 by William Stafford. Reprinted by permission of Harper & Row, Publishers, Inc.

"The End of the Trail" by J. Monroe Thorington, from *The Glittering Mountains of Canada* (Philadelphia: John W. Lea, 1925).

Prologue

The Land of Spirits

The Indians have given to the main range of the Rocky Mountains the appropriate name "Backbone-of-the-World".

Walter McClintock,
The Old North Trail

These Mountains Are Our Sacred Places

Chief John Snow

Century after century the rugged Rocky Mountains sat there in majesty, and nature seemed to say: "Your thoughts must be as firm as these mountains, if you are to walk the straight path. Your patience and kindness must be as solid as these mountains, if you are to acquire understanding and wisdom."

The old Stoney medicine man had said: "You must continue to go to the sacred mountains. You must fast and pray for many days and nights, and perchance you will see a vision upon the mountains." Before he went to the beautiful land of the spirits beyond the sunset, the old man with a century of experience spoke these words: "You must search and search and you will find ancient truths and wisdom that shall guide you in the future." He continued: "My grandfathers told me these things when I was just a little boy and in my youth it was told to me over and over again by the campfire and in the tribal encampment, so it has been imprinted in my heart ever since that time."

And the medicine man stated further: "My grandchildren, you must search and continue to search in order to find them. When a revelation is open to you, you will become a special person to our tribe. It may be that you will gain courage and bravery and become a hero in many battles. It may be that you will be given understanding and wisdom and become a Chief amongst Chiefs. It may be that you will become a great hunter, knowing the paths and circling of the four winds, knowing where the animals roam and birds migrate at the seasons appointed for them by the Creator. It may be that you will be given the gift of prophecy, see into the future, and will advise and guide your people along the straight path."

2

Upon these lofty heights, the Great Spirit revealed many things to us. Some of my people received powers to heal. They could heal the physical body with herbs, roots, leaves, plants, and mineral spring waters. They could also heal the broken and weary soul with unseen spiritual powers. Others received powers over the weather. These gifted religious men and women could call for a great storm or calm the weather; they could call on the winds, rain, hail, snow, or sleet, and they would come. From these mountain-top experiences my fellow tribesmen and women were given unique tasks to perform to help the tribe prepare for things to come.

Therefore the Rocky Mountains are precious and sacred to us. We knew every trail and mountain pass in this area. We had special ceremonial and religious areas in the mountains. In the olden days some of the neighbouring tribes called us the "People of the Shining Mountains." These mountains are our temples, our sanctuaries, and our resting places. They are a place of hope, a place of vision, a place of refuge, a very special and holy place where the Great Spirit speaks with us. *Therefore, these mountains are our sacred places.*

The Thunderbird
Chief Brings-down-the-Sun (as told to Walter McClintock)

"I was once camped with my grandfather and father on the Green Banks (St. Mary's River), close to the Rocky Mountains. They were digging out beavers, which were very plentiful. My father went off for a hunt to supply our camp with meat. He followed the trail of some elk up the side of a steep mountain, until he came to timberline, where he saw a herd of mountain sheep. He followed them towards Nin-ais-tukku (Chief Mountain). When he drew near the summit, he discovered a dense, foul-smelling smoke rising from a deep pit. He pushed a huge boulder into it to hear it fall. There came back no sound, but a cloud of smoke and gas arose so dense and suffocating, that he turned to flee, but it was only to meet a black cloud coming up the mountain side. He was frightened and tried to escape, but suddenly there came a terrible crash, and my father fell to the ground. He beheld a woman standing over him. Her face was painted black and red zig-zag streaks like lightning were below her eyes. Behind the woman, stood a man holding a large weapon. My father heard the man exclaim impatiently, 'I told you to kill him at once, but you stand there pitying him.' He heard the woman chant, 'When it rains the noise of the Thunder is my medicine.' The man also sang and fired his big weapon. The report was like a deafening crash of thunder, and my father beheld lightning coming from the big hole on the mountain top. He knew nothing more, until he found himself lying inside a great cavern. He had no power to speak, neither could he raise his head, but, when he heard a voice saying, 'This is the person who threw the stone down into your fireplace,' he realised that he was in the lodge of the Thunder Maker. He heard the beating of a drum, and, after the fourth beating, was able to sit up and look around. He saw the Thunder Chief, in the form of a huge bird, with his wife and many children around him. All of the children had drums, painted with the green talons of the Thunder-bird and with Thunder-bird beaks, from which issued zig-zag streaks of yellow lightning.

"We call the thunder Isis-a-kummi (Thunder-bird). We believe that it is a supernatural person. When he leaves his lodge to go through the heavens with the storm-clouds, he takes the form of a great bird with many colours, like the rainbow, and with long green claws. The lightning is the trail of the Thunder-bird.

"Whenever the Thunder Maker smoked his pipe, he blew two whiffs upwards toward the sky, and then two whiffs towards the earth. After each whiff the thunder crashed. Finally the Thunder-bird spoke to my father, saying, 'I am the Thunder Maker and my name is Many Drums (expressive of the sound of rolling thunder). You have witnessed my great power and can now go in safety. When you return to your people, make a pipe just like the one you saw me smoking, and add it to your bundle. Whenever you hear the first thunder rolling in the spring-time, you will know that I have come from my cavern, and that it is time to take out my pipe. If you should ever be caught in the midst of a heavy thunder-storm and feel afraid, pray to me, saying, "Many Drums! pity me, for the sake of your youngest child," and no harm will come to you.' (This prayer is often used by the Blackfeet during dangerous storms.) As soon as my father returned, he added to his Medicine Bundle a Pipe similar to the one shown to him by the Thunder-bird."

4

Spirit Legends
George McLean

There is a place on the Crowsnest Pass, along in the mountain, where the cliff overhangs. Above the place where a man can reach, there are designs in paint in different colours. They are made like rainbows. And then there are buffaloes, and Indians on horses chasing them, and war dances shown on them, sun dances, pictures of them. It is where nobody could have made them. Every year when you are there, there is a different picture. The Indians believe that the pictures they see, when they are there, represent things that are going to happen. Every year it is a different picture. The pictures always change.

The old people thought that mud, red paint, was a medicine. We still use it as a medicine. I heard it myself that they know when there are some spirits around there, at Vermilion Springs. We have been told, if ever we go to this place and get some of this mud, to drop some gifts into this spring — any kind of gift, such as tobacco, pipes, rings, or any other things a man would like. They burnt sweet incense, some sweet roots that we use for smoking. Several kinds. They are mixtures. (And I don't like to tell.) We used to burn incense, as a sweet-smelling sacrifice. If we take this red earth, it will appear to have life. When we want to decorate someone, or to give a sign of peace, it will seem to give life to it. We don't know what kind of spirit is in there. Some saw things or could hear singing. It sounded like a flute, an Indian flute, a whistle, and singing. And it talks, but *we* can never see anything.

We believe that there are little human beings, *makutibi,* that live under the ground in some mountains north of here. Some hunters, when tracking bears or ptarmigans into caverns, have heard a great noise, and then it is as if they hear a lot of people talking. These are the little people.

The Great Lizard of the Mountains

Shuswap medicine song (as recorded by Marius Barbeau)

Very well, very well, child, I will sing for thee!
I will sing to the Lizard, the great one of the mountains.
I will sing to the many Lizards, his sons and daughters.
Let them roll along the mountain slopes;
let them come down the steep hill-sides!
As they glide down, the trees are crushed to dust,
the snow turns into water,
and the rocks are pulverized into grains of sand.
Child, look at him coming, the great Lizard.
He is followed by his children, every one.
Now they sit in a ring at the bottom,
and the bands around their heads have come undone.
The bands are blown upward by the wind from the canyon.
Child, look, and look with me!
The bands are like rainbows in the air.
What wonderful rainbows!
They stand up on end and reach up into the sky.
The rainbows are their breaths,
the breaths of the Lizards from the mountain-tops,
and this is what they sing,
"Child, the breath of our mouths are rainbows.
The power of rainbows is what saves our health.
We are never, never sick.
Look at us, look at the rainbows, child,
and you will be well again."

The First White Men
Shuswap legend (as recorded by
Marius Barbeau)

This took place long ago, in the mountains. Two hunters of our own tribe were travelling along the trails, in the passes. The name of one was Rain-drop, and of the other, Cloven-hoof. As they were preparing to ford a deep creek, two men unlike anybody else approached them. "These are People from the Sky," they thought to themselves. But they could not move away; their legs were as if stiffened by the cold. Rain-drop said, "I will kill them." Cloven-hoof retorted, "Beware! it means disaster for us!" They had only hafted stone axes in their hands. When they saw that the ghost-like strangers were not afraid but drew nearer, they thought, "We cannot do anything, we cannot help ourselves."

One of the two men — they were white like peeled logs — took a cup and a crystal-like bottle from his pocket and poured out a drink. Rain-drop was too frightened to try the cup. So was Cloven-hoof. The white man then swallowed a mouthful himself. "If he can drink it," thought Cloven-hoof, "it may not be hurtful." Rain-drop's idea was. "If we drink it, we may become as white as they are. We may get the power of spirits." Now they were both willing. Rain-drop took the cup first. Then it was his friend's turn. They found it good, very good, much better than anything they had ever known. After one cupful, another. They felt jolly. "We will turn into white beings from the sky." The change was so wonderful that they clamoured for more. They sat down to rest and fell into a stupor. When they knew no more, the white men departed.

They must have stayed there a long while, a day or more. Their limbs were stiff and cold and their stomachs sick when they came to. Rain-drop was the first to stand up. What he did was to look at one of his hands. It was not white, but the same shade as before. The other hand was not different. He had not had enough to drink. The change had only begun. Cloven-hoof was sick when he came to. He fell to sleep again, and when he awoke his friend was gone. "It is all very strange," he said; "Rain-drop is surely gone to the sky, and I am left alone here. I did not get enough to drink; that is the whole trouble." He was disappointed to find the shade of his skin

7

unchanged. After crawling a short distance, he found his friend asleep on the trail. "He stopped only half-way," he thought; "not enough drink!" And he also lay down to sleep again.

Before a few days had passed, they were much disappointed. The change had left nothing but regret to them. When they reached home and told their experience, the old men laughed and said, "You fools! These were not ghosts, but white men."

The Great
Lone Land

The First Explorers
and Travellers
1793–1885

An immense plain stretched from my feet to the mountain — a plain so vast that every object of hill and wood and lake lay dwarfed into one continuous level, and at the back of this level, beyond the pines and the lakes and the river-courses, rose the giant range, solid, impassable, silent — a mighty barrier rising midst an immense land, standing sentinel over the plains and prairies of America, over the measureless solitudes of the Great Lone Land. Here, at last, lay the Rocky Mountains.

W. F. Butler, *The Great Lone Land*

Whitewater
Alexander Mackenzie

*Alexander Mackenzie's epic voyage to the Pacific Ocean in 1793 is a
landmark in the history of North American exploration, yet the journey
nearly ended in disaster in a valley on the western edge of the Rocky
Mountains. After successfully traversing the main range of the Rockies via
the Peace River Canyon, Mackenzie ascended the Parsnip River to its
head-waters. He crossed the divide to the Pacific watershed on June 12th
and together with his crew of nine nosed his 25-foot birchbark canoe into
the timber-choked waters of James Creek. The following day the party
attempted to run this snow-fed mountain stream.*

Thursday, 13. — At an early hour of this morning the men began to
cut a road, in order to carry the canoe and lading beyond the rapid;
and by seven they were ready. That business was soon effected, and
the canoe reladen, to proceed with the current which ran with great
rapidity. In order to lighten her, it was my intention to walk with
some of the people; but those in the boat with great earnestness
requested me to embark, declaring, at the same time, that, if they
perished, I should perish with them. I did not then imagine in how
short a period their apprehension would be justified. We accordingly
pushed off, and had proceeded but a very short way when the canoe
struck, and notwithstanding all our exertions, the violence of the
current was so great as to drive her sideways down the river, and
break her by the first bar, when I instantly jumped into the water,
and the men followed my example; but before we could set her
straight, or stop her, we came to deeper water, so that we were
obliged to re-embark with the utmost precipitation. One of the men
who was not sufficiently active, was left to get on shore in the best
manner in his power. We had hardly regained our situations when

we drove against a rock which shattered the stern of the canoe in such a manner, that it held only by the gunwales, so that the steersman could no longer keep his place. The violence of this stroke drove us to the opposite side of the river, which is but narrow, when the bow met with the same fate as the stern. At this moment the foreman seized on some branches of a small tree in the hope of bringing up the canoe, but such was their elasticity that, in a manner not easily described, he was jerked on shore in an instant, and with a degree of violence that threatened his destruction. But we had no time to turn from our own situation to enquire what had befallen him; for, in a few moments, we came across a cascade which broke several large holes in the bottom of the canoe, and started all the bars, except one behind the scooping seat. If this accident, however, had not happened, the vessel must have been irretrievably overset. The wreck becoming flat on the water, we all jumped out, while the steersman, who had been compelled to abandon his place, and had not recovered from his fright, called out to his companions to save themselves. My peremptory commands superseded the effects of his fear, and they all held fast to the wreck; to which fortunate resolution we owed our safety, as we should otherwise have been dashed against the rocks by the force of the water, or driven over the cascades. In this condition we were forced several hundred yards, and every yard on the verge of destruction; but, at length, we most fortunately arrived in shallow water and a small eddy, where we were enabled to make a stand, from the weight of the canoe resting on the stones, rather than from any exertions of our exhausted strength. For though our efforts were short, they were pushed to the utmost, as life or death depended on them.

This alarming scene, with all its terrors and dangers, occupied only a few minutes; and in the present suspension of it, we called to the people on shore to come to our assistance, and they immediately obeyed the summons. The foreman, however, was the first with us; he had escaped unhurt from the extraordinary jerk with which he was thrown out of the boat, and just as we were beginning to take our effects out of the water, he appeared to give his assistance. The Indians, when they saw our deplorable situation, instead of making the least effort to help us, sat down and gave vent to their tears. I was on the outside of the canoe, where I remained till every thing was got on shore, in a state of great pain from the extreme cold of the water; so that at length, it was with difficulty I could stand, from the benumbed state of my limbs.

The loss was considerable and important, for it consisted of our whole stock of balls, and some of our furniture; but these considerations were forgotten in the impressions of our miraculous escape. Our first inquiry was after the absent man, whom in the first moment of danger, we had left to get on shore, and in a short time his appearance removed our anxiety. We had, however, sustained no personal injury of consequence, and my bruises seemed to be in the greater proportion.

All the different articles were now spread out to dry. The powder had fortunately received no damage, and all my instruments had escaped. Indeed, when my people began to recover from their alarm, and to enjoy a sense of safety, some of them, if not all, were by no means sorry for our late misfortune, from the hope that it must put a period to our voyage, particularly as we were without a canoe, and all the bullets sunk in the river. It did not, indeed, seem possible to them that we could proceed under these circumstances. I listened, however, to the observations that were made on the occasion without replying to them, till their panic was dispelled, and they had got themselves warm and comfortable, with an hearty meal, and rum enough to raise their spirits.

I then addressed them, by recommending them all to be thankful for their late very narrow escape. I also stated, that the navigation was not impracticable in itself, but from our ignorance of its course; and that our late experience would enable us to pursue our voyage with greater security. I brought to their recollection, that I did not deceive them, and that they were made acquainted with the difficulties and dangers they must expect to encounter, before they engaged to accompany me. I also urged the honour of conquering disasters, and the disgrace that would attend them on their return home, without having attained the object of the expedition. Nor did I fail to mention the courage and resolution which was the peculiar boast of the North men; and that I depended on them, at that moment, for the maintenance of their character. I quieted their apprehension as to the loss of the bullets, by bringing to their recollection that we still had shot from which they might be manufactured. I at the same time acknowledged the difficulty of restoring the wreck of the canoe, but confided in our skill and exertion to put it in such a state as would carry us on to where we might procure bark, and build a new one. In short, my harangue produced the desired effect, and a very general assent appeared to go wherever I should lead the way.

Journey to the Bow River and Rocky Mountains

David Thompson

In the autumn of 1800, the North West Company fur traders Duncan McGillivray and David Thompson with a small party of men and an Indian guide ascended the Bow River from a Piegan encampment near today's Calgary. They reached the eastern front of the Rocky Mountains on November 30th at a point near present-day Exshaw, Alberta, where McGillivray, Thompson, and a voyageur named Dumond ascended one of the more accessible mountains on the north side of the river.

Nov 30 Sunday A very fine Day. At 7.50 AM we set off for the Rocky Mountains, and went in S 30 W 4$^{1}/_{2}$ m — at end of Co we left our Horses, and went up along the River on Foot S 15 W 2$^{1}/_{2}$ m to a Point of the Mountain, which we thought practicable — for the Mountain all this last Course presents an inaccessible steep — from where we set out this Morn to the end of the first Course the River gradual widens, and the Banks lower, until there is hardly any Bank at all — in the distance very few Rapids and for the last Mile of the first Course the River may be abt 250 yds to 300 yds over with several small Islands — abt the last Course it has the same Appearance — beyond that it winds in the Mountain about WSW for 3 or 4 miles as seen from the Heights — At end of the last Course Mr. McGillivray, Dumond & myself began to ascend the Mountain, we found it very steep with much loose small Stones very sharp, but as we got higher & the loose Stones became less frequent, where the Rock was solid, it was extremely rough and full of small sharp Points like an enormous Rasp. This enabled us to mount Places very steep, as the footing was good & sure but it cut our Shoes, Socks etc all to pieces in a Trice. The Rock of the Mountain all the way to the Top is one and the same, of a dark Gray, with few or no Veins, very hard & glassy, and upon rubbing Two Pieces of it together for a Moment produces when held near the Nose a strong disagreeable Smell, somewhat Sulphurous; our view from the Heights to the Eastward was vast & unbounded. The Eye had not Strength to discriminate it's Termination — to the Westward Hills & Rocks rose to our View covered with

Snow, here rising, there subsiding, but their Tops nearly of an equal Height every where. Never before did I behold so just, so perfect a resemblance to the waves of the Ocean in the wintry Storm — when looking upon them and attentively considering their wild order and appearance, the Imagination is apt to say, these must once have been Liquid, and in that State when swelled to its greatest agitation, suddenly congealed and made Solid by Power Omnipotent. There are low Shrubs of Fir & Canadian Pine almost to the very Top — in Places we also found the Dung of Cows for about two thirds up the Mountain, tho' we saw no Grass; After having spent 4 Hours there, we returned to our Horses from whence we set out with Expedition and having come below the Falls we recrossed the River and went down on the South side to our Gully, where we arrived at $5^1/_4$ PM all well Thank God.

The Discovery of Athabasca Pass
David Thompson

When the Piegan Indians prevented him from crossing the Rocky Mountains by the traditional Howse Pass route, David Thompson led a party of men north to the Athabasca River. There, in January of 1811, he made the first recorded crossing of Athabasca Pass, establishing a trail that would serve the transcontinental fur trade for the next forty years.

Jany 5th. Thermometer -26 very cold. Having secured the goods and provisions we could not take with us, by 11 AM set off with eight Sleds, to each two dogs, with goods and Provisions to cross the Mountains, and three Horses to assist us as far as the depth of the Snow will permit. We are now entering the defiles of the Rocky Mountains by the Athabasca River, the woods of Pine are stunted, full of branches to the ground, and the Aspin, Willow &c not much better: strange to say, here is a strong belief that the haunt of the Mammoth, is about this defile, I questioned several, none could positively say, they had seen him, but their belief I found firm and not to be shaken. I remarked to them, that such an enormous heavy Animal must leave indelible marks of his feet, and his feeding. This they all acknowledged, and that they had never seen any marks of him, and therefore could show me none. All I could say did not shake their belief in his existence.

January 6th. We came to the last grass for the Horses in Marshes and along small Ponds, where a herd of Bisons had lately been feeding; and here we left the Horses poor and tired, and notwithstanding the bitter cold, [they] lived through the winter, yet they have only a clothing of close hair, short and without any furr.

January 7th. Continuing our journey in the afternoon we came on the track of a large animal, the snow about six inches deep on the ice; I measured it; four large toes each of four inches in length to each a short claw; the ball of the foot sunk three inches lower than the toes, the hinder part of the foot did not mark well, the length fourteen inches, by eight inches in breadth, walking from north to south, and having passed about six hours. We were in no humour to follow him: the Men and Indians would have it to be a young mammoth and I held it to be the track of a large old grizled Bear; yet the shortness of the nails, the ball of the foot, and it's great size was not that of a Bear, otherwise that of a very large old Bear, his claws worn away; this the Indians would not allow. Saw several tracks of Moose Deer. 9 PM Ther -4.

Janu[ar]y 8th. A fine day. We are now following the Brooks in the open defiles of the secondary Mountains; when we can no longer follow it, the road is to cross a point of high land, very fatigueing, and come on another Brook, and thus in succession; these secondary Mountains appear to be about 2 to 3000 feet above their base, with patches of dwarf pines, and much snow; we marched ten miles today; and as we advance we feel the mild weather from the Pacific Ocean. This morning at 7AM Ther +6 at 9 PM +22. One of my men named Du Nord beat a dog to death, he is what we call a "flash" man, a showy fellow before the women but a coward in heart, and would willingly desert if he had courage to go alone; very glutinous and requires full ten pounds of meat each day. And as I am constantly ahead [I] cannot prevent his dog flogging and beating: We saw no tracks of Animals.

January 9th. Ther +32. SE wind and snowed all day which made hauling very bad. We could proceed only about four miles, this partly up a brook and then over a steep high point with dwarf pines. We had to take only half a load and return for the rest. The snow is full seven feet deep, tho' firm and wet, yet the Dogs often sunk in it, but our snow shoes did [not] sink more than three inches; and the weather so mild that the snow is dropping from the trees, and everything wet; here the Men finished the last of the fresh and half dried Meat which I find to be eight pounds for each man p^r day. Ther +22.

January 10th. Ther +16. A day of Snow and southerly Gale of wind, the afternoon fine, the view now before us was an ascent of deep snow, in all appearance to the height of land between the Atlantic and Pacific Oceans, it was to me a most exhilarating sight, but to my uneducated men a dreadful sight, they had no scientific object in view, their feelings were of the place they were; our guide Thomas told us, that although we could barely find wood to make a fire, we must now provide wood to pass the following night on the height of the defile we were in, and which we had to follow; my men were the most hardy that could be picked out of a hundred brave hardy Men, but the scene of desolation before us was dreadful, and I knew it, a heavy gale of wind much more a mountain storm would have buried us beneath it, but thank God the weather was fine, we had to cut wood such as it was, and each took a little on his sled, yet such was the despondency of the Men, aided by the coward Du Nord, sitting down at every half mile, that when night came, we had only wood to make a bottom, and on this to lay wherewith to make a small fire, which soon burnt out and in this exposed situation we passed the rest of a long night without fire, and part of my men had strong feelings of personal insecurity, on our right about one third of a mile from us lay an enormous Glacier, the eastern face of which quite steep, of about two thousand feet in height, was of a clean fine green color, which I much admired but whatever was the appearance, my opinion was, that the whole was not solid ice, but formed on rocks from rills of water frozen in their course; westward of this steep face, we could see the glacier with it's fine green color and it's patches of snow in a gentle slope for about two miles; eastward of this glacier and near to us, was a high steep wall of rock, at the foot of this, with a fine south exposure had grown a little Forest of Pines of about five hundred yards in length by one hundred in breadth, by some avalanche they had all been cut clean off as with a scythe, not one of these trees appeared an inch higher than the others. My men were not at their ease, yet when night came they admired the brilliancy of the Stars, and as one of them said, he thought he could almost touch them with his hand: as usual, when the fire was made I set off to examine the country before us, and found we had now to descend the west side of the Mountains; I returned and found part of my Men with a Pole of twenty feet in length boring the Snow to find the bottom; I told them while we had good Snow Shoes it was no matter to us whether the Snow was ten or one hundred feet deep. On looking into the hole they had bored, I was surprised to see the color of the sides of a beautiful blue; the surface was of a very light color, but as it descended the color became more deep, and at the lowest point was of a blue, almost black. The altitude of this place above the level of the Ocean, by the point of boiling water is computed to be eleven thousand feet (Sir George Simpson). Many reflections came on my mind; a new world was in a manner before me, and my object was to be at the Pacific Ocean before the month of August, how were we to find Provisions, and how many Men would remain with me, for they were dispirited, amidst various thoughts I fell asleep on my bed of Snow.

"I'll take my oath . . ."
Ross Cox

Athabasca Pass, 1816.

At one P.M. we arrived at two small lakes, between which we encamped. They are only a few hundred feet each in circumference, and the distance between them does not exceed twenty-five or thirty feet. They lie on the most level part of the height of land, and are situated between an immense cut of the Rocky Mountains. From them two rivers take their rise, which pursue different courses, and fall into separate oceans: the first winds into the valley we had lately left, and, after joining the upper part of the Columbia, empties itself into the North Pacific; while the other, called the Rocky Mountain River, a branch of the Athabasca, follows first an eastern and then a northern course, until it forms a junction with the *Unjiga*, or Peace River. This falls into Great Slave Lake, the waters of which are ultimately carried by Mackenzie's River to the Arctic Ocean.

The country round our encampment presented the wildest and most terrific appearance of desolation that can be well imagined. The sun shining on a range of stupendous glaciers, threw a chilling brightness over the chaotic mass of rocks, ice, and snow, by which we were surrounded. Close to our encampment one gigantic mountain of a conical form towered majestically into the clouds far above the others, while at intervals the interest of the scene was heightened by the rumbling noise of a descending *avalanche;* which, after being detached from its bed of centuries, increased in bulk in its headlong career downwards, until it burst with a frightful crash, more resembling the explosion of a magazine than the dispersion of a mass of snow.

One of our rough-spun unsophisticated Canadians, after gazing upwards for some time in silent wonder, exclaimed with much vehemence, "I'll take my oath, my dear friends, that God Almighty never made such a place!"

The Committee's Punch Bowl
George Simpson

George Simpson, the governor of the Hudson's Bay Company, made his first trip across the Athabasca Trail in October, 1824, travelling up the Whirlpool River, over Athabasca Pass, and down to Boat Encampment on the Columbia River.

The Mountains now encrease to a stupendous Size; the Summits of many obscured from our sight by Clouds and of others covered by eternal Snows. We crossed the River once to Day the ford bad and the current strong and Encamped at the Grand Traverse. 15th Left our Encampment after Breakfast; the road hilly craggy & rugged and in many places dangerous but the Horses are accustomed to it and rarely make a false step; one of them however, my wardrobe forming part of his Load Slipped from the bank of the River and was swept down by the current some Hundred Yards but saved by the activity of his Driver; forded the River twice to Day and put up at Campement D'Orignal. After a thorough drenching of Sleet & Rain we renewed our March on the Morning of the 16th the Weather continuing exceedingly bad throughout the Day; as we proceed the Road gets worse and the mountains rise perpendicular to a prodigious height; the scenery Wild & Majestic beyond description; the track is in many places nearly impassable and it appears extraordinary how any human being should have stumbled on a pass through such a formidable barrier as we are now scaling and which nature seems to have placed here for the purpose of interditing all communication between the East and West sides of the Continent. We forded the river about a Doz times to Day and put up at Campement Fusel near the height of Land.

Sunday, October 17th. We had a regular fall of Snow of about 8 inches last night with severe frost; started from our encampment early; towards the height of Land the Road is as bad and dangerous as it can well be and Glaciers are seen which have bidden defiance to the rays of the Sun since the beginning of time wherever the Snow & Ice has room to collect in the face of the mountains and the valleys or passes underneath exhibiting the ravages of the avalanches which sweep down every tree and shrub also loose rocks that happen to be in their way.

At the very top of the pass or height of Land is a small circular Lake or Basin of Water which empties itself in opposite directions and may be said to be the source of the Columbia & Athabasca Rivers as it bestows its favors on both these prodigious Streams, the former falling into the Pacific at Lat. 46½ north and the latter after passing through Athabasca & Great Slave Lakes falling into the Frozen Ocean at about 69 North Lat. That this basin should send its Waters to each side of the Continent and give birth to two of the principal Rivers in North America is no less strange than true both the Dr. & myself having examined the currents flowing from it east & West and the circumstance appearing remarkable I thought it should be honored by a distinguishing title and it was forthwith named the "Committee's Punch Bowl." From hence the descent is extremely rapid down the West side, in many places nearly perpendicular and the changes of climate and consequent difference in the character of the country and its productions which takes place in the course of a few minutes walk would to a person who had not experienced it appear almost incredible. About the height of land and on the East side thereof for several Days Journey the Timber is small and stunted but no sooner do we begin to descend the West side than we fall on the most noble trees I ever beheld, principally Cedar, Hemlock White & Red Pine and Ash all of prodigious size. From the Committee's Punch Bowl to the Base of the Mountain on the West side we occupied 4½ hours in

19

walking, 2 hours of which were consumed in what is called the Grande Côte where our descent could not be less than 40 feet p minute; the other part is not so steep but the descent may be safely reckoned at 15 to 20 feet p minute so that after making a fair allowance for time lost in falls breathing &c. I think without exaggeration I may estimate the height of this single mountain at not less than 4500 feet; this is the lowest pass in the mountain behind which and on each side thereof are immence masses of mountain piled upon and overlooking each other, the principal of which is a huge mountain known by the name of McGillivray's Rock in honor of the Hon[ble] W[m] McGillivray the top of which was enveloped in fog but as far as we could judge by the eye double the height of that described which would make it exceeding 13,000 feet. At and before reaching the height of Land the Cold was intense but immediately after we began to descend the difference of climate was as great as between Summer & Winter and in vegetation the contrast was fully as much.

This was a most harrassing Day to our poor horses and many a cruel blow they got from their unfeeling Drivers, it was evident that the Hon[ble] member for Galway's Bill against cruelty to Animals was not in force in the Rocky Mountain.

The Botanist and the Bear
Thomas Drummond

When John Franklin arrived in western Canada to begin his second exploration to the Arctic Ocean in 1825, one member of the expedition, a botanist name Thomas Drummond, was sent west with the fur trade brigades to spend a year of biological collecting and cataloguing in the Rocky Mountains.

I agreed to accompany the brigade as far as Jasper's House, and accordingly set out with them on horseback. Having crossed the Assinaboyne River, the party halted to breakfast, and I went on before them for a few miles, to procure specimens of a *Jungermannia*, which I had previously observed in a small rivulet on our track. On this occasion I had a narrow escape from the jaws of a grisly bear; for, while passing through a small open glade, intent upon discovering the moss of which I was in search, I was surprised by hearing a sudden rush and then a harsh growl, just behind me; and on looking round, I beheld a large bear approaching towards me, and two young ones making off in a contrary direction as fast as possible. My astonishment was great, for I had not calculated upon seeing these animals so early in the season, and this was the first I had met with. She halted within two or three yards of me, growling and rearing herself on her hind feet, then suddenly wheeled about, and went off in the direction the young ones had taken, probably to ascertain whether they were safe. During this momentary absence, I drew from my gun the small shot with which I had been firing at ducks during the morning, and which, I was well aware, would avail me nothing against so large and powerful a creature, and replaced it with ball. The bear, meanwhile, had advanced and retreated two or three times, apparently more furious than ever; halting at each interval within a shorter and shorter distance of me, always raising herself on her hind legs, and growling a horrible defiance, and at length approaching to within the length of my gun from me. Now was my time to fire: but judge of my alarm and mortification, when I found that my gun would not go off! The morning had been wet, and the damp had communicated to the powder. My only resource was to plant myself firm and stationary, in the hope of disabling the bear by a blow on her head with the butt end of my gun, when she should throw herself on me to seize me. She had gone and returned ten or a dozen times, her rage apparently increasing with her additional confidence, and I momentarily expected to find myself in her gripe, when the dogs belonging to the brigade made their appearance, but on beholding the bear they fled with all possible speed. The horsemen were just behind, but such was the surprise and alarm of the whole party, that though there were several hunters and at least half-a-dozen guns among them, the bear made her escape unhurt, passing one of the horsemen, (whose gun, like mine, missed fire,) and apparently intimidated by the number of the party. For the future, I took care to keep my gun in better order, but I found, by future experience, that the best mode of getting rid of the bears when attacked by them, was to rattle my vasculum, or specimen box, when they immediately decamp. This is the animal described by Lewis and Clark in their Travels on the Missouri, and so much dreaded by the Indians. My adventure with the bear did not, however, prevent my accomplishing the collecting of the *Jungermannia*. It is No. 17 of the "American Mosses."

The Ascent of Mount Brown
David Douglas

On May 1st, 1827, the botanist David Douglas, travelling eastward with a Hudson's Bay Company brigade, made a solo climb of 9,183-foot Mount Brown above Athabasca Pass. While his 16,000-foot estimate of the peak's elevation would lead later mountaineers astray, his was undoubtedly the highest ascent in the Canadian Rockies at the time.

After breakfast at one o'clock, being as I conceive on the highest part of the route, I became desirous of ascending one of the peaks, and accordingly I set out alone on snowshoes to that on the left hand or west side, being to all appearance the highest. The labour of ascending the lower part, which is covered with pines, is great beyond description, sinking on many occasions to the middle. Half-way up vegetation ceases entirely, not so much as a vestige of moss or lichen on the stones. Here I found it less laborious as I walked on the hard crust. One-third from the summit it becomes a mountain of pure ice, sealed far over by Nature's hand as a momentous work of Nature's God. The height from its base may be about 5500 feet: timber, 2750 feet; a few mosses and lichen, 500 more; 1000 feet of perpetual snow; the remainder, towards the top 1250, as I have said, glacier with a thin covering of snow on it. The ascent took me five hours; descending only one and a quarter. Places where the descent was gradual, I tied my shoes together, making them carry me in turn as a sledge. Sometimes I came down at one spell 500 to 700 feet in the space of one minute and a half. I remained twenty minutes, my thermometer standing at 18°; night closing fast in on me, and no means of fire, I was reluctantly forced to descend. The sensation I felt is beyond what I can give utterance to. Nothing, as far as the eye could perceive, but mountains such as I was on, and many higher, some rugged beyond any description, striking the mind with horror blended with a sense of the wondrous works of the Almighty. The aerial tints of the snow, the heavenly azure of the solid glaciers, the rainbow-like hues of their thin broken fragments, the huge mossy icicles hanging from the perpendicular rocks with the snow sliding from the steep southern rocks with amazing velocity, producing a crash and grumbling like the shock of an earthquake, the echo of which resounding in the valley for several minutes.

The British botanist David Douglas, who climbed to the summit of Mount Brown in 1827. Archives of the Canadian Rockies

Simpson's Pass
George Simpson

During the summer of 1841, the Hudson's Bay Company's governor led a small party through the Rocky Mountains by a totally new route. They entered the mountains from the east by way of Devil's Gap, passed by Lake Minnewanka (Peechee's Lake) and Cascade Mountain (the Spout), crossed the Bow River just a few miles upstream from present-day Banff, and ascended Healy Creek to the pass which now bears Simpson's name.

In the afternoon, we emerged from the woods on a long open valley terminating in a high ridge, whence we obtained one of those majestic views, found only " 'midst mountain fastnesses." As far as the eye could reach, mountain rose above mountain, while at our feet lay a valley surrounded by an amphitheatre of cold, bare, rugged peaks. In these crags, which were almost perpendicular, neither could tree plant its roots nor goat find a resting-place; the "Demon of the Mountains" alone could fix his dwelling there. On the stony bosom of the valley in question we pitched our tents for the night. Here we found one of the sources — in spring, a torrent, but now almost dry — of the river La Biche; and here we bade adieu to that stream, which, during the last three days, we had crossed at least forty times. One of the overhanging peaks, from its bearing a rude resemblance to an upturned face, is called the Devil's Nose.

The path, which we had been following, was a track of the Assiniboines, carried, for the sake of concealment, through the thickest forests. The Indians and Peechee were the only persons that had ever pursued this route; and we were the first whites that had attempted this pass of the mountains.

In the morning, we entered a defile between mountainous ridges, marching for nine hours through dense woods. This valley, which was from two to three miles in width, contained four beautiful lakes, communicating with each other by small streams; and the fourth of the series, which was about fifteen miles by three, we named after Peechee, as being our guide's usual home. At this place he had expected to find his family; but Madame Peechee and the children had left their encampment, probably on account of a scarcity of game. What an idea of the loneliness and precariousness of savage life does this single glimpse of the biography of the Peechees suggest!

Having marched for nine hours over broken rocks and through thick forests, we found, on halting for breakfast, that six of our horses, three of them with packs, were missing; and we instantly despatched all our men but two in quest of them, determining at the same time to remain for the rest of the day in order to await their return. The beauty of the scenery formed some compensation for this loss of time. Our tents were pitched in a level meadow of about five hundred acres in extent, enclosed by mountains on three sides, and by Peechee's lake on the fourth. From the very edge of the water, there rose a gentle ascent of six or eight hundred feet, covered with pines, and composed almost entirely of the accumulated fragments of the adamantine heights above; and on the upper border of this slope there stood perpendicular walls of granite, of three or four thousand feet, while among the dizzy altitudes of their battlemented summits the goats and sheep bounded in playful security.

As ill luck would have it, one of the missing horses carried our best provisions; but, by stewing two partridges and making a little pemmican into a kind of burgoo, we contrived to produce both breakfast and supper for eight hungry travellers. Though we had considerably increased our elevation by this morning's march, yet the heat was great, reaching as high as 70° in the shade.

The defile, through which we had just passed, had been the scene of an exploit highly characteristic of savage life. One of the Crees, whom we saw at Gull Lake, had been tracked into the valley, along with his wife and family, by five youths of a hostile tribe. On perceiving the odds that were against him, the man gave himself up for lost, observing to the woman that, as they could die but once, they had better make up their minds to submit to their present fate without resistance. The wife, however, replied that, as they had but one life to lose, they were the more decidedly bound to defend it to the last, even under the most desperate circumstances; adding that, as they were young and by no means pitiful, they had an additional motive for preventing their hearts from becoming small. Then, suiting the action to the word, the heroine brought the foremost warrior to the earth with a bullet, while the husband, animated by a mixture of shame and hope, disposed of two more of the enemy with his arrows. The fourth, who had by this time come to pretty close quarters, was ready to take vengeance on the courageous woman, with uplifted tomahawk, when he stumbled and fell; and, in the twinkling of an eye, the dagger of his intended victim was buried in his heart. Dismayed at the death of his four companions, the sole survivor of the assailing party saved himself by flight, after wounding his male opponent by a ball in the arm.

It was six o'clock next morning before our people returned with the missing horses, which they had found about fifteen miles behind. On starting, we proceeded up a bold pass in the mountains, in which we crossed two branches of the Bow River, the south branch, as already mentioned, of the Saskatchewan. From the top of a peak, that rose perpendicularly at least two thousand feet, there fell a stream of water, which, though of very considerable volume, looked like a thread of silver on the gray rock. It was said to be known as the Spout, and to serve as a landmark in this wilderness of cliffs.

About two in the afternoon, we reached, as Peechee assured us, the Bow River Traverse, the spot at which a fresh guide from the west side of the mountains, of the name of Berland, was to meet us with a relay of horses. But, whether this was the Bow River Traverse or not, no Berland was here to be found. Thinking that the two guides might have different notions as to the precise place of rendezvous, we despatched two men to another crossing-place about two miles farther up the stream, instructing them, according to circumstances, either to return to this point and pursue our track, or else to cut across the country in order to join us. The river, the same as that which we crossed before reaching Carlton, was here about a hundred and fifty yards in width, with a strong and deep current. We conveyed baggage and horses, and everything else, on a raft covered with willows; and, as we finished the operation only at sunset, we encamped for the night on the south or right bank of the stream.

As we were always glad to make our guns save our pemmican, we had to-day knocked down a porcupine which, being desperately hungry, we pronounced to be very good fare. We had also tried, but in vain, to get within shot of some of the goats and sheep that were clambering and leaping on the peaks; the flesh of the latter is reckoned a great delicacy; but that of the former is not much esteemed.

The water of the river was cold, being formed chiefly of melted snow; and the temperature of a small tributary in the neighbourhood of our camp proved to be only 42°, while, in the course of the afternoon, the mercury had stood at 70° in the shade. We enjoyed the coolness both for drinking and bathing, though the water, like that of the Alps, was known to give the goitres, even as far down as the fork of the two grand branches of the Saskatchewan, to such as might habitually and permanently use it. Our men, poor fellows, had had quite enough of the luxury, in the swimming way, for, in managing the raft, they had been three or four hours in the current.

Next morning, we began to ascend the mountains in right earnest, riding where we could, and walking where the horses found the road too steep to carry us, while by our side there rushed downwards one of the sources of the Bow River. We were surrounded by peaks and crags, on whose summits lay perpetual snow; and the only sounds that disturbed the solitude were the crackling of prostrate branches under the tread of our horses, and the roaring of the stream, as it leaped down its rocky course. One peak presented a very peculiar feature in an opening of about eighty feet by fifty, which, at a distance, might have been taken for a spot of snow, but which, as one advanced nearer, assumed the appearance of the gateway of a giant's fortress.

About seven hours of hard work brought us to the height of land, the hinge, as it were, between the eastern and the western waters. We breakfasted on the level isthmus, which did not exceed fourteen paces in width, filling our kettles for this our lonely meal at once from the crystal sources of the Columbia and the Saskatchewan, while these feeders of two opposite oceans, murmuring over their beds of mossy stones as if to bid each other a long farewell, could hardly fail to attune our minds to the sublimity of the scene. . . .

In addition to the physical magnificence of the scene, I here met an unexpected reminiscence of my own native hills in the shape of a plant, which appeared to me to be the very heather of the Highlands of Scotland; and I might well regard the reminiscence as unexpected, inasmuch as, in all my wanderings of more than twenty years, I had never found anything of the kind in North America. As I took a considerable degree of interest in the question of the supposed identity, I carried away two specimens, which, however, proved, on a minute comparison, to differ from the genuine staple of the brown heaths of the "land o' cakes." We made also another discovery, about which there could be no mistake, in a troublesome and venomous species of winged insect, which, in size and appearance, might have been taken for a cross between the bull-dog and the house-fly.

Rundle's Climb
Robert Rundle

In the autumn of 1844, the Wesleyan missionary Reverend Robert Rundle attempted to climb a mountain along the Bow River just inside the eastern front of the range (not the mountain which bears his name today).

Nov. 9 — Saty morning. Am now climbing a mountain. Here are two veins, perhaps of spar, in the bed of rock where I am now sitting. I became quite ill thro' fatigue &c. but was in good spirits when climbing, until I was very high up. I made two attempts to get up an elevation but could not succeed. Rocks very steep — felt very weak, so weak, that at last I was near fainting whilst passing over a projecting ledge of rock. What a moment of anxiety. I have some recollection of calling to the Almighty to assist me & praised be His name, my prayer was heard. I descended to the next stage. It was presumptuous of me I know but I began again to see if I could not find a way to scale higher' but I could not succeed so I now abandoned my design & commenced descending. I was not careful about the road & had great difficulty in descending. I was very weak from want of food, having left without breakfast, & began to feel afraid ever & anon too I heard the moving stones which terrified me. How hard, too, to pass along the steep sloping sides sloping away to fearful descent. At length, however, I reached the bottom, but how was I to get to the encampment? I had lost the road. Very tired, weak, & unwell. Heard gun fired!! & so guided!! Reached at last, thanks to Providence. Took some medicine & had *breakfast* abt sunset. Started on little Black; felt quite different. Snowing; reached encampment about 11 o'clock or so.

The Reverend Robert Rundle. Archives of the Canadian Rockies

The Mountain Man
Father Pierre De Smet

Headwaters of the Columbia, September, 1845.

The Canadian! Into what part of the desert has he not penetrated? The monarch who rules at the source of the Columbia is an honest emigrant from St. Martin, in the district of Montreal, who has resided for twenty-six years in this desert. The skins of the rein and moose deer are the materials of which his portable palace is composed: and to use his own expressions, he EMBARKS on horseback with his wife and seven children, and LANDS wherever he pleases. Here, no one disputes his right, and Polk and Peel, who are now contending for the possession of his dominions, are as unknown to our carbineer, as the two greatest powers of the moon. His *sceptre* is a beaver trap — his *law* a carbine — the one on his back, the other on his arm, he reviews his numerous furry subjects the beaver, otter, musk-rat, marten, fox, bear, wolf, sheep, and white goat of the mountains, the black-tailed roe-buck, as well as its red-tailed relative, the stag, the rein and moose deer; some of which *respect his sceptre* — others *submit to his law*. He exacts and receives from them the tribute of *flesh* and *skins*. Encircled by so much grandeur, undisturbed proprietor of all the sky-ward palaces, the strong holds, the very last refuge which Nature has reared to preserve alive liberty in the earth — solitary lord of these majestic mountains, that elevate their icy summits even to the clouds — Morigeau (our Canadian) does not forget his duty as a Christian. Each day, morning and evening, he may be seen devoutly reciting his prayers, midst his little family.

Many years had Morigeau ardently desired to see a priest; and when he learned that I was about to visit the source of the Columbia, he repaired thither in all haste to procure for his wife and children the signal grace of baptism. The feast of the Nativity of the Blessed Virgin, this favor was conferred on them, and also on the children of three Indian families, who accompany him in his migrations. This was a solemn day for the desert! The august sacrifice of Mass was offered; Morigeau devoutly approached the Holy Table; — at the foot of the humble altar he received the nuptial benediction; and the mother, surrounded by her children and six little Indians, was regenerated in the holy waters of baptism. In memory of so many benefits, a large cross was erected in the plain, which, from that time, is called the *Plain of the Nativity*.

I cannot leave my good Canadian without making an honorable mention of his royal CUISINE A LA SAUVAGE. The first dish he presented me contained two paws of a bear. In Africa, this ragout might have given some alarm; in effect, it bears a striking resemblance to the feet of a certain race. A roast porcupine next made its appearance, accompanied by a moose's muzzle; the latter I found delicious. Finally, the great kettle containing a sort of hotch-potch, or salmagundi, was placed in the midst of the guests, and each one helped himself according to his taste.

Some remains of beef, buffalo, venison, beavers' tails, hare, partridges, &c., made an agreeable, substantial, famous soup.

With the Stoney Indians
Father Pierre De Smet

On the eastern slope of the Rockies, September, 1845.

Cleanliness is a virtue which has no place in the Indian catalogue of domestic or personal duties. The Assiniboins are filthy beyond conception; they surpass all their neighbours in this unenvied qualification. They are devoured by vermin, which they, in turn, consume. A savage, whom I playfully reprehended for his cruelty to these little invertebral insects, answered me: "He bit me the first, I have a right to be revenged." Through complacency, I overcame natural disgust, and assisted at their porcupine feast. I beheld the Indians carve the meat on their leathern shirts, highly polished with grease — filthy, and swarming with vermin, they had disrobed themselves, for the purpose of providing a table-cloth! — They dried their hands in their hair — this is their only towel — and as the porcupine has naturally a strong and offensive odor, one can hardly endure the fragrance of those who feast upon its flesh and besmear themselves with its oil.

A good old woman, whose face was anointed with blood, (THE INDIANS' MOURNING WEEDS,) presented me a wooden platter filled with soup; the horn spoon destined for my use was dirty and covered with grease; she had the complaisance to apply it to the broad side of her tongue, before putting it into my unsavory broth.

If a bit of dried meat, or any other provision is in need of being cleansed, the dainty cook fills her mouth with water and spirts it with her whole force upon the fated object. A certain dish, which is considered a prime delicacy among the Indians, is prepared in a most singular manner, and they are entitled to a patent for the happy faculty of invention. The whole process belongs exclusively to the female department. They commence by rubbing their hands with grease, and collecting in them the blood of the animal, which they boil with water; finally, they fill the kettle with fat and hashed meat. But — HASHED WITH THE TEETH! Often half a dozen old women are occupied in this mincing operation during hours; mouthful after mouthful is masticated, and thus passes from the mouth into the cauldron, to compose the choice ragout of the Rocky Mountains. Add to this, by way of an exquisite desert, an immense dish of crusts, composed of pulverized ants, grass-hoppers and locusts, that had been dried in the sun, and you may then be able to form some idea of Indian luxury.

The Last of the Snake Indians
Henry John Moberly

At Jasper I induced a young halfbreed to join me and try his luck in British Columbia. We started in company across the pass to Tete Jaune Cache, the snow a foot deep on the ground and the streams frozen over but not solid enough to bear us. We were obliged, therefore, to cut our way through brush and fallen timber at points where we should otherwise have followed a creek-bed. Six days of this brought us to Tete Jaune, where we planned to embark.

At the Cache we found encamped a small band of Shushwaps, among them a woman, the last member of a petty tribe called the Snake Indians. . . .

The Snake woman . . . had lived through one of the most remarkable experiences of which I have ever heard. Eighteen or nineteen years before her tribe had consisted of some twenty families, living entirely in the mountains and for decades at war with the Wood Assiniboines. The Snakes at the time of which I write were camped on the side of a mountain west of the post [Jasper House], and a band of Assiniboines at Lac Brule, just below the entrance to the pass. The Assiniboines proposed a meeting at the head of the lake for the purpose of ratifying a peace, each band to come unarmed.

The Snakes agreed, and the men of the band, leaving their guns, arrived and were placed in the inner circle round the council fire. The Assiniboines, however, concealed their guns under their blankets and at a prearranged signal drew them and shot down in cold blood every man of their ancient enemies. They then rushed to the Snake camp and wiped out the rest of the band, with the exception of three young women whom they brought as prisoners to Fort Assiniboine. Here they were stripped, bound and placed in a tent, to be tortured and finally dispatched at a great scalp dance to be held next day.

During the night a French halfbreed, Bellerose by name, crept into the lodge where the prisoners lay and cut their bonds. All he could provide them with was his scalping knife and a fire bag containing flint, steel and punk. The women made their escape and followed the Athabasca River to its junction with the Baptiste. Here they could not agree as to their further course. Two decided to follow the Athabasca, the third the Baptiste. The two, making a raft and taking with them the fire bag, crossed the Baptiste and were never afterwards heard of.

The third, left only with the knife, travelled up the Baptiste some thirty miles and there made preparations for wintering. Berries were still to be had, she managed to kill a few squirrels and with the sinews from their tails made snares for rabbits. She killed some porcupines and groundhogs, too, dried them and out of the rabbit skin made herself a dress. She kindled a fire in the primitive way, by revolving the point of one dry stick rapidly in a hole made in another, and collected a large pile of dry wood. By the time winter had set in she was prepared for it.

Thus she lived until midsummer, gathering gum from the poplars and making dried meat from rabbits and other small animals she killed. Then she removed several days' journey to another good hunting ground.

Three months later an Iroquois hunter wandering far from his accustomed haunts came upon a series of strange tracks and traces. They puzzled him. He was unable to decipher what kind of animal could have made them. So many tales of "*weetigoes*" and other mysterious beings were current that none thought it worth while to travel so far to look into this one, and for a time the whole matter died out.

Next summer, however, when the hunters were in camp some little distance from the Baptiste, this man decided to return to the spot and try to find out what animal had made the mystifying tracks. He struck the river where the Snake woman was living, saw snares set, trees barked and fresh prints in the ground that resembled those of a human being. He was sure he had now run upon a real *weetigo* (cannibal) and, being a plucky man, determined to hunt and kill him.

Creeping round cautiously, with his gun at full cock, and prepared at any moment to be pounced upon, he came to a high bank where an immense collection of dry wood with a little fire near it was piled not far from the entrance to a small cave. He could see no other signs of life.

He hid himself close to the cave, and presently a wild creature in a short skirt of rabbit skins approached with a load of rabbits. Throwing down the pack, this grotesque object picked up some sticks with which to replenish the fire, and recognizing the sex the hunter knew at once that she must be one of the three women who had escaped two years before from the Assiniboines.

Noticing him at length she made a frenzied effort to escape but was soon overtaken. She had become perfectly wild, and he had much difficulty in bringing her to camp. She remained with his family for two years. Then the officer in Jasper House kept her for another two years as servant to his wife, at the end of which time she married a Shushwap. She was the only survivor of her tribe.

A small stream to the north-west of Jasper House still bears on some maps the name of Snake Indian River.

An Artist on the Athabasca Trail
Paul Kane

Autumn 1845.

Oct. 30th. — We had a fine view of the mountains from the boat for the first time; the men greeted them with a hearty cheer.

Oct. 31st. — The atmosphere clear but very cold. I made a sketch of the river and the mountains in the distance.

November 1st. — We entered Jasper's Lake in the morning. This lake is about twelve miles long, and from three to four miles wide, but at this season of the year very shallow, on account of its sources in the mountains being frozen. We had to land three men on the south shore for the purpose of decreasing the draft of our boat; but even then we proceeded with great difficulty. Shortly after we had put them on shore, it began to blow a perfect hurricane, which drove us to the north side, and a snow storm coming on, we were compelled to encamp. This was unfortunate, as it was impossible to communicate with the men whom we had left at the other side, and who were without either provisions or blankets, and we knew from the intense cold that they must be suffering severely.

Nov. 2nd. — We were now close upon the mountains, and it is scarcely possible to conceive the intense force with which the wind howled through a gap formed by a perpendicular rock called "Miëtte's Rock," 1500 feet high, on the one side, and a lofty mountain on the other. The former derives its appelation from a French voyageur, who climbed its summit and sat smoking his pipe with his legs hanging over the fearful abyss. M'Gillveray and the guide went on to Colin Frazer's, distant about fourteen or fifteen miles, to procure horses, as we found that further progress in the boat was impossible, both on account of the shallowness of the water and the violence of the wind.

Nov. 3rd. — The hurricane still continued, accompanied by very heavy snow; indeed, from what I heard, I believe it is always blowing at this place. The forest is composed entirely of very high pine trees, small in circumference, and growing thickly together; these had a very curious appearance in the storm, as they waved in the wind like a field of grain. The immense long roots seemed to be especially provided them by nature to prevent their being blown over; and, as the soil is very light, and upon a rocky foundation, these roots formed a net work near the surface, which was in constant motion, and rocked us to sleep as we lay round our camp fires.

Meanwhile, our guide returned from Jasper's House with several horses. We found our boat blown out of the water, and lying fifteen feet distant from it on the shore although its weight was so great, that the strength of our remaining nine men could not return it to its element.

I selected a horse, and, taking the guide with me, started for the establishment in advance of the rest of the party. After a severe ride of four hours, and having forded the river four times, dangerously crowded with drift ice borne down by a rapid current, sometimes coming over the saddle, I arrived at Jasper's House cold, wet, and famished. But I was soon cheered by a blazing fire and five or six pounds of mountain sheep, which I certainly then thought far more delicious than any domestic animal of the same species. About 10 o'clock that evening, to our great joy, the three men whom we had left on the south shore, came in. Their sufferings had been very great, as they had been wandering through the woods for three days without food, endeavouring to find the house, which none of them had been at before. One of them had not even taken his coat with him, and it was only by lying huddled together at night that they escaped being frozen. Another suffered dreadfully from the swelled state of his legs, caused by the strings usually tied round their leggings being too tight, and which, owing to his benumbed condition, he did not perceive. We had some difficulty in cutting them off, as they were buried in the swollen flesh.

Nov. 4th. — Mr. Lane and party arrived safe in the evening with the loaded horses. Jasper's House consists of only three miserable log huts. The dwelling-house is composed of two rooms, of about fourteen or fifteen feet square each. One of them is used by all comers and goers: Indians, voyageurs, and traders, men, women, and children being huddled together indiscriminately; the other room being devoted to the exclusive occupation of Colin and his family, consisting of a Cree squaw, and nine interesting half-breed children. One of the other huts is used for storing provision in, when they can get any, and the other I should have thought a dog-kennel had I seen many of the canine species about. This post is only kept up for the purpose of supplying horses to parties crossing the mountains. I made a sketch of the establishment.

Nov. 5th. — We started with a cavalcade of thirteen loaded horses,

A lithograph of Paul Kane's sketch of Jasper House. Archives of the Canadian Rockies

but as we did not expect to be able to get the horses across the mountains, I got an Indian to make me a pair of snow shoes. The Indians about here do not number above fifteen or twenty; they are the Shoo-Schawp tribe, and their chief, of whom I made a sketch, is called "Capote Blanc" by the voyageurs — in their own language it is Assannitchay, but means the same. His proper location is a long distance to the north-east; but he had been treacherously entrapped, whilst travelling with thirty-seven of his people, by a hostile tribe, which met him and invited him to sit down and smoke the pipe of peace. They unsuspectingly laid down their arms, but before they had time to smoke, their treacherous hosts seized their arms and murdered them all except eleven, who managed to escape, and fled to Jasper's House, where they remained, never daring to return to their own country through the hostile tribe. Capote Blanc was a very simple, kind-hearted old man, with whom I became very friendly.

We left this inhospitable spot about noon, and crossed the river in a small canoe to where the men were waiting for us, with the horses, which they had swam across the river in the morning. We rode on till 4 o'clock, and encamped in a small prairie, of which I made a sketch.

Nov. 6th. — We made but few miles of progress to-day, being obliged to encamp at La Row's Prairie in order to pasture our horses, our next stopping place being too distant to reach that evening.

Nov. 7th. — We made a *long day*; our route lay sometimes over almost inaccessible crags, and at others through gloomy and tangled forest; as we ascended, the snow increased in depth, and we began to feel the effects of the increasing cold and rarefaction of the atmosphere.

Nov. 8th. — We saw two mountain goats looking down on us from a lofty and precipitous ledge of rock, not exceeding, to all appearance, a few inches in width. One of the Indians who accompanied us from Jasper's House to take back the horses, started to attain a crag above them, as these animals cannot be approached near enough to shoot them from below, their gaze being always directed downwards. They chanced, however, to see him going up, and immediately escaped to an inaccessible height.

Nov. 9th. — Finding the snow so deep, and knowing, not only that we were late, but that our further progress must be slow, we became apprehensive that the party who should be waiting for us with boats and provisions from Fort Vancouver, at the other side of the mountains, would give up all hopes of meeting us and might leave. This would have entailed the most fearful hardships upon us, if it did not produce actual destruction, as we should have had to recross the mountains with scarcely any or no provisions. We, therefore, despatched the guide and M'Gillveray, to hasten on to Boat Encampment. We encamped at the "Grand Batteur," where we found some snow shoes, which had been hidden by the party that had come out in the spring.

Nov. 10th. — We had not proceeded far before the horses stuck fast in the snow, and we were obliged to encamp on the spot to give those men who were unprovided time to make snow shoes, without which they could not proceed. We remained here all day, and sent the horses back with everything we could dispense with, our provisions and blankets being quite as much as the men could carry; and some of the new hands, who had only come into the country that year, were now so knocked up by their long and fatiguing voyage from Montreal, which they had left in the spring, as to be quite useless.

Nov. 11th. — We sent two experienced men in advance to beat the track for the new beginners, and made our first essay on snow shoes. Some of our men succeeded but indifferently in the attempt, having never used them before; and the shoes, which we made the day before not being of the best description, materially impeded our progress. The shoes which the Indian had made for me at Jasper House were particularly good ones, and I found little difficulty in their use. Mrs. Lane had also taken the precaution to bring a pair with her and as she had been accustomed to them from her childhood at Red River, where they are a great deal used, she proved one of our best pedestrians. We encamped early, making for the first time what is called a regular winter encampment. This is only made where the snow is so deep that it cannot be removed so as to reach the ground. The depth to which the snow attains can be calculated by the stumps of the trees cut off at its former level for previous camp fires; some of these were twelve or fifteen feet above us at the present time, and the snow was nine or ten feet deep under us. Some of the old voyageurs amused themselves by telling the new hands or *Mangeurs du Lard*, that the Indians in those parts were giants from thirty to forty feet high, and that accounted for the trees being cut off at such an unusual height.

It is necessary to walk repeatedly with snow shoes over the place chosen for the encampment until it is sufficiently beaten down to bear a man without sinking on its surface. Five or six logs of green timber, from eighteen to twenty feet long, are laid down close together, in parallel lines, so as to form a platform. The fire of dry wood is then kindled on it, and pine branches are spread on each side, on which the party, wrapped in their blankets, lie down with their feet towards the fire. The parallel logs rarely burn through in one night, but the dropping coals and heat form a deep chasm immediately under the fire, into which the logs are prevented from falling by their length. Into this hole an Iroquois, who had placed himself too near the fire, rolled a depth of at least six or seven feet, the snow having melted from under him while asleep. His cries awoke me, and after a hearty laugh at his fiery entombment, we succeeded in dragging him out.

Nov. 12th. — To-day we attained what is called the Height of Land. There is a small lake at this eminence called the Committee's Punch-bowl; this forms the head waters of one branch of the Columbia River on the west side of the mountains, and of the Athabasca on the east side. It is about three quarters of a mile in circumference, and is remarkable as giving rise to two such mighty rivers; the waters of the one emptying in the Pacific Ocean, and of the other into the Arctic Sea. We encamped on its margin, with difficulty protecting ourselves from the intense cold.

Nov. 13th. — The lake being frozen over to some depth, we walked across it, and shortly after commenced the descent of the grand côte, having been seven days continually ascending. The descent was so steep, that it took us only one day to get down to nearly the same level as that of Jasper's House. The descent was a work of great difficulty on snow shoes, particularly for those carrying loads; their feet frequently slipped from under them, and the loads rolled down the hill. Some of the men, indeed, adopted the mode of rolling such loads as would not be injured down before them. On reaching the bottom, we found eight men waiting, whom M'Gillveray and the guide had sent on to assist us to Boat Encampment, and we all encamped together.

Nov. 14th. — I remained at the camp fire finishing one of my sketches, the men having made a very early start in order to reach Boat Encampment, where they would get a fresh supply of provisions, ours being nearly exhausted. As soon as I had finished my sketch I followed them, and soon arrived at a river about seventy yards across, and with a very rapid current.

Having followed their track in the snow to the edge of the river, and seeing the strength of the current, I began to look for other tracks, under the impression that they might possibly have discovered a way to get round it. But I was soon undeceived by seeing in the snow on the other side the path they had beaten down on the opposite bank; nothing, therefore, remained but for me to take off my snow shoes, and make the traverse. The water was up to my middle, running very rapidly, and filled with drift ice, some pieces of which struck me, and nearly forced me down the stream. I found on coming out of the water my capote and leggings frozen stiff. My difficulties, however, were only beginning, as I was soon obliged to cross again four times, when, my legs becoming completely benumbed, I dared not venture on the fifth, until I had restored the circulation by running up and down the beach. I had to cross twelve others in a similar manner, being seventeen in all, before I overtook the rest of the party at the encampment. The reason of these frequent crossings is, that the only pass across the mountains is the gorge formed by the Athabasca at one side, and the Columbia at the other; and the beds of these torrents can only be crossed in the spring before the thaws commence, or in the fall after the severe weather has set in. During the summer the melting of the mountain snow and ice renders them utterly impracticable.

Nov. 15th. — It will be easily imagined with what regret we left a warm fire and comfortable encampment, to plunge at once into one of the deepest crossings we had yet encountered, covered like the preceding with running ice. Here, as in many other of the crossings, our only means of withstanding the force of the current was for all to go abreast shoulder to shoulder, in a line parallel with it, each man being supported by all below him. Mrs. Lane, although it was necessary to carry her in the arms of two powerful men across the river, acquitted herself in other respects as well as any of us. One of the greatest annoyances accompanying the use of snow shoes, is that of having to take them off on entering a river, and replacing them over the wet and frozen moccasins on coming out of it.

Before stopping to breakfast this morning, we crossed the river twenty-five times, and twelve times more before camping; having waded it thirty-seven times in all during the day.

The Columbia here makes long reaches, to and fro, through a valley, in some parts three miles wide, and backed with stupendous mountains, rearing their snowy tops above the clouds, and forming here and there immense glaciers, reflecting the rays of the sun with extreme brilliancy and prismatic beauty. The last part of the route lay through a slimy lake or swamp, frozen over, but not with sufficient solidity to bear us, so that we had to wade above our knees in a dense mass of snow, ice, and mud, there being no such thing as a dry spot to afford a moment's respite from the scarcely endurable severity of the cold, under which I thought I must have sank exhausted.

At length, however, we arrived at Boat Encampment, about 5 P.M., almost perishing with cold and hunger, having tasted nothing since what I have already termed breakfast, which consisted only of a small supply of soup made of pemmi-kon, this being the mode of making the most of a small quantity of it. On our arrival we found a good fire blazing, and some soup made from pork and corn, brought from Fort Vancouver, boiling in the pot, which I attacked with so much avidity, that one of the men, fearing I might take too much in my present exhausted state, politely walked off with the bowl and its contents.

The men had been here waiting our arrival for thirty-nine days, and would have returned to Fort Vancouver the next day, had not the guide and M'Gillveray opportunely arrived in time to prevent them, as they thought we had either been cut off by the Indians, or that we had found it impossible to cross the mountains. In fact, they were clearing the snow out of the boats preparatory to starting. Had our messengers not arrived in time, it would most likely have proved fatal to us all, as we could not have re-crossed the mountains without provisions.

A Hard Crossing
Henry James Warre

The Athabasca Trail, May, 1846.

Besides our cumbersome snowshoes (to prevent one from sinking into the yielding snow), every man has to carry his own provisions as well as from 60 lbs. to 70 lbs. of necessary articles viz. rifles, spades, pick axes, blankets, cooking utensils, etc. All such impediments were equally divided, packed in bundles and were carried on a framework, which fitting pretty fairly on a man's back is supported by a band which crosses the forehead and keeps the load high upon the shoulders.

Crossing without difficulty a narrow ridge of hills covered with small cottonwood, bursting into leaf under the shelter of lofty pine trees, we entered upon the flat stony valley of the Canoe [Wood] River. Up this stream we ascended for three days, wading twenty or thirty times a day through the rapid current that loaded with ice and blocked by floating timber flowed from side to side of the valley, and remaining throughout the day in our saturated garments, half frozen and wholly wet, until the bright fires of huge pine logs were kindled to scare away the wild animals at night and prevent ourselves from being frozen.

One day a grizzly bear crossed our path, but did not show his vaunted courage. I only got a snap shot at him as he lumbered up the rocks over which it was impossible to follow. Our hunter kept us pretty well supplied with venison ranging from elk to deer. These, by keeping about an hours march in front of our noisy party, he managed to stalk and kill.

On the third evening we encamped under an apparently inaccessible scarp of rock upon which the glaciers seemed to hang and over

Fur traders ascending to Athabasca Pass from Boat Encampment on the Columbia — a watercolour made by Henry James Warre in 1846. Public Archives of Canada

which innumerable cascades tumbled, glistening in the bright moonlight. The scene was grand but awful in its savage solitude. Not a vestige of human life was to be seen, nay, so far as we knew existed for miles around, beyond our own party. As for them, the three days wading had told so severely upon the men that few cared to look upon the hardships they yet had to surmount.

With daylight we commenced our march, in single file — the leading man stopping and falling in, in rear, every ten minutes. Every forward pace seemed to carry us two steps backwards until by hard work and patience we had cut a flight of stairs out of the yielding snow. At night we encamped in the summit of those rocks we had contemplated from below on the previous day. But the sun had set, and our men were too much exhausted to dig the usual shelter out of the snow. We had nothing to cook for hard pemmican (buffalo meat and suet pounded into a cake) had now become our only food. However, a noble mountain pine that rose in its evergreen pride close by offered us a capital living tent, under the hanging branches of which we endeavoured to make ourselves happy. But the night air was cold, so breaking off a few branches from a decaying tree we lighted our fire. In a moment the flames extended to the hanging foliage and the whole tree was in a blaze! Having discarded our snowshoes, we were powerless to walk, but we plunged in all haste into the deep snow for safety. In spite of our misery the scene was ludicrous. The burning tree made a magnificent torch — lighting up the surrounding desolation — but our rest was destroyed and the snow swallowed up every article of our equipment. Happily the fire did not extend, so we made the best of it for the night, and a glorious sunrise, reflected from the snow-clad pinnacles of the surrounding mountains, enabled us to collect our scattered things and start once more upon our weary march.

The scenery through which we passed onwards was grand beyond description, but oh how desolate! Mountains upon mountains raised their naked heads high above the mists which rolled upwards from the valleys below. Pine and fir trees broken by storms and wonderfully picturesque in shape grew thick together in the ravines or stood like mountain sentinels scattered amidst the rugged rocks. The trackless valleys were smooth with unbroken snow. No living thing dared to brave the awful loneliness that surrounded the "Lake of the Mountains" [The Committee's Punch Bowl] from whence flow the mighty rivers which water the eastern plains of America. . . .

Our hunter could find us no food and our small stock of pemmican was becoming exhausted. Day after day we still crept on, toiling over the frozen snow while the mountains thundered down their avalanches beside us "as from some mountains craggy forehead torn, a rock's round fragment flies, with fury borne" and as the "mass precipitate" descended we were obliged to pass, climbing over the still shaking fragments and expecting every hour to be buried in the ruins.

Human nature is very enduring but must be supported by food. Our nine days provisions had lasted for *fifteen*, at the end of which time we still found ourselves surrounded by snow-covered mountains, far from our destination! There was now no possibility of disguising the truth that stared in our pinched and hungry visages. We were all on the brink of dying with hunger. If any of us dropped in the track as weary and faint we trekked through the snow on these fearful heights, woe to that luckless me! The rest were all too exhausted to give help, and in the pangs of hunger what famishing wretch would part with his last small ration even to a dying comrade.

Our fate would have been no unusual tale. Several parties of snow hunters or emigrants ere ours have perished thus in the snow. And if their traces were found later by chance in summer, signs might not be wanting that before starvation had done its fell work, the ghastly expedient of cannibalism had been resorted to by the last survivors.

It was fearful to witness the silent agony of starvation already among us. Two or three little dogs which followed with the party had long since disappeared. The men were completely exhausted, and unless food could be obtained, death was drawing very near. Selecting two men who seemed more capable than the rest, I now resolved to leave the party in the hope of obtaining food with which to return as speedily as possible. We might perish even more speedily than the others but the chance was worth the risk. . . .

Dividing our last morsel of pemmican, we started off upon our terrible journey. Necessity lent strength to our legs and bright sunshine cheered our downward progress. We had travelled rapidly for about six hours when the tinkling of sleigh bells suddenly astonished our delighted ears. Coming up the valley with three sledges drawn by dogs, we encountered Pere De-Smet, our friend the Jesuit missionary who had been supposed murdered. He was safe and alive and as usual on a mission of beneficence to relieve some Indians who were also "frozen up" in the mountains. We quickly persuaded him to divide a part of his food to rescue our starving comrades, and before the day closed our poor famished voyageurs had gorged themselves in true Indian fashion after their late enforced fast.

I and my companions went on to Fraser's [Jasper] House on the Athabasca River, from whence we crossed a narrow neck of land to the Saskatchewan River, down which we descended for 300 miles meeting many Indians and some wild adventures on our way.

The Emigrants
James Sinclair

In the autumn of 1854, James Sinclair and a party of Red River emigrants crossed the Rockies on their way to the Oregon Territory. In a letter to his son-in-law, Dr. William Cowan of Fort Garry, Sinclair provides a glimpse of the hardships they endured as an inexperienced guide led men, women, children, and livestock through what was most probably North Kananaskis Pass — one of the most difficult and lofty passes in the Great Divide.

> Kootanais River (2 miles from the Lake,
> the Source of the Columbia)
> Oct. 24th, 1854

My Dear Doctor,

As my Guide Broken Arm returns from hence I have merely time to say we are all well. We have been a long time on our journey, so far, but I expect to be at Walla Walla in 20 days hence. Our rascally Guide took us by a pass over the Mountains (known only to himself) which he represented as the best and the shortest, but which took us 30 days and this with hard work in cutting our way and hunting after cattle through a dense forest, wind-fall timber, deep ravines, steep side hills, following up one River (the Strong Current River, which falls into the Bow River, near the old Fort) to its source, and following down another, the Kootanais, to this point where it is 200 yds wide. Altogether it is the worst road I ever travelled. Had we taken the Route by the Red Rock, my old Route, we should now have been near Walla Walla — eight head of cattle were left or lost on the way (but none of mine) belonging to Moon & Sutherland — I am only surprised we were able to bring a single animal here. Had I seen this road before I should never have dreamt of driving Horned Cattle by such a rascally route — Our Guides have all turned out a set of Confounded rascals from Beacon Creek to this place — to them we attribute the slow progress of our movements — at Bow River the Blackfeet shot seven of our cattle (with arrows) two of which died on the spot. The others have since recovered — about 40 men hovered about our camp the night before but of this we were not aware until the following morning. I presume they saw that we were on our guard, and that it would not be safe to molest us. They therefore kept their distance, of which we were not sorry. I still think the cattle were shot by a few young scamps, and that they were prevented by some others from molesting us — the same night they stole 3 Horses. The owners of which took no trouble to take care of them — neither the cattle or Horses belonged to me — Our animals are in pretty good order — even now some would be good beef — I have no apprehension of any being left between this and Walla Walla.

Agnes Lucy thrives well and sucks her pemmican soup as well as any other in the party — but all are tired of the Journey — however. I feel we are now over the worst part of it — I will write by Panama —

Yours Sincerely,

The Discovery of the Kicking Horse Pass
James Hector

During the summer of 1858, Dr. James Hector, geologist with the Palliser Expedition, discovered the Kicking Horse Pass — the eventual route for the Canadian Pacific Railway. Hector crossed the pass with a party of four men: Nimrod, a Stoney hunter; Peter Erasmus, a Métis interpreter; and two Red River men named Sutherland and Brown. The journey up the Kicking Horse River to the pass and down to the Bow River on the eastern side was the most gruelling made by Hector during his extensive Rocky Mountain explorations.

August 29th. — For the last few days, since leaving the lakes, our horses have fared badly, as there is no fine grass in the valley excepting in the swampy bottom, but there it is too soft for them to feed. Their legs are also getting very badly cut by the constant leaping and scrambling over the fallen timber, so that on the whole they have their tempers and patience tried a good deal. We had travelled a few miles when we came to a large flat, where the wide valley terminated, dividing into two branch valleys, one from the north-west and the other to the south-west. Here we met a very large stream, equal in size to Bow River where we crossed it. This river descends the valley from the north-west, and, on entering the wide valley of Beaverfoot River, turns back on its course at a sharp angle, receives that river as a tributary, and flows off to the south-west through the other valley. Just above the angle there is a fall about 40 feet in height, where the channel is contracted by perpendicular rocks.

A little way above this fall, one of our pack horses, to escape the fallen timber, plunged into the stream, luckily where it formed an eddy, but the banks were so steep that we had great difficulty in

*Captain John
Palliser (left) and
Dr. James Hector.*
Provincial
Archives of
British Columbia

getting him out. In attempting to recatch my own horse, which had strayed off while we were engaged with the one in the water, he kicked me in the chest, but I had luckily got close to him before he struck out, so that I did not get the full force of the blow. However, it knocked me down and rendered me senseless for some time. This was unfortunate, as we had seen no tracks of game in the neighbourhood, and were now without food; but I was so hurt that we could not proceed further that day at least. My men covered me up under a tree, and I sent them all off to try and raise something to eat. Peter I sent up the mountain in the angle of the valley, to take bearings, and to see what the mountains were like to the west. He ascended 3,500 feet by the aneroid, but did not get to the highest part of the mountain, which is quite a low one compared to those north of the valley. It is composed of the grey limestone, and splintery iron shale, all dipping 35° to the E.N.E. The mountains seen to the N.W. were high and snow-clad, but beyond those forming the side of the valley there were more seen to the S.E. The men all returned at night without having killed anything. Nimrod had tracked some wapiti, but there were traces of Indians having been in the neighbourhood in spring, probably Shouswaps or Kootanies, and they found a very bad trail leading down the valley to the S.W. Nimrod, who had been that way, found the river soon became hemmed in by high rocks, so that the trail had to go high up over the mountain. There had only been two trails, with very few horses, and they appear to have returned from this post by the same road they came. At one of these camps he found wool of the mount goat, and also wapiti hair. The deer tracks he had seen were leading up the valley to the N.W., and were not fresh. This evening we saw several flocks of geese flying down the valley to the S.W.

August 30. — I was so much better by noon, that I took a meridian altitude, and found the latitude to be 51° 10' N. The men were again hunting to-day, and Peter and Brown found a large flock of white goats, but the only one they shot managed to get to the edge of a precipice and fell over, so that they got none of the meat.

Nimrod went a long distance after the deer, and came back quite lame, having run a sharp spike into his foot. He had seen the wapiti and missed a fine buck. We were now in a bad way, as, although I had kept a private *caché* of about five pounds of pemican, which I now produced, it was only enough for one meal for us all. I intended however to make it last for three days, by which time we should, from the look of the stream which I intended to ascend, be about to reach the height of land, and get back to the east slope of the mountains where we would be sure to find game.

August 31st. — Every morning just now we have dense fogs, that generally last till nine or ten o'clock, but the evenings are fine and clear. After travelling a mile along the left bank of the river from the N.W., which because of the accident the men had named Kicking Horse River, we crossed to the opposite side. It was 90 to 100 yards wide, and almost too deep to ford. The motion on horseback gave me great pain, but we managed to get along slowly till noon. We left the river a considerable distance to our right, following notched trees that Nimrod had marked the day before when out hunting in order to show us the best way, as an Indian soon finds out the right direction to carry a trail in.

At nightfall we again struck the river, where it passes through a narrow defile, and through which we found a well-marked trail. This is generally the case whenever the valleys are narrow, as there, whenever Indians have passed in former times, they have been limited to the same track; while in wider parts of the valley they hunt about in search of game, without leaving distinct traces of where they pass.

The deposits of red and grey sand, with clay and gravel, are at least 600 feet thick in the valley. Our course had changed almost to due north, and we passed over the grey slate strata, dipping first to the N.E. at 5°, and then changing to a high angle in the same direction. Where we encamped the river is hemmed by high precipices of blue limestone. The river is very muddy, and with the imperfect tackle we have, consisting of some large cod hooks and twine, we cannot catch any trout.

September 1st. — Started early, sending Nimrod and Peter ahead to hunt. The valley soon after starting got very wide, with extensive swampy flats and clumps of fine timber. The willows fringing the margins of these grassy swamps exactly resembled hedgerows enclosing green fields.

Halt at noon, in latitude 51° 16' 30" N., a little way below where the river receives two large tributaries, one from the east and the other from the N.W.

Above this point the main stream makes a large bend to the east, to avoid which we crossed a high rocky spur of the mountain, and again met the river by descending into a magnificent cañon, where we encamped.

The higher portions of the mountains we passed this day are capped with a great thickness of slate rock with ferruginous bands. The valley or cañon in which we encamped is about half a mile wide, enclosed by rocky walls, that often rise nearly perpendicularly 4,000 to 5,000 feet. They are composed of the white slate rock, on which rests unconformably enormous beds of limestone, much dislocated; while the banded slate rock and ferruginous shales form the higher parts of the mountains.

September 2nd. — Started very early, as our only hope of getting any game was by reaching the east side of the mountain. Nimrod had indeed again seen wapiti yesterday, but the fallen woods were so difficult to hunt in, that with his lame foot he only got a long shot, which he missed. We travelled on the shingle flat, which occupies the full width of the valley, crossing and recrossing the river, which must during the spring floods cover the whole valley bottom. After five miles the valley terminated in a sudden slope, covered with heavy pine forests. Entering these we began to ascend rapidly, but loitered a good deal to eat large blueberries, that grew in abundance, and which we were very glad to get, although not very substantial food, when we had been fasting altogether for the past day, and living on only very short allowance for the previous five. After gaining a considerable height, we found it necessary to cross the stream, which was boiling and leaping through a narrow channel of pink quartzose rock. It was with much difficulty that we effected a crossing, and then we had much climbing over moss-covered rocks, our horses often sliding and falling. One, an old grey, that was always more clumsy than the others, lost his balance in passing along a ledge, which overhung a precipitous slope about 150 feet in height, and down he went, luckily catching sometimes on the trees; at last he came to a temporary pause by falling right on his back, the pack acting as a fender; however, in his endeavours to get up he started down hill again, and at last slid on a dead tree that stuck out at right angles to the slope, balancing himself with his legs dangling on either side of the trunk of the tree in a most comical manner. It was only by making a round of a mile that we succeeded in getting him back, all battered and bruised, to the rest of the horses. In the lower part of the ascent we passed much cedar and birch, but as we rose we got into forests exclusively composed of spruce fir. We travelled eight hours before camping, the last two being over fine level ground through open forest. We passed many small lakes, and at last reached a small stream flowing to the east, and were again on the Saskatchewan slope of the mountains. The large stream we had been ascending takes its rise from a glacier to the east of the valley through which we had passed. We encamped in a beautiful spot beside a lake, with excellent pasture for the horses. I had killed a grouse, and we were glad to boil it up with some ends of candles and odd pieces of grease, to make something like a supper for the five of us after a very hard day's work. We were now 1,275 feet above our encampment of last night, and the cold was very sharp, and we felt it more severely in our famished state.

September 3rd. — This morning all the swamps were covered with ice. As I was now nearly recovered from the accident, I started with Nimrod at daylight to hunt, leaving the men and horses to follow a prescribed course to the east. We took our horses with us, and after a few miles we came to a large stream from the west, up the valley of which we saw a great glacier. Following it down, we came after five miles to a large river, which Nimrod at once recognized as Bow River, and then I began to recognize the mountains down the valley, 15 or 20 miles to the east, as the Castle Mountains.

The descent from our camp at the height of land of the pass which we had just traversed is very slight to Bow River, and cannot amount to more than 100 feet. We crossed Bow River, and leaving our horses tethered in a swamp, set off to hunt on foot. We saw several fresh moose tracks, and followed one for more than two hours, but failed in coming up with it. Towards noon, on coming to the river, I found our party had crossed, so I made for them in order to get the latitude. Nimrod soon started again into the woods, and had not been long gone, when we heard most furious firing, and in a short time he returned in a high state of glee, having shot a moose. We at once moved our camp to where it lay, about one mile distant, in a thicket of willows. It was a doe, and very lean, but, notwithstanding, we soon set about cooking and eating to make up for our long fast. It was not till we got the food that we all found out how depressed and weak we were, as desperation had been keeping us up. I had three days before promised that if nothing was killed by to-day I would kill one of the horses, and this evening, if Nimrod had not killed the moose, the old grey that fell over the cliff would have been sacrificed. I had refrained from killing a horse sooner, as I have been warned by experienced travellers that once the first horse is killed for food many more are sure to follow, as the flesh of a horse out of condition is so inferior as merely to create a craving for large quantities of it, without giving the strength or vigour to induce the hunters to exert themselves to kill other game. The prospect of starving is then looked on with indifference, as they know it will be avoided by killing another horse, until at last too few are left to carry the necessaries for the party, who then undergo great sufferings, and, as in the case of several American expeditions, some may even perish.

Memories of Dr. Hector and the Kicking Horse
Peter Erasmus

Peter Erasmus, who travelled with Dr. James Hector through the trials of the Kicking Horse crossing in the late summer of 1858, many years later told his own story of the party's struggles.

I was to learn later that Dr. Hector alone of all the men of my experience asked no quarter from any man among us, drivers or guides. He could walk, ride, or tramp snowshoes with the best of our men, and never fell back on his position to soften his share of the hardships, but in fact gloried in his physical ability after a hard day's run to share in the work of preparing camp for the night, building shelters from the wind, cutting spruce boughs, or even helping get up wood for an all-night fire. He was admired and talked about by every man that travelled with him, and his fame as traveller was a wonder and a byword among many a teepee that never saw the man.

We had been travelling through the mountains for about two weeks; our progress was very slow as sometimes we had to retrace our steps because of some impassable obstruction in our way. The doctor wanted to cross over to the Columbia River and to establish the latitude and longitude of the divide, going by compass as much as possible and only consulting the guide as a last resort.

Our food was getting low; Nimrod could find no game to replenish our dwindling supplies. Finally we were on short rations and gave up compass-reading for Nimrod's guidance north to where he promised better hunting.

We were following along a river bank as the easiest way in the direction we wanted to go when one of the horse's packs came loose. The horse lost his balance and tumbled backward into the river. The clumsy brute had been giving us trouble all the way. The river was quite deep and the banks steep. We all left our saddle-horses and rushed down to save the brute. Losing the pack would have been quite serious in our present situation as it contained most of our food supplies. Sutherland, an old cow puncher, roped the horse and we were able to finally get him on safe ground.

The doctor went to pick up his own horse which was feeding among some spruce with his lines trailing. The instant the doctor reached for the lines, the horse whirled and kicked him with both feet in the chest. The doctor was knocked unconscious.

We all leapt from our horses and rushed up to him, but all our attempts to help him recover his senses were of no avail. We then carried him to the shade of some big evergreens while we pitched camp. We were now in serious trouble, and unless Nimrod fetched in game our situation looked hopeless. One man stayed and watched the unconscious doctor. The rest of us took turns trying to catch trout that we could see in the clear mountain water of the river. Dr. Hector must have been unconscious for at least two hours when Sutherland yelled for us to come up; he was now conscious but in great pain.

54

He asked for his kit and directed me to prepare some medicine that would ease the pain. I had him sign a document stating the facts of the accident in case his illness might prove serious. He readily agreed that it would be the proper thing to do. I asked and got permission to try to find something to shoot. The accident happened in the early forenoon, and it was late in the afternoon before I got started.

I found some fresh deer tracks shortly after I left camp, but was too anxious, and startled them before I could get a good shot. Following them I had another running shot, drew blood, but did not knock the buck down. I kept after the wounded deer, and before I realized that I had gone so far, it was dark, and I had lost my directions. It was hopeless to try to find the way in the dark so I built a fire and tried to forget that I was hungry, cold, and worried over the doctor. Nights in the mountains get pretty cold and that one was the longest and most miserable of any time I ever spent on the trail.

Early next morning I climbed a high place and got my directions from the fog rising from the river. There were no rabbits or bird game of any kind and I decided the deer had not been hurt enough to be worthwhile chasing again. Although I watched for any moving object I could not find any sign of a squirrel. The area was totally barren of any game. Nimrod had gone on the hunt long before I got back empty-handed and tired to the party. The doctor was still in pain but feeling much better, for which I was thankful.

"Peter, you must rest up today to conserve your strength and make another try tomorrow. It'll be impossible for me to ride for a day or two. It'll be up to you and Nimrod to get us food, for we're nearly at the end of our rations."

Late that evening our hunter hobbled into camp, empty-handed. He had fallen when he missed his footing while stalking some sheep. The doctor said he had a badly sprained ankle. It was already swollen, and looked bad. The doctor gave me instructions to treat the man's ankle, and then said, "Now, Peter, it's entirely up to you; that man cannot walk for a few days."

Nimrod gave me directions to where he had last tracked the sheep. I had not yet reached the place when I spotted some of the animals across a deep ravine. They had not seen me or scented my presence. Taking advantage of every cover I could, crawling on my knees for the most part, I reached a point directly opposite. Trembling with excitement and weakness, I slowly raised my head above cover and looked. There in plain sight was a big sentinel sheep, his head raised watching something in the opposite direction. He was standing dead still. I slowly pushed my gun across a dead log and tried to take aim, but my eyes watered and the gun shook so I had to wait to calm my nerves.

Biting my lips in vexation at my foolish nerves, I finally got a grip on myself, took aim, and fired. He gave a tremendous leap and landed twenty feet below, tumbling and rolling to the bottom of the ravine. I knew the sheep would be dead. The others disappeared in a twinkling of an eye. I lay for a moment stunned at the effectiveness of my long shot, then with a yell that echoed back from the mountain, scrambled and slid down the slope after my kill.

It was hard to keep from dancing and holding my gun in triumph as I had seen some of my Indian friends do after some extraordinary shot. I quickly skinned the animal, cut off a thigh for my carrying sack and hit back for camp, anxious to carry the good news to the others. Nimrod got up and hobbled over to where I had placed the meat. After examining the meat he turned to me in disappointment, "No good, Peter. No good. Can't eat." Then I remembered: I had killed a buck, and at that time of year, during the rutting season, they were not fit for human consumption.

My disappointment was the keener because of my early exultation over the kill. In my eagerness to get food I had completely forgotten one of the first lessons I learned from the Pigeon Lake Indians. This was the last straw, and I sat in silent misery. The others tried to cheer me up. "Never mind, Peter. If you can kill a buck, you can just as easily kill a doe. You try again tomorrow." But nothing the doctor said was any help in my misery.

Brown said, "Hell, you're the only man among us who would have the guts to try. The rest of us will give our rations to keep you on your feet. Nimrod sure can't travel with that ugly black ankle of his." The other men echoed their agreement to his suggestion.

The Stony did his best to prepare some of the meat but none of us could get it down. Sutherland kept on trying for trout; he gave a tremendous shout, finally landing one. One trout for six men was not a big meal but it helped a lot, especially with the Stony's herbs to add taste to the fish soup.

Nimrod, who knew of a salt lick only ten miles away where he felt sure he would get a moose, also wanted to try again next morning, but the doctor ordered him to stay in camp. "Erasmus will go out again today, and tomorrow I will try to ride; we will go together to where you think you might get a moose. We'll ride within a mile of the place; maybe you can walk that far."

That morning, fortified with the rations of all three men and I suspect the doctor's share as well, I felt like a new man. I didn't see a thing all day, but on my way back to camp shot a partridge. I ate the gizzard raw and felt much better. It was a temptation to eat the rest of that small bird, but the thought of the men's sacrifice that morning was enough to overcome my greed.

The Stony immediately took charge of the bird for cooking, taking elaborate care that not a morsel would be wasted; he added his own mountain ingredients and apportioned the meat with the same care as he used in its preparation. "Drink the soup," he said, "it will do you more good than tea." The doctor took his share that night, the first nourishment since his accident. There was more cheerful talk that night than any of the last five nights, as we prepared to make an early start next morning.

Nimrod had been busy the previous evening preparing some kind of contraption that, he said, he would use the next morning on his moose hunt. He was humming a little song as he prepared to leave. I could see the contraption was to be a foot strap to take some of the weight off his foot. I rigged up a back strap for him to carry his gun and leave his hands free. "You know," said Brown, "that little beggar might just do what he says, kill a big moose, and he still can sing while the rest of us hate to talk; it takes too much energy."

We put the doctor on the quietest horse we had and started for Nimrod's promised land of the moose. I was somewhat doubtful that such could be possible in an area barren of game prospects. However, he took the lead and we soon came to a well marked pack trail which took a northerly direction, and after travelling about eight or nine miles, Nimrod mentioned that we had reached the place to stop. We quickly stripped the animals of their gear, while the Stony made ready for the hunt. My companions lay down and were asleep almost at once. I helped our hunter get into his foot sling and gun carrier, slightly irritated at the monotonous little humming song of his. I watched him, curious to see how he managed that foot. Every time he put the lame foot forward, he pulled on the knee strap, giving him a kind of rolling motion. It worked, and he was still singing in a low tone hardly noticeable fifty yards away. Walking must have been painful, for his ankle was still black and swollen, yet he was cheerful and as determined as ever.

About four o'clock in the afternoon we heard a shot, then another.

"Nimrod has shot a moose," I yelled. "Come on, let's go and find him."

"Go ahead," said the doctor. "If he has had any luck, we can move the camp later."

It was tough going through the heavy brush and timber as we tried to go straight towards where we thought the sound came from. It sounded close but it was more than a mile before we got there. Brown followed close behind and when we saw our hunter, we both yelled together.

"What did you get, did you kill anything?"

"Moose, of course, moose," pointing with his pipe at the same time to where a big moose lay, close to the salt lick.

Smiling happily between puffs, he explained how he had nearly lost the moose when his foot sling had caught a stick and almost threw him into a pile of dry brush. The noise would have scared the moose, and it would have been out of sight before he could have gotten a shot. He had to wait a long time before the moose quieted down and he could approach to gun range.

We were proud of him, the smallest but the most courageous of us all. Brown walked up to him where he was sitting on a rock and said, "From now on, Nimrod, you're my brother. If my name was White instead of Brown, I'd give you my name, for I think you are the whitest friend any man could have."

When I interpreted Brown's long speech, Nimrod laughed and said, "I would rather be Red than White; it is closer to your colour than White, and tell him I am proud to be his friend, for he is more like my people than his own." Brown was a dark, swarthy man, with black hair and bristling black eyebrows. Brown got a big laugh out of my interpretation and shook the Stony's hand again.

A Sportsman in the Rocky Mountains
The Earl of Southesk

In the late summer of 1859, the Earl of Southesk and his hunting party of fur trade employees entered the front ranges of the Rockies, south of Jasper House, where they spent several days hunting sheep and other game on the headwaters of the Medicine Tent and Cairn (North) rivers.

September 6th. — Having determined to move the camp to another valley, I made a rough sketch of the opposite mountains as a remembrance of the scene. This finished, I marked my name on a fir-tree, a matter easily accomplished by blazing off part of the bark, and drawing the letters on the exposed surface with the black end of a half-burnt stick. The resin dries soon afterwards, and forms a sort of varnish which preserves the inscription for years.

The place we are leaving is known as the "Height of Land," being just where the waters divide, — the Athabasca head-stream rising in the snows of a great mountain (which stands towards the left in my sketch), and flowing northwards, while the the North River (I have heard no other name for it) flows southwards, to the north branch of the Saskatchewan, from a point not far distant. This country is very little known. The Iroquois, the Assiniboines, and others, hunt as far as the small lake near which we camped on the 2d, but strangely enough, they do not traverse the few miles farther, which would bring them from where game is scarce and wild, to where it abounds and is easy of approach. Perhaps superstitious reasons may keep them away, as the name "Medicine Tent River" indicates magic and mystery.

I am the first European who has visited this valley, and if I might have the geographical honour of giving my name to some spot of earth, I should choose the mountain near which the two rivers rise. . . .

The view from the Earl of Southesk's camp in the Medicine-tent River Valley, 1859. Archives of the Canadian Rockies

After my name had been marked on the fir-tree, we moved the camp a few miles, passing down into the neighbouring valley of the North River. Antoine and I rode forward together, but stopping for a while at the turn of the hill, we heard the rest of the party approaching, and waited for their arrival. As my men came into view, dashing up at a brisk pace, or galloping here and there to drive in the straggling horses, I was greatly struck with their picturesque appearance; having, indeed, hardly seen them on the march together since we left Edmonton, for the thick woods and narrow winding tracks keep a large party always in detachments.

All of them carried guns, all, except three, were dressed in fringed leather hunting-shirts, — of every colour, from the yellow of newness, and the white of new-washedness, to the blood-stained brown of extreme antiquity, as displayed in Antoine's venerable garment. M'Kay, powerful in form and strong of muscle, broad-chested, dark, and heavily bearded, with a wide-brimmed black hat and unfringed buff coat, and bestriding a large brown horse, resembled some Spanish cavalier of old; while Matheson, mounted on an active little dun pony, — with a blue Saskatchewan cap, gay with bright ribbons, over his long fair hair, and broad belts of scarlet cloth across his chest, — tall, straight, and merry, — was the image of a gallant young troubadour, riding in smart undress to the tournament.

M'Beath, lengthy of stature, dark, moustached and bearded, grave and calm, with a military belt and a rifleman's sword, looked like an ex-Life Guardsman, half in uniform; and this martial resemblance was heightened by the red blanket that served as his saddle-cloth, and contrasted richly with the coal-black horse that carried him. Kline, wiry and active, riding Lane — that fine old white mountain-horse, which few but he could capture when loose on the plains, — made a gay and cheerful show; his broad-brimmed white hat, with its wavy blue-ribbon streamers, perched upon long curly black hair, and shading a clever, well-bearded face; his chest surmounted by belts of silver and red brocade.

Next came Munroe, — tall, strongly yet lightly framed, wearing a short canvas hunting-shirt belted round the waist with leather, and cross-belted with much-embroidered cloth of black; then Short, formed like a Greek statue, strong and very active, but of no great height, wearing a handsome pouch of leather ornamented with blue and white beads; — hardy fellows both, of showy dashing air, ready to do aught that might become a man.

Duncan, dressed in strong sand-grey shooting-suit and flannel shirt, wearing a stout wide-awake hat, and carrying a double gun in its plain waterproof cover, looked every inch the worthy Scotsman that he is. Near him rode Toma, the brave Iroquois canoe-man, leather-shirted, darkly and simply dressed, slow in the movement of his massive limbs, with swarthy face, and small black eyes, grave in their expression though often twinkling with humour, — a most faithful and excellent fellow.

Then Lagrace, that original and amusing old man, in a purple cotton shirt, tight but very long and wrinkled trousers, a white blanket skull-cap enriched with peak and ears, and decorated with streamers of scarlet cloth, beneath a battered eagle-feather which probably once adorned some Indian horse's tail, — that keen-witted ancient traveller who did everything differently from other men, — led when they drove, woke when they slept, drank cans of strong tea at dead of night, walked out alone and slew queer animals with sticks and stones while all the rest were at their meals, — that quaint old jester who enlivened our halts, after the weariest marches on the dullest days, by all manner of strange devices, — scalp-dances round the kettle lid, Cree war-songs, sudden wrestling matches with Antoine (in which this old aggressor always got the worst), jokes in the most astonishingly broken English, — to whom or what shall he be likened, with his brown parchment skin, his keen aquiline nose, his piercing black eyes, long wild locks, and half-mockingly smiling, small and thin-lipped mouth? I know not — unless Mephistopheles have an American twin-brother . . .

As this gallant party topped the crest of a low hill fair in my view, ribbons streaming, guns swaying, whips flashing, gay colours sparkling in the sun, some approaching at a quick trot, others dashing after vagrant steeds, or urging the heavy-laden pack-horses, who jogged along like elephants with castles on their backs — all life, dash, rattle, and glitter, — they formed so bright a picture, so grandly back-grounded by the stately rocks, so gaily fore-grounded by the crisp green sward, that I could not refrain from attempting to describe it, though the ablest pen or pencil would fail to do justice to the scene.

We all halted together, and camped, and in the afternoon Antoine and I went out to the hills. Coming to a rocky ravine, we observed a herd of female sheep on the opposite side, and opened fire on them. The old hunter killed one ewe and two lambs, I killed two of the ewes and wounded another, and afterwards getting a long running chance at the wounded one, I knocked it over also.

After "arranging" the slain (to use Antoine's expression) we proceeded to the highest part of a steep narrow ridge, a spur of the principal range, and looking over the rocky wall that formed its upper edge, saw close by, just upon the other side, a small herd of rams, two of which had remarkably fine horns. The nearest of these I shot quite dead, the other struggled on severely wounded. Antoine ran after it to finish it off, but his flint-lock missed fire, and, before he was ready again, the fine old ram dropped lifeless, and rolled down the slope of the hill. The horns of this pair were very good indeed, larger even than those brought in by Munroe the day before but, as usual, somewhat worn and broken at the points.

Returning to our horses, which we had left below, we got home in excellent time. On our arrival, Short reported that he had come close upon a large grisly bear, in the valley below the ridge where I had been shooting the rams. It looked at him, and he at it, but neither cared to begin the fight, so each went his own way. At the time, Short's behaviour seemed to me rather over-cautious; with a good double-barrelled gun in his hand, I thought he ought not to have declined the combat. But, on reflection, I believe he acted rightly, having no sufficient inducement for such a hazardous venture. So fierce, strong, active, and tenacious of life is the grisly bear, that even for the best marksman, supported by trustworthy companions, it is the height of imprudence to risk a long shot at him, and a failure at close quarters leaves a solitary hunter small chance indeed of escape.

Talking about grislies, one day, with a good authority on the subject (I forget whom — it might have been James M'Kay), he informed me that if that animal perceives a man in an open plain or glade he will generally advance towards him, and when about a hundred yards distant will rear himself up on his haunches to reconnoitre, after which he will either move away, or continue his advance. In the latter case, he stops again when about thirty yards from the hunter, and again rears himself on end. The hunter, meanwhile, steadily waits, reserving his fire, and the grisly, having finished his inspection, again advances, until he is ten yards from his opponent, when for the third time he rises in all his gigantic height, prepared to hurl himself forth in the last terrible spring. Now is the hunter's moment: quick as thought his bullet passes into the chest of the bear, sped at that short range with such precision that it carries with it instantaneous death — woe to the hunter if it does not!

In the Rocky Mountains, though probably not north of the Bow River and its head-waters, there exists a savage and treacherous wild beast, more dangerous in some respects than even the grisly himself. This is the puma — or some feline animal closely resembling it in colour and general appearance — which, while nearly as fierce and tenacious of life as the grisly bear, greatly excels him in activity, besides possessing an advantage denied to him — the cat-like power of climbing the highest trees.

But it is not owing to these formidable qualities that the puma is an object of some dread, it is on account of its stealthy habits of nocturnal aggression. Marking out a small party of hunters or travellers, it will follow them secretly for days, and watch by their camp at night, till at last it discovers one of their number resting a little separate from his companions. Then, when all is dark and silent, the insidious puma glides in, and the sleeper knows but a short awakening when its fangs are buried in his throat.

One consolation is left to the survivors — if they kill the eater they may eat him in return; for the puma is considered the most delicately-flavoured animal in the Territories.

These details I gathered from my men, and I see no reason to doubt their truth, for, though such ferocious practices are not, to my knowledge, attributed to the puma of the Atlantic States, the jaguar of South America — a beast of kindred species — is written of as attacking sleepers in the very manner described. One of my party amused us exceedingly by a story concerning a certain expedition to which he had been lately attached: — how some of the people belonging to it had noticed a puma in a tree, and immediately saluted it with a volley; but how, instead of securing the victim, they had simultaneously taken to their heels at the moment of drawing trigger, and run so fast and far that they never felt inclined to go back to claim their trophy, — which they most shrewdly suspected might have claimed them, for, while the death of the enemy was doubtful, its indignation, if alive, was not.

The Last Monument
Charles Wilson

*In the summer of 1861, after more than three summers of tough travel
through the dense British Columbia bush, the British Boundary
Commission surveying the international boundary between the U.S. and
Canada reached the Rockies. The terrain offered an almost idyllic relief
from the drudgery of past mountain ranges. The final monument on the
crest of the Great Divide above Cameron Lake and present-day Waterton
National Park brought an end to one of the toughest surveying tasks ever
undertaken in North America.*

July 26th.   Just as we were starting in the morning for Haig's camp
we met Lyall & Bauerman on their way out to the plains, so I determined not to lose such a good opportunity & turned off for a couple
of days journey with them. Turning up to the left & following the
Indian hunting trail, after a scramble over fallen timber & up a very
steep ascent for about 3 miles we at last reached the summit of the
mountains & had a capital view of the pass & surrounding mountains. To the west we could see right up the pass through the Galton
mountains & towards the east we could see the faint outline of the
plains through the mouth of the rocky gorge that led to them. They
are well called Rocky mountains, the range as far as we saw them
being rugged peaks of bare rock of all shapes & sizes & many of them
seemingly inaccessible; I went up to the top of one of the peaks about
8200 ft high with some of our party & we had a glorious view, a
perfect sea of peaks all around us & running off to the North & South,
whilst on the west we looked down into the valley of the Flathead,
small lakes of the most brilliant blue, with their borders of bright
green herbage lay scattered in all directions in the hollows, hundreds
of feet beneath us & (where it could still cling) some patches of snow
& small glaciers heightened the beauty of the scene; so rugged &
precipitous are the mountains that at this great altitude no snow
remains except in hollows & on some benches, which have a tolerably
level surface, in the spring the snow must all come off at once or
nearly so; the effects of the avalanches appears to be tremendous &
the rocky glens are in some places piled high up with the débris of
tree & rock; after spending some time on the top of the ridge, we
commenced to descend on the other side & after about 10 miles

camped on the banks of the Saskatchewan. The descent on the eastern side was much more gradual than on the western & the trees rapidly disappeared & what there were of them were very stunted & badly grown, very different from the magnificent fellows we have been accustomed to see in the west. At our camp we had quite got out of the trees & were in a fine grassy valley & here too we came upon the first traces of buffalo in the shape of some old skulls & bones lying bleaching in the sun; the eastern end of the pass is far finer than the western, the peaks being more rugged & rising more abruptly, towering right overhead. We spent the evening in a rather excited state of mind, thinking of the morrow when we were to reach the far famed plains & hoping that we might stumble upon some old buffalo bull who had withdrawn from the herd, for the latter we knew that the Indians had driven far out on to the plains where we had no time to follow them. During the day we crossed the great watershed of America, for in the morning we had quenched our thirst with the waters of the Columbia & the Pacific & were now robbing Hudson's bay of a mite of the waters which the Saskatchewan after its long wanderings pours into it. We used to think we had capital fishing in the Cascade Mountains, but this year has quite beaten anything we have seen before, the streams are literally alive with the most delicious trout of all weights, from about 4 oz to $2^1/_2$ lbs & they are the most ravenous fish I ever met with, the greatest catch was made by Dr Lyall, (our surgeon), who caught 9 dozen in about 4 hours; of course our fishing is done in a very rough way, as we cannot carry about rods, reels & all the etceteras of a fisherman, a young larch tree or a piece of willow for a rod, some 15 or 20 feet of line & a roughly tied fly of grouse feathers are our weapons & though rough are very effectual.

July 27$^{th.}$ On getting up in the morning at about 5, we had a beautiful sight, the deep gorge we were in being still in the dark shade of night, with the moon shining gloriously overhead, whilst the high peaks around us were tipped with the bright gold of the rising sun. For about 6 miles we kept down the valley which was open & grassy though closed in on either side by high mountains, when, taking a sharp turn to the left we suddenly came out on the plains; rolling prairie as far as the eye could reach, without a tree, save where a bright belt of green marked the course of the Waterton river & the green border round the Waterton or chief mountain lake, which lay sparkling at the foot of the lofty mountains on our right. We followed the Waterton river down for some distance, camped on its bank & then went out to see if we could find anything, but though we saw numerous signs of buffalo that had been here in the spring & the ground was littered with skulls, bones & a few remnants that the Indians & wolves had left, we were not fortunate enough to get a sight of a living animal, indeed the only living things we saw, were wolves & a few deer, however I was glad to have had even such a peep at the plains & the scenery was I think finer than any we had yet come across, the mountains being bare of trees, rugged & rising in one long unbroken line abruptly from the plain.

*July 28*th. As I had no more spare time, I left Lyall & Bauerman to continue their journey & returned up the pass & we camped for the night on a small prairie near the head of the eastern side of the pass, at a good height, for on awaking in the morning we found that there had been a sharp frost, covering our buffalo robes & hair with sparkling crystals.

*July 29*th. We again crossed over the summit, where there was a gale of wind blowing nearly strong enough to take the hair off one's head & passing our camp of the 25th we followed the Kishenehu up for another 4 miles, where we were again lucky enough to come upon Anderson with whom we camped. During the latter part of our journey we passed through a large fire which was burning away at a great rate & rapidly spreading up the mountain side.

*July 30*th. A ride of about 8 miles brought us to Haig's camp & the end of the boundary which is to be marked at present. The valley through which we travelled was covered with one immense network of fallen timber, the effect of the tremendous gales which are always blowing up here, through all of which a trail had to be cut before the station could be reached. Up this valley there is a much better pass to the plains than the one we had gone by, there being hardly any ascent on either side but it is so much choked up with piles of fallen timber & driftwood, that it would require a great deal of labour to cut a trail through it, there would be no difficulty however in bringing a railroad through. Haig's camp we found close to a small lake, from which the Kishenehu rises & in a recess formed by a steep rocky ridge.

*July 31*st. Three of us started off to pay our devoirs to the final monument on the boundary, after a short scramble we got on to the summit or divide, some distance north of the line, the divide being at that point comparatively low & covered with grass, here we stirred up a Ptarmigan & her chicks, the mother was most ruthlessly slaughtered with a big stone & I became the possessor of the chicks, poor things their end soon followed their mother's! for after carrying them about the whole day & bringing them safely into camp, (with the intention of rearing them,) while my back was turned, their box was broken into by some lean hungry hound who made very short work of my pets. Leaving the grassy ridge, we commenced a fresh ascent & after a good climb over bare rock where hands & feet were well employed, a steady eye needed & an occasional halt to watch the course of a stone sent rolling by the foot into a little lake some 1500 ft below us, we stood upon the narrow shoulder beside the cairn of stones which marked the end of our labours & here we found tokens of previous visitors in the shape of sundry Anglo Saxon names engraved on the stones, to which truly English record we refrained from adding ours. The view from this point was very fine, precipices & peaks, glaciers & rocks all massed together in such a glorious way, that I cannot attempt to describe it. Fancy our delight at finding on a grassy spot, close to a huge bank of snow, real "London Pride" & the dear old "Forget-me-not" which carried our thoughts far away from the wild mountains to many a pleasant spring day of "Auld lang syne" in "merrie England", I send you some which I gathered right on the summit. After this we ascended a curious pyramidal peak over 8000 ft high which concluded our days work & is the highest altitude I have been at. We returned to camp by an easier but much longer route than the one by which we had ascended, being principally down a steep grassy slope too slippery for foot hold, so we sat down, cast off our moorings & made all sail for the bottom which we reached in safety though much to the detriment of our unmentionables.

The Rock Whistler
John Keast Lord

While the British Boundary Commission surveyors made their way up to the last monument on the Great Divide in 1861, naturalists assigned to the commission roamed the surrounding peaks observing and collecting the resident flora and fauna.

THE HOARY MARMOT (*Arctomys okanaganus*), or, as styled by the fur-traders, the "Rock Whistler," lives on the very summit of the Rocky Mountains.

The Rock Whistler

If there is a spot on the face of the globe more dismal, solitary, inhospitable, and uninviting than another, that spot is where this most accomplished siffleur resides; and it is not by any means a matter to be wondered at, that so very little is to be found, in works on Natural History, relating to this little anchorite's habits.

My purpose being to climb the craggy ascent that led up to the watershed — not by any means a dangerous thing to do; it was simply leg-aching, tiresome, scrambling work. The grass being dry, it polished the soles of my mocassins, until they became like burnished metal; so that progression, up the long green slopes, was much the same as it would have been up an ice-slant, with skates on. I got up at last, and feeling somewhat fagged, seated myself on a flat rock, unslung my gun, lighted my pipe, and had a good look at everything round about me.

The sun had crept steadily up unto the clear sky, unflecked by a single cloud; the mists, that in the early morning hung about the ravines, and partially veiled the peaks and angles of the vast piles of rocks, had vanished, revealing them in all their immensity. Below me was a lake, smooth as a mirror, but the dark-green cold look of the water hinted at unfathomable depth. Tiny rivulets, fed by the snow, wound their way, like threads of silver, between the rocks and through the grass, to reach the lake.

I was not so much impressed with the beauty of the landscape, as awed by its substantial magnificence. Few living things were to be seen save a group of ptarmigan, sunning themselves on a ledge of rocks, a couple of mountain-goats browsing by the lake, and a few grey-crowned linnets, — birds seldom seen but at great altitudes. There were also the recent traces of a grizzly, or black bear, that had been munching down the wild angelica. A solemn stillness intensified the slightest sound to a supernatural loudness — even a loosened stone rattling down the hillside made me start; there was no buzz and hum of busy insects, or chirp of birds, or splash of torrents, to break the silence; the very wind seemed afraid to moan: it was deathlike silence to the very letter.

As I smoked away, silent as all about me, suddenly a sharp clear whistle, that awoke the echoes far and near, thoroughly roused me, and sent all other thoughts to the rout. As I could see nothing, I deemed it expedient to remain quiet. Cocking my rifle, I lay on the grass, and waited patiently for a repetition of the performance. I had not long to tax my patience: again came the same sound, then others joined in the refrain, until the place, instead of being steeped in silence, resembled the gallery of a theatre on boxing-night.

I very soon spied one of the performers, seated on the top of a large rock; its position was that of a dog when begging. With his forefeet he was busy cleaning his whiskers, smoothing his fur, and clearly going in for a somewhat elaborate toilet: perhaps he was going a wooing, or to a morning concert, or for a constitutional, or a lounge on the "Marmot's mile;" but whatever his intentions were, I regret to say they were frustrated. Solely in the cause of science I had to stop him; resting my rifle on a flat rock, as I lay on the ground, I fired, and the sharp crack, as it rang amid the rocks, was the whistler's death-knell.

Rapidly reloading, I scampered off to secure my prize. I am afraid there was not much pity felt — delight at getting a new animal was uppermost. Smoothing his fur, I plugged the shot-holes, examined him closely, measured him; admired his handsome shape, bright-grey coat, and brushy tail; investigated his teeth and claws, walked back, and had a look at him from a distance; then set to work, and skinned him. You can see him also, if you like to visit the British Museum, where this very victim is "set up," and placed amidst the Marmots; his name, together with that of his destroyer, black-lettered on the board to which he is affixed. At the sound of the rifle, every one of his companions took sensation-headers into their holes, and did not come out again during my stay on this occasion.

Across the Rockies with Mr. O'B.
Viscount Milton and W. B. Cheadle

By the 1860s travel across the Athabasca Pass had declined and a new route over the Rockies via Yellowhead Pass started receiving greater use. In 1862 over one hundred emigrants to the Cariboo gold fields crossed the pass, and in 1863 two British adventurers, Viscount Milton and W. B. Cheadle, followed. They were accompanied by a Métis guide (The Assiniboine), his wife and son, and a hitchhiker they had acquired at Fort Edmonton — an itinerant Irishman named Felix O'Byrne (Mr. O'B.).

We arrived opposite Jasper House on the 29th of June. The Fort was evidently without inhabitants, but as the trail appeared to lead there only, we purposed to cross the river at this point, and set to work to cut timber for a raft. On the 30th we laboured hard with our two small axes, felling the dry pine-trees, while Mr. O'B. devoted himself to the study of Paley, over a pipe. It was late in the afternoon before sufficient timber was cut down, and it had then to be carried several hundred yards to the river's edge. Mr. O'B. was required to assist in this, but he had disappeared. We made diligent search for him, and at last found him, squatted behind a bush, still enjoying his book and pipe. We apologised for interrupting his studies, and informed him that all hands were now required in order to get the wood down to the river's edge as quickly as possible, so as to be able to cross before dark. Mr. O'B. assured us that he had been looking forward with eager impatience for an opportunity of giving his assistance, but got up and followed us with evident reluctance, and impressed upon us that his weak and delicate frame was quite unfit for heavy work. A few of the largest trunks were carried with difficulty by the united strength of our whole party, and we were then detailed into parties of two, for the transport of the rest. Milton paired off with O'B., Cheadle with The Assiniboine, and the woman with the boy, for the lesser trees. Mr. O'B. shouldered, with a sigh, the smaller end of the log, his fellow-labourer the other, and they proceeded slowly towards the shore. After the first few steps O'B. began to utter the most awful groans, and cried out, continually, "Oh, dear! Oh, dear! this is most painful — it's cutting my shoulder in two — not so fast, my lord. Gently, gently. Steady, my lord, steady; I *must* stop. I'm carrying all the weight myself. I shall drop with exhaustion directly — *triste lignum te caducum.*" And then, with a loud "Oh!" and no further warning, he let his end of the tree down with a run, jarring his unhappy partner most dreadfully. A repetition of this scene occurred on each journey, to the great amusement of every one but the unfortunate sufferer by the schoolmaster's vagaries. At last, hurt repeatedly by the sudden dropping of the other end of the load, Milton dispensed with Mr. O'B.'s assistance, and dragged the trunk alone. The Assiniboine coming up at the moment, indignantly vituperated Mr. O'B., and, shouldering the log, carried it off with ease. The sun was setting when this portion of our task was over, and we decided to defer crossing until the morning. As we were engaged discussing Mr. O'B.'s delinquencies, and commenting rather severely upon his pusillanimity, he overheard us, and came up, with the imperturbable confidence which he always displayed in all social relations, remarking it was all very well for Cheadle, who had "shoulders like the Durham ox, to treat gigantic exertion of this kind so lightly, but I assure you it would very soon kill a man of my delicate constitution." Cheadle remarked that Milton was of slighter build than himself, and he did his share without complaint. "Ah! yes," replied Mr. O'B., "he is fired with emulation. I have been lost in admiration of his youthful ardour all the day! *Optat ephippia bos* — but you see I am older, and obliged to be cautious; look how I have suffered by my exertions to-day!" — showing us a small scratch on his hand. We exhibited our palms, raw with blisters, which caused him to turn the conversation by dilating on his favourite topic — the hardships of the fearful journey we were making.

Milton and the boy had volunteered to swim across with horses, in order to carry ropes to the other side with which to guide the raft — a somewhat hazardous adventure, as the river was broad, and the stream tremendously rapid; but before our preparations were completed on the following morning, a half-breed made his appearance in our camp — a welcome sight after our solitary journey of three weeks. He informed us that he was one of Mr. Macaulay's party who were out hunting. The party had divided at McLeod River, and were to meet at the Fort that day. He advised us to cross the river some miles higher up, beyond the lake, where the stream was more tranquil, and thereby avoid the River Maligne on the other side, which it was very hazardous to attempt to ford at this season.

We accordingly raised camp, and proceeded, under his guidance, along the bank of the river for four or five miles. On the way we forded several streams, or more probably mouths of one river, flowing into the Athabasca from the south, very swollen and rapid. We crossed them on horseback without much difficulty, by carefully following our guide; but Mr. O'B., having taken a rooted dislike to equitation, since his horse lay down with him when ascending the mountain, perversely resolved to wade across. We pulled up on the further side and watched him, as he followed, cautiously and fearfully, steadying himself by the stout stick which he invariably carried. He went on with great success until he gained the middle of the stream, when he suddenly plunged into a hole, where the water was nearly up to his arm-pits. He cried out wildly, "I'm drowning! Save me! save me!" then, losing his presence of mind, applied, in his confusion, the saying of his favourite poet, "*In medio tutissimus ibis,*" and struggled into deeper water still, instead of turning back to the shallow part. He was in imminent danger of being carried off, and

71

Milton dashed in to the rescue, and brought him out, clinging to his stirrup. He was dreadfully frightened, but gradually recovered composure when assured we had no more rivers to ford for the present.

In a short time we reached a sandy plain, richly clothed with flowers, and camped close to a clear shallow lake, communicating by a narrow outlet with the upper Athabasca Lake. Here we decided to remain until Mr. Macaulay arrived. On scanning the heights beyond the lake with a glass, we saw a large flock of bighorns on the loftiest crags, and The Assiniboine and his son went out to hunt, but returned unsuccessful, having been so enveloped in the mountain mists that they found it impossible to proceed. . . .

On the 3rd of July Mr. Macaulay arrived, and set up his tent close to our lodge. His hunt had not been a very successful one, and as he had only a few days' supply of bighorn mutton, would be compelled to set out again almost immediately. He was therefore quite unable to replenish our stock, but invited us to sup on some delicious trout which he had caught in one of the mountain lakes the day before. He informed us that a winter rarely passed now without a great scarcity of provisions at Jasper House, and their being driven to horse-flesh as a last resource. From him we also heard another anecdote of our old enemy, the wolverine. When returning to the Fort from a hunting expedition at the beginning of the previous winter, Mr. Macaulay was surprised to find that all the windows of the building, which are of parchment, were gone. He fancied that some one had broken in to rob the place. On entering he searched about, yet found nothing; but hearing a noise in the room overhead, he went up and there discovered a wolverine, which was chased and killed. He had lived on the parchment windows in default of more usual food, and had been so satisfied with his diet, that his natural curiosity had slept, and strangely enough, he had not investigated the packages of goods which lay about.

We learnt from Mr. Macaulay that the three miners, of whom we had heard at Edmonton as having gone to prospect the sources of the North Saskatchewan, and whose notice we had seen on the tree when we first struck the Athabasca, had already passed on their way across the mountains to Cariboo. At Mr. Macaulay's suggestion, we engaged an old Iroquois half-breed to accompany us as far as Tête Jaune Cache. As we had no money, he was to receive one of our pack-horses in payment. We tried to persuade him to go forward to the end; but he did not know anything of the country beyond the Cache and would not venture further.

At this point Mr. O'B.'s provisions came to an end. His 40 lbs. of pemmican, which he was very positive would last him until the end of the journey, had rapidly disappeared before his vigorous appetite. Mr. Macaulay kindly furnished him with a little tea and tobacco, and we supplied the necessary pemmican, with many exhortations to him to use it carefully, for a prospect of starvation was discernible even now.

On the 4th of July, we started again, under the guidance of the Iroquois, and were accompanied by Mr. Macaulay and two of his men to the point where we were to cross the Athabasca. The path lay through water, often up to the horses' girths, or along the steep sides of the narrowing valley, and it was already dusk when we reached our destination. We camped for the night by the river's edge, at a place where was plenty of dry timber, some of which had been already cut down for a raft by the Canadian emigrants. On one of the trees the names of those of whom we had heard from Mr. Macaulay as being just before us, were inscribed, and a statement that they crossed on the 16th June, or nearly three weeks before.

In the morning all set to work, cutting and carrying timber, Mr. Macaulay working with the rest; but Mr. O'B., as before, could not be found. As the last log was carried down to the water, he suddenly came up with — "Oh! dear, *can* I be of any use, my lord? — can I help you, Doctor?" We expressed our sorrow that he was too late, but The Assiniboine was very angry, and vowed he should not come on board the raft. It required the exercise of all our authority to overrule his determination, and we saw in this occurrence signs pregnant of future trouble. By noon the raft was ready, and we drove our horses into the stream. When we had seen them safely across, we rewarded our half-breed friends by dividing the last remains of our rum amongst them — a treat they appreciated above everything — and bidding a hearty good-bye to Mr. Macaulay and the rest, pushed off on our adventure. The stream at this place was deep, wide, and tranquil, and we crossed without difficulty or mishap. Before we were fairly over we found that we had left one of our two remaining axes behind; but we did not turn back to regain it, since it was no light matter to navigate so large a raft. Had we known how sorely we should need this axe afterwards, we should not have spared any trouble to obtain it.

We landed on a sparsely timbered flat, where the trees had all been destroyed by fire, packed the horses, and travelled a few miles before sundown. By noon on the following day, and still following the Athabasca, we reached a beautiful little prairie, surrounded by fine hills green almost to their summits, and overtopped by lofty snow-clad peaks. One of these, which has received the name of the Priest's Rock, was of curious shape, its apex resembling the top of a pyramid, and covered with snow. The prairie was richly carpeted with flowers, and a rugged excrescence upon it marked the site of the old Rocky Mountain Fort, Henry's House.

The track, leaving the valley of the Athabasca at this point, turned towards the north-west, and entered a narrow rocky ravine, the valley of the river Myette. The stream was not more than thirty yards in width, but deep and rapid, and its bed beset with great rocks and boulders. The path was obstructed by large stones and fallen timber, lying so thickly that our two men were kept hard at work all the afternoon, and the horses progressed only by a succession of jumps. We made but a short distance with great labour, and camped for the night on the banks of the stream.

For the whole of the next morning the road presented the same difficulties, and our advance was as slow as on the preceding day. At mid-day we reached the place where we were to cross the river, and pulled up to make a raft. After crossing by this means, we toiled on through a ravine so narrow, and where the mountains came down so close to the water's edge, that, in order to pass them we were compelled to traverse the stream no less than six times more before evening. In each of these cases we crossed on horseback, the river now being a succession of rapids, not more than four or five feet deep. These passages of the river were difficult, and many of them dangerous, for the water was very high, and the current extremely powerful.

At the last fording-place, the waters rushed down a swift descent in a foaming cataract, raging and boiling so fiercely round great rocks which studded the channel, that we hesitated before we ventured to urge our horses forward. But the Iroquois led the way, and crossed safely, although his horse staggered about and hardly held his own. We then drove the pack-horses before us, and plunged in. The water streamed over our horses' shoulders, as they struggled against the current, and slipped amongst the smooth boulders, tumbling about and regaining their footing in the most wonderful manner. Mr. O'B. was compelled to mount his steed again for this occasion, and, judging from the despairing expression of his countenance, he did so with little hope of reaching the other side in safety. He was exhorted carefully to follow the line taken by the guide, and Milton and the woman rode on either side of him. Clutching the mane with both hands, he did not attempt to guide his horse, but employed all his powers in sticking to the saddle, and exhorting his companions, "Steady, my lord, please, or I shall be swept off. *Do* speak to Mrs. Assiniboine, my lord; she's leading us to destruction; what a reckless woman! *'varium et mutabile semper femina!'* Mrs. Assiniboine! — Mrs. *Assiniboine!* oh, dear! oh, dear! what an awful journey! I'm going! I'm going! Narrow escape that, my lord! very narrow escape, indeed, Doctor. We can't expect to be so lucky every time, you know." And the moment he gained the shore, he scrambled off and left his horse to its own devices.

Many of the pack-horses were carried off far down the stream, and we fully expected some of them would be lost, but they eventually all struggled ashore. The only damage we suffered was the wetting of the flour and pemmican, but by immediate care the injury was in great measure repaired. . . .

On the 10th we struck the Fraser River, sweeping round from the south-west through a narrow gorge, to expand some miles lower down into Moose Lake. Our route now lay along the north bank of the Fraser, and the travelling was exceedingly difficult and harassing. The river had overflowed its banks up to the almost perpendicular sides of the straitened valley in which it is confined. The track was completely under water up to the horses' girths, and we spent the greater part of the day in wading and the rest in toiling through swamps beset with fallen timber. It was impossible to stop, for there was neither dry place in which to camp nor pasture for the horses, and we therefore travelled on until dark, very thankful to find a place of rest at last. All agreed that it was the hardest day we had yet gone through, and Mr. O'B. had two of his hair-breadth escapes, which formed a text for him to discourse about the perils and sufferings which he encountered "on this most extraordinary journey." Since his successful crossing of the Myette, he had been somewhat more reconciled to horseback, and on this day mounted his steed rather than wade on foot.

Soon after we set out, he dropped behind the rest of the cavalcade, and before long, Cheadle, who was driving some of the hindmost horses, was arrested by a most tremendous bawling for help from the rear. He ran back in haste, and found Mr. O'B., in rather muddy condition, and with very disconsolate air, leading his horse by the bridle. It appeared the horse had shied and pitched him off amongst the logs and *débris* around, and he imagined himself severely hurt. But no important injury could be found, and, by dint of great persuasion, and active assistance, Cheadle induced him to re-mount, and exhorted him to keep close up to the rest. But he was too much afraid of his horse to urge him on by any but the most gentle, verbal persuasion, and tender pattings on the neck. He was soon left behind again, and the ears of the party saluted by another succession of piteous cries from the rear. Cheadle again went back to his assistance, in very unamiable mood, but was unable to resist a burst of laughter when he came upon the unfortunate Mr. O'B. He was driving his horse before him, with the saddle under its belly, and the bridle trailing on the ground. He was covered with mud, his long visage scratched and bleeding, and his clerical coat, split asunder to the neck, streamed from his shoulders in separate halves. "Very nearly killed, Doctor, this time. I thought it was all over. *'Semel est calcanda via lethi,'* you know. My horse fell and rolled on to me, tearing my coat, as you see. I've had a most providential escape." He could not be persuaded to mount again, and had a wearisome time with his horse, which, if he offered to lead it, hung back and refused to budge, and when he drove it before him, persisted in going the wrong way.

But if this 10th of July was a hard and harassing day, the 11th was still worse. In the first place, we were delayed a long time in starting, for Bucephalus was not to be found. He was, at length, discovered by The Assiniboine on the other side the Fraser, and the man was obliged to strip and swim the ice-cold river to fetch him back. Soon after we started, we came to Moose River, which was somewhat difficult to ford, for the water was high and rapid, pouring over the horses' shoulders in the deepest part. Mr. O'B. lost nerve and steered badly, his horse lost its footing, and nearly took a voyage into the Fraser; the rider, however, gripped mane and saddle firmly, and both got ashore together, adding another "hair's-breadth escape" to Mr. O'B.'s list. . . .

A few hours' travelling in the morning of the 14th brought us to the Grand Fork of the Fraser, where an important branch from the north or north-east flows by five separate mouths into the main body of the Fraser, which we had been following thus far. Here we pulled up, in order to search carefully for safe fords by which to cross these numerous swollen streams. This Grand Fork of the Fraser is the original Tête Jaune Cache, so called from being the spot chosen by an Iroquois trapper, known by the *sobriquet* of the Tête Jaune, or "Yellow Head," to hide the furs he obtained on the western side. The situation is grand and striking beyond description. At the bottom of a narrow rocky gorge, whose sides were clothed with dark pines, or, higher still, with light green shrubs, the boiling, impetuous Fraser dashed along. On every side the snowy heads of mighty hills crowded round, whilst, immediately behind us, a giant among giants, and immeasurably supreme, rose Robson's Peak. This magnificent mountain is of conical form, glacier-clothed, and rugged. When we first caught sight of it, a shroud of mist partially enveloped the summit, but this presently rolled away, and we saw its upper portion dimmed by a necklace of light feathery clouds, beyond which its pointed apex of ice, glittering in the morning sun, shot up far into the blue heaven above, to a height of probably 10,000 or 15,000 feet. It was a glorious sight, and one which the Shushwaps of The Cache assured us had rarely been seen by human eyes, the summit being generally hidden by clouds. After leaving the old Cache, we entered upon fresh difficulties — deep streams to cross, timber to jump every ten yards, and the whole valley flooded. The horse which carried our flour took to swimming about in deep water, and one packed with pemmican wandered into the Fraser, and was borne down the stream for some distance. However, he managed to find foothold at last under the bank, and we were able to haul him out with ropes.

The next day, the 15th of July, still found us struggling through floods, logs, and *débris*, and was signalised by the occurrence of an irremediable misfortune. In order to prevent the possible loss or damage of provisions by the horses disporting themselves in deep water, we led those which carried flour and pemmican. Two of the others, however, who were running loose — a horse most aptly named Gisquakarn, or "The Fool," and Bucephalus — strayed over the true river-bank into the stream, and were swept off in a moment. They soon disappeared from our view, and the Iroquois and boy went in pursuit, whilst we followed with the rest of the horses. About a mile down stream we caught sight of the animals, standing in a shallow in the middle of the stream, and as we came just at this time to one of the rare natural gardens of the mountains, brilliant with flowers and rich in strawberries, we camped in the open ground. We were in full view of the two animals in the river, and hoped they would be tempted to join their companions on shore. Bucephalus began to neigh, and eventually commenced swimming towards us; but Gisquakarn, "The Fool," instead of following in the right direction, steered down mid-stream, and Bucephalus, after a moment's hesitation, turned away and followed him into the fiercest strength of

77

The Assiniboine rescuing the packhorse Bucephalus from the waters of the Fraser River during the crossing of the Rockies by Viscount Milton and W. B. Cheadle in 1863. Glenbow Archives

the irresistible flood. Away both went, far outstripping our utmost speed in pursuit, their packs only being visible in the distance, bobbing about like corks in the rolling waters.

The Assiniboine led the chase, and soon left all the rest of us far behind, for he had a wonderful facility in getting over obstructions, and the way in which he vanished amidst the closely-set trunks, and past the barriers of fallen timber, was marvellous. He did not rush and tear along, but glided out of sight, apparently unhindered by the obstacles which opposed our progress. We struggled on far in the rear, and occasionally caught a glimpse of the horses like specks in the distance, still borne down the middle of the torrent. About two miles below, another shallow gave them resting ground for a moment, and enabled The Assiniboine to come up. The current was so strong, however, that they were soon swept off again; but Bucephalus, observing The Assiniboine, attempted to reach the shore. The place was a fearful rapid, where the water poured madly in rolling billows over immense boulders. As the horse neared the land for an instant in passing, The Assiniboine leaped in, threw his arms round the animal's neck, who neighed gratefully when he saw his deliverer come to the rescue, and the two, mutually supporting each other, eventually gained the shore. The escape of The Assiniboine seemed marvellous, and we did not fail amply to reward him for the intrepidity he had displayed. Few men would have dared to plunge into such a boiling torrent, and as we looked at the huge rolling waves after it was over, we could hardly believe it possible that the thing had in reality occurred.

Having unpacked Bucephalus, and spread all the soaked baggage out to dry in the sun, we started forward again to learn the fate of the other horse Gisquakarn, who had obstinately pursued the middle course — in this case certainly not the safest. After another mile's run, we descried him under the opposite bank, where it was too abrupt to climb, his head buried in the bushes which fringed the shore, and hardly able to stand against the rush of water. It seemed madness to attempt to cross the stream on a raft in its present swollen state, and we were reluctantly compelled to abandon him to his fate for the present. The Iroquois started immediately for Tête Jaune Cache, which he calculated could not be more than seven or eight miles distant, in order to obtain the assistance of the Shushwaps there, who possessed canoes in which the river might be crossed. The rest of us returned to camp with our injured property, and employed ourselves in investigating the extent of our losses. Early the next morning the Iroquois returned with two young Shushwaps, who crossed the river, and proceeded to the place where the horse had been last seen. From the marks on the bank it was evident that the animal had made frantic but futile endeavours to climb the bank, but had at last rolled back and been carried off, nor did we ever find any further traces of him.

This misfortune was no light one. We had now neither tea, salt, nor tobacco, for our whole store of these luxuries had been carried by the horse which was lost. All our clothes, matches, and ammunition were gone, except what we carried on our persons at the time. All our papers, letters of credit, and valuables, Milton's buffalo robe and blanket, Cheadle's collection of plants, the instruments and watches, had set out on their voyage towards the sea. But there was much reason for congratulation as well as lamentation. No actual necessaries of life had gone; we had still the pemmican and flour. The journals, too, without which the present valuable history could never have been published, were saved with Bucephalus.

Mr. O'B. lost his letters of introduction, his tin kettle, and a pair of spectacles; but his Paley, carefully carried in his breast-pocket, still remained to him. The loss of the spectacles, however, obliged him to pursue his studies under great disadvantages, for he was now reduced to reading with one eye only, for the only pair he had left boasted of but a single glass. As we sat over the camp fire at night, talking about our losses, drinking the last of our tea, and smoking some of the last pipes we were destined to enjoy for many weeks, Mr. O'B. improved the occasion with a certain characteristic philosophy. He directed our attention to the consideration of how much worse the misfortune would have been if he, or one of us, had been riding the animal which was lost. Then the loss of his kettle was, after all, of little consequence, for the tea to use in it was gone too. "No," said he, "what grieves me is the loss of your tobacco; it's a very serious thing to me, as well as you; for, do you know, my own was just finished, and I was on the very point of asking you to lend me some till we get through." Milton being the only man who had any tobacco left, some four small plugs, smilingly took the hint, and shared it with the rest of the party.

On the following day we moved on towards The Cache with the Iroquois and Shushwaps, whilst The Assiniboine and his son searched the river closely for traces of the lost horse or baggage. As we were following along the track with the train of horses, in single file, Cheadle, who was driving some of the rearmost pack-horses, heard loud cries behind — "Doctor, Doctor! Stop, stop!" and was presently overtaken by Mr. O'B., who came up out of breath, gasping out, "Doctor, Doctor! you had better go back directly, something's happened; don't you hear some one shouting for assistance? I expect it is Mrs. Assiniboine with one of the horses fast in a bog." Anathematising Mr. O'B. for not having himself gone back to help her, and receiving in reply a tribute to the greater value of his own aid, Cheadle ran hastily back a few hundred yards and there came upon the woman, endeavouring perseveringly, but vainly, to extricate a horse, which was almost buried in a morass, by first beating him vigorously, and then hauling at his tail. By cutting off the packs, and one hauling at the head and the other the tail, the horse was at last got out, and then Mrs. Assiniboine relieved her feelings by a torrent of violent language in the Cree tongue, eminently abusive of Mr. O'B., who she declared was close behind her when the accident happened, but instead of coming to her, took to his heels and bolted, afraid lest he should be left behind with only a female protector! She was very indignant, and declared she would never lift a finger to help him in anything for the future; and from that time neither the man, his wife, or son could ever be induced to oblige "Le Vieux" in the smallest matter, and were quite unable to understand the considerations of humanity which prevented us at once from abandoning Mr. O'B. to his fate —far the wisest course, they assured us, to take with so timid and useless a member of the party.

The Death of the Moose
William Francis Butler

William Francis Butler, a British officer on leave, travelled through the northern Rockies via the old Peace River fur trade route in 1873.

On the 8th of May we reached, early in the morning, the entrance to the main range. A short rapid marks it, a rapid easy to run at all stages of water, and up which we towed our canoe, carrying the more perishable articles to save them from the spray — a precaution which was, however, not necessary, as no water was shipped.

We were now in the mountains. From the low terrace along the shore they rose in stupendous masses; their lower ridges clothed in forests of huge spruce, poplar, and birch; their middle heights covered in dense thickets of spruce alone; their summits cut into a thousand varied peaks, bare of all vegetation, but bearing aloft into the sunshine 8000 feet above us the glittering crowns of snow which, when evening stilled the breezes, shone reflected in the quiet waters, vast and motionless.

Wonderful things to look at are these white peaks, perched up so high above our world. They belong to us, yet they are not of us. The eagle links them to the earth; the cloud carries to them the message of the sky; the ocean sends them her tempest; the air rolls her thunders beneath their brows, and launches her lightnings from their sides; the sun sends them his first greeting, and leaves them his latest kiss. Yet motionless they keep their crowns of snow, their glacier crests of jewels, and dwell among the stars heedless of time or tempest.

For two days we journeyed through this vast valley, along a wide, beautiful river, tranquil as a lake, and bearing on its bosom, at intervals, small isles of green forest. Now and again a beaver rippled the placid surface, or a bear appeared upon a rocky point for a moment, looked at the strange lonely craft, stretched out his long snout to sniff the gale, and then vanished in the forest shore. For the rest all was stillness; forest, isle, river and mountain — all seemed to sleep in unending loneliness; and our poles grating against the rocky shore, or a shot at some quick-diving beaver, alone broke the silence; while the echo, dying away in the vast mountain cañons, made the relapsing silence seem more intense.

Thus we journeyed on. On the evening of the 8th of May we emerged from the pass, and saw beyond the extremity of a long reach of river a mountain range running north and south, distant about thirty miles from us. To the right and left the Rocky Mountains opened out, leaving the river to follow its course through a long forest valley of considerable width.

We had passed the Rocky Mountains, and the range before us was the central mountain system of North British Columbia.

It was a very beautiful evening; the tops of the birch-trees were already showing their light green leaves amidst the dark foliage of the spruce and firs.

Along the shore, where we landed, the tracks of a very large grizzly bear were imprinted freshly in the sand. I put a couple of bullets into my gun and started up the river, with Cerf-vola for a companion. I had got about a mile from the camp when, a few hundred yards ahead, a large dark animal emerged from the forest, and made his way through some lower brushwood towards the river. Could it be the grizzly? I lay down on the sand-bank, and pulled the dog down beside me. The large black animal walked out upon the sand-bar two or three hundred yards above me. He proved to be a moose on his way to swim the river to the south shore. I lay still until he had got so far on his way that return to the forest would have been impracticable; then I sprang to my feet and ran towards him. What a spring he gave across the sand and down into the water! Making an allowance for the force of the current I ran towards the shore. It was a couple of hundred yards from me, and when I gained it the moose was already three-parts across the river, almost abreast where I stood, swimming for his very life, with his huge unshapen head thrust out along the surface, the ears thrown forward, while the large ripples rolled from before his chest as he clove his way through the water.

It was a long shot for a rifle, doubly so for a smooth-bore; but old experience in many lands, where the smooth-bore holds its own despite all other weapons, had told me that when you do get a gun to throw a bullet well, you may rely upon it for distances supposed to be far beyond the possibilities of such a weapon; so, in a tenth of the time it has taken me to say all this, I gave the moose the right barrel, aiming just about his long ears. There was a single plunge in the water; the giant head went down, and all was quiet. And now to secure the quarry. Away down stream he floated, showing only one small black speck above the surface; he was near the far side, too. Running down shore I came within calling-distance of the camp, from which the smoke of Kalder's fire was already curling above the tree-tops. Out came Kalder, Jacques, and A————. Of course it was a grizzly, and all the broken flint-guns of the party were suddenly called into requisition. If it had been a grizzly, and that I had been retiring before him in skirmishing order, gods! what a support I was falling back upon! A————'s gun is already familiar to the reader; Kalder's beaver-gun went off about one shot in three; and Jacques possessed a weapon (it had been discarded by an Indian, and Jacques had resuscitated it out of the store of all trades which he possessed an inkling of) the most extraordinary I had ever seen. Jacques always spoke of it in the feminine gender. "She was a good gun, except that a trifle too much of the powder came out the wrong way. He would back her to shoot 'plum' if she would only go off after a reasonable lapse of time, but it was tiring to him to keep her to the shoulder for a couple of minutes after he had pulled her trigger, and then to have her go off when he was thinking of pulling the gun-coat over her again." When she was put away in the canoe, it was always a matter of some moment to place her so that in the event of any sudden explosion of her pent-up wrath, she might discharge herself harmlessly along the river, and on this account she generally lay like a stern-chaser projecting from behind Jacques, and endangering only his paddle.

All these maimed and mutilated weapons were now brought forth, and such a loading and priming and hammering began, that, had it really been a grizzly, he must have been utterly scared out of all semblance of attack.

Kalder now mastered the position of affairs, and like an arrow he and Jacques were into the canoe, and out after the dead moose. They soon overhauled him, and, slipping a line over the young antlers, towed him to the shore. We were unable to lift him altogether out of the water, so we cut him up as he lay, stranded like a whale.

Directly opposite a huge cone mountain rose up some eight or nine thousand feet above us, and just ere evening fell over the scene,

William Francis Butler's moose being butchered beneath the artistically exaggerated Mount Selwyn. Butler shot the moose following his traverse through the Peace River Pass in 1873. Archives of the Canadian Rockies

his topmost peak, glowing white in the sunlight, became mirror'd in most faithful semblance in the clear quiet river, while the life-stream of the moose flowed out over the tranquil surface, dyeing the nearer waters into brilliant crimson.

If some painter in the exuberance of his genius had put upon canvas such a strange contrast of colours, people would have said it is not true to nature; but nature has many truths, and it takes many a long day, and not a few years' toil, to catch a tenth of them. And, my dear friend with the eye-glass — you who know all about nature in a gallery and with a catalogue — you may take my word for it.

And now, ere quitting, probably for ever, this grand Peace River Pass — this immense valley which receives in its bosom so many other valleys, into whose depths I only caught a moment's glimpse as we floated by their outlets — let me say one other word about it.

Since I left the Wild North Land, it has been my lot to visit the chief points of interest in Oregon, California, the Vale of Shasta, and the Yosemite. Shasta is a loftier mountain than any that frown above the Peace River Pass. Yosemite can boast its half-dozen waterfalls, trickling down their thousand feet of rock; but for wild beauty, for the singular spectacle of a great river flowing tranquilly through a stupendous mountain range, — these mountains presenting at every reach a hundred varied aspects, — not the dizzy glory of Shasta nor the rampart precipices of Yosemite can vie with that lonely gorge far away on the great Unchagah.

Ordeal in the Mountains
Pierre Berton

In 1871 the search for a pass through the Rockies that would accommodate the Canadian Pacific Railway began in earnest. One of the first parties was despatched by Walter Moberly to survey the Howse Pass.

For Moberly, a surveyor's life might have been disappointing but it was at least stimulating. For the men under him — axemen, packers, chainmen, levellers, rodmen — it could be pitiless.

One such man, who left a record of his feelings, was Robert M. Rylatt, a former sergeant with the Royal Engineers, who had been hired by Moberly to take charge of the commissariat and pack train for Party "S" to survey the Howse Pass in the Rockies in the summer of 1871.

Rylatt had won three medals fighting with the Turkish army under Omar Pasha on the Danube and later in the battle of Inkerman during the Crimean war. He arrived in Canada as part of the engineering detachment under Col. R. C. Moody, who laid out New Westminster, the first capital of the new colony of British Columbia. For all of his five years in Canada his wife had been a hopeless invalid and Rylatt badly needed money. Not without misgivings, he signed on for the ordeal of his life.

He was to be gone a year and his description of "the painful hour of parting" is heart-rending: how his wife Jane, rising from her pillow, cried, "Oh, Bob, I shall never see you again"; and how, on the steamboat, "as every stroke of the paddles bore me further from her, I felt as if I had ruthlessly abandoned her."

If Rylatt had known what lay ahead he would never have signed a contract with the Canadian Pacific Survey; but there was no way in which he could quit once he began. He was virtually a prisoner, walled off by a five-hundred-mile barrier of mountain and forest which few men could dare to penetrate alone. The job, he thought, would take a year but Rylatt, who left New Westminster in July of 1871, did not return until June of 1873.

Party "S" was under the charge of E. C. Gillette, an American engineer of good reputation whom Moberly had known for many years. It consisted of four officers, who were surveyors, and sixteen men — mainly axemen — together with eight Mexican and Indian packers and one hunter. The forty-five pack animals carried almost seven tons of food and equipment.

To reach the Rockies, the party had to struggle over hills choked with loose boulders and through mudholes so deep the horses were mired to the girth. Over and over again Rylatt had to go through the laborious business of unloading each animal, hauling him out of the mud and reloading him again. Some had to be left to their fate:

"How worried would be any member of the Humane society, could he see the treatment animals in a Pack Train receive, where the animals themselves are only a secondary consideration, the open sores on their backs, from hard and incessant packing, angry and running with humour, over which the Packer, too often, if not closely watched, without washing throws the heavy *apparajos* or Pack saddle, and as the sinch [sic] is tightened . . . the poor beast groans, rears and plunges and not unfrequently sinks down under the pain, only to be whipped again into position."

Ahead of the horses moved the axemen, hacking their way through the massive network of prostrate cedars, cutting tunnels in a green tangle as thick as any Borneo jungle and laying down patches of corduroy for the animals to cross.

The party pushed straight across the Selkirk Mountains into the Kootenay country and did not reach the upper Columbia until late in September. They started down it on rafts and in small canoes, watching with growing alarm as it swelled in size with every mile. On the third day, the raft on which Rylatt was travelling hit a submerged log in the rapids and was sucked under. The five men on the raft leaped for the shore; one, James Malloy, fell short. The current pulled him under with the raft and he was never seen again.

At the mouth of the Blaeberry River, which flows down from the summit of the Howse Pass to join the Columbia, the axemen were faced with a Herculean task. They must cut a pathway to the top through forests untrodden since Palliser's associate, Hector, had passed that way a dozen years before. The fall winds had already reduced the country to a mire so thick that one mule could not be pulled from the gumbo; Rylatt was forced to shoot him in his swampy prison.

Yet there were moments of great beauty and mystery here among the silent peaks and Rylatt, who was a sensitive man, was not unmoved. On his first Sunday in the mountains he found himself alone — the others were working five miles farther up the pass. It was his first such experience in the wilderness and he made the most of it. He watched the sun dropping down behind the glaciers on the mountain tops, tipping the snows with a gold that turned to red while, in the shadowed gorges, the ice could be seen in long streaks of transparent blue. He watched the glow leave the peaks and the gloom fill up the valleys. He watched velvet night follow ghostly twilight and saw the pale rays of the aurora compete with the stars to cast "softening hallows [sic] of light around these everlasting snows." Suddenly, he began to shiver and a sense of irreconcilable loneliness overcame him. It was the silence — the uncanny and overpowering silence of the Canadian wilderness: "Not a leaf stirred; not the hum of an insect; not even the noise of the water in the creek — this being too distant . . . I listened for a sound but did not hear even the rustle of a falling leaf. . . ."

He made a fire, as much to hear the crackling of the wood as for the warmth. It came to him that no one who had not experienced what he was going through could ever really understand what it was like to be truly alone:

"Your sense of being alone in the heart of a city, or even in a village, or within easy distance of fellow beings . . . gives you no claim to use the term 'alone.' You may have the feeling peculiar to being alone — that is all. Listen sometime when you think you are alone. . . . Can you hear a footfall; a door slam in the distance; a carriage go by? Or the rumble of one . . . ? Can you hear a dog bark? Have you a cricket on the hearth or even the ticking of a clock . . . ?"

Rylatt realized that the tiniest of sounds can give a feeling of relief — "the sense of knowing your species are at no great distance" — but here, in the solitude of the Rockies, there was only silence.

The sense of isolation was increased by the onset of winter and the absence of mail. Goaded by Walter Moberly, who had rejoined the party, Gillette and his men began chopping their pathway to the summit of the pass. By the time the trail was opened, on October 26, the snow was already falling. The following day, with eight inches blanketing the mountainside, the surveyors gathered at the summit, ready at last to start work, but the instruments were so full of water they were useless and the slopes so slippery with wet snow that no man could maintain a footing. The following day another foot of snow fell, the engineers realized that nothing could be done, and the party settled down for the long winter. It would be May before the mountain trails would be passable again and for those sections that ran through the canyons it would be considerably later. It was not really safe to travel with loaded pack horses before June; even then the mountain torrents could be crossed only with difficulty, being swollen with melting snow from above. The twenty-nine members of the party, including two ex-convicts, were faced with each other's company for six or seven months.

At the very outset the party was beset by worries over mail and pay. It was months before they saw a pay-cheque. A government official in Victoria — another political appointee — had withheld the money, banked it and appropriated the interest to himself. Nor was the mail forwarded. It lay for months in various post offices because no arrangements had been made to handle it. One of the packers set off in late November for Wild Horse Creek, a five-hundred-mile journey on snowshoes, and returned with a few letters, but nothing for Rylatt, who was beside himself with anxiety over his wife's condition.

"Poor wife, are you dead or alive?" he confided to his diary. "Have the two deposits of money I sent reached her? It may easily be understood in my case how hard it is to receive no word, no sign, and altogether I am very miserable."

On December 4, Walter Moberly, accompanied by his Indian guides, left the camp on his long trek across the Selkirks. He took with him one of the party, a Frenchman named Verdier who had just learned that his wife had eloped leaving their five children alone. "He was like a crazy man," Rylatt observed; he sent a note with some money to his own wife with Verdier, knowing there would be no further communication with the world until the following May or June.

A few days later he cut his thumb and opened a small roll of bandage material his wife had stowed in his kit. "When I saw scraps of oiled silk, fingers of old gloves, and the softest of lint, how tenderly I felt towards her, but when a slip of paper came to light, on which were the words 'God bless you, Bob,' it made me feel wretched. . . ."

On Christmas Day, the thermometer dropped to 34 below zero and the following day the mercury in it froze solid. Though Christmas dinner was served piping hot, the food was frozen to the plates before the men could consume it.

By New Year's Eve, 1871, Rylatt felt he had reached the bottom. He and four others sat in their cabin, seeing the old year out and trying to keep warm. Though a rousing fire had been lit it was necessary for each man to change position constantly as the side of the body away from the heat became numbed with cold.

'We talked of our wives, adventures, etc.; but there was no mirth; and when the New Year was announced by the watch, we crept into our blankets. It was quite a time before I slept, my brain being busy with past remembrances. This was the first time the anniversary of the New Year had not been kept in the company of my wife."

Ahead of the party stretched four more months of this prison-like existence. The tensions, which had beeen simmering beneath the surface, began to burst out more frequently. Already Rylatt and the chief surveyor, Gillette, were speaking to each other only when necessary. Earlier in the season they had had an altercation in which Gillette had thrown a grouse bone in Rylatt's face. Rylatt had responded with a cup of hot coffee and Gillette had threatened to shoot him. By February Rylatt had conceived a deadly hatred for the surveyor, who he was convinced was going crazy. This raging antipathy was returned in kind. "That man, Gillette, is not only a fool but an unmanly cur, deserving the sympathy of none, and the power that pitchforked such a being into even our rough society, and placed him pro tem at the head of it, ought to be blackballed," Rylatt wrote in his diary. Gillette, on his part, promised Rylatt he would drill a hole in him before they parted.

"The men are growing rusty for want of activity and biliousness has soured their tempers," Rylatt recorded on February 25. Two weeks later he noted in his diary that "the roughs of the party are in open mutiny. Growling at their food, cursing me for being out of sugar; all this I care little for . . . but my pent up feelings have found vent today, and the leader of the roughs will carry my mark to his grave. I have passed through a somewhat exciting scene and don't care to have it repeated."

Seven of the most mutinous of the party had gathered at the cookhouse door, intent on rushing it and seizing the food including the non-existent sugar, which they believed Rylatt was secretly hiding. In the altercation that followed, Rylatt was threatened by Roberts, the ringleader, an Australian ex-convict. Rylatt snatched up a hatchet and when Roberts made a move, chopped off three of his fingers. This drove off the mob but they returned again in an hour, armed with axes. Rylatt held them off with his Henry rifle and stayed on guard until the threat diminished and the camp returned to a state of sullen tension.

As the sun grew warmer in April and the river ice showed signs of breaking up, much of the ill-humour disappeared. Some mail arrived in May, but still Rylatt had no word of his wife; the white man who had undertaken to carry letters from Wild Horse Creek to Hope on the Fraser the previous fall had perished in the snows, his body discovered in the spring with the mailbag beside it. "I cannot understand why no line has reached me from my wife," Rylatt wrote. "Is she dead? . . . this suspense is terrible . . . surely some one of our many acquaintances would have let me know. . . . Generally people are ready to signal bad news. My chum Jack had some bad news; his house being burned down. His wife it would appear was enjoying herself at a Ball. . . . He lost everything. . . ."

May 6: "I have somehow got it into my head my wife is not dead, but out of her mind — this thought haunts me."

On May 15, Walter Moberly arrived with the news that the Howse Pass route had been abandoned and that the party must quit its quarters on the Columbia and move north. In his pocket he carried a letter from Rylatt's wife. It had been on his person so long that the cover had been worn away. It was dated October 9, 1871.

Moberly dealt swiftly with the mutineers and with Gillette, who had surreptitiously countenanced the attack on Rylatt: "If Gillette has sown the seed of this discontent, damn him, he shall reap the harvest." Four of the malcontents were dismissed; Gillette was suspended and his assistant, Ashdowne Green, put in charge of the party.

"I cannot forget the look of hatred on Roberts' face as, upon my leaving in the boat, he held up to my sight his mutilated hand and exclaimed: 'You see this; it will help me to remember you!' "

Gillette tried to carry out his threat to shoot Rylatt but as his hand reached for the Smith and Wesson on his belt, Rylatt staggered him with a heavy blow and another member of the party pinioned his arms.

Guided by Kinbasket, the Chief of the Kootenays, a "daring little shrivelled up old fellow," the party started on the long journey northward, breaking trail for the pack horses as they moved through dense clouds of mosquitoes. "I have smothered my face with mosquito muslin, smeared my hands with bacon grease, but bah! nothing keeps them off, and the heat only melts the grease and sends it beneath my clothing," Rylatt wrote in disgust.

In mid-August Chief Kinbasket came to grief when a grizzly bear attacked him. "The old chief had barely time to raise the axe and aim a blow . . . 'ere the weapon was dashed aside like a flash and he was in the embrace of the monster; the huge forepaws around him, the immense claws dug into his back, the bear held him up. Then fastening the poor chief's shoulders in his iron jaws, he raised one of his hind feet, and tore a fearful gash, commencing at the abdomen, and cutting through to the bowels, he fairly stripped the flesh and muscles from one of his thighs, a bloody, hanging mass of rent flesh and clothing." Kinbasket was not found until the following morning. Miraculously he was still alive; more miraculously, he survived; but the party had lost its trailblazer.

In late September, the party reached the Boat Encampment at the Big Bend of the Columbia River. The route now took a right angle towards the Rockies and the foot of the Athabasca Pass. It seemed impossible to reach the Yellow Head before winter set in. The party hesitated. And here, in the shadow of the glowering peaks, with the brooding forest hanging over them and the moon glistening on the great, rustling river they indulged in a weird charade. On September 28, they held a Grand Ball.

"Think of it," Rylatt wrote in his diary, "a dance — and an enjoyable dance at that."

The "orchestra" consisted of the best whistler in the party, a man who knew all the latest dance tunes ("Little Brown Jug," "The Man on the Flying Trapeze" and "Shoo, Fly, Don't Bother Me" were all popular during the early years of the decade). "He puckered his mouth, beat loud time on an empty soap box with a stick, and the graceful forms began to whirl."

The dancers were deadly serious. Some were assigned the role of lady partner — and later allowed to change about. Rylatt described his assistant, the bespectacled Dick White, dancing with one such "lady" — a great six-footer, hairy-faced and with a fist like a sledge, pants tucked carelessly into boots still covered with river mud, "while Dick, with eyeglasses adjusted, held the huge hand gingerly, and by the tips of his fingers, then circling the waist of this delicate creature with the gentleness due to modesty and the fair sex, his lovely partner occasionally letting out a yell of hilarity, would roll the quid of tobacco to the other cheek of the sweet face, discharging the juice beneath the feet of the dancers."

The dancing grew wilder as the full moon shed its eerie light over the scene. Whenever the whistler gave out the dancers themselves supplied the music, shouting the tunes aloud. The entire crew, "panting like pressure engines," seemed to have forgotten where they were and saw themselves in some vast, chandeliered ballroom, far from the dripping forests, the mires and the deadfalls.

"They were now in the last dance, and appeared to have gone mad, and when at last the orchestra stopped, and Dick White doffed his cap with the indispensable flourish, and the moon shone on his bald scalp as he offered his arm to the fair one at his side, preparatory to leading her to a seat on a log, I fairly screamed with laughter, and then to see that modest young lady suddenly throw out one of her number eleven boots, and sledge hammer arm, and place Dick in an instant on his back and to observe the lady dancing a jig around him, yelling at the same time that made the distant hills echo, was glorious fun."

Thus did Party "S" by temporary madness save itself from a larger insanity.

The following day, Rylatt received three letters from his wife, the last written by a neighbour, she being too ill to hold a pen. It ended with an earnest appeal: "Oh, Bob, come home, I can't bear it!"

He could not go home; Moberly had already refused to release him from his two-year contract. As the fall rains began, pouring down in such sheets that it was impossible to cook a meal, the party, reduced in numbers, moved north again, spurred on by Moberly who had returned from his interview with Fleming at the Yellow Head to find them settling in for the winter.

"The whole valley is like a lake," Rylatt noted. "Thus, under the present state of affairs, I exist. My drenched clothing is taken off at night, wrung out, and I turn in to my equally wet blankets. When resuming my clothing in the morning, I shiver all over, my teeth chatter, as I dolefully reflect how difficult it will be to prepare a meal."

There were no more warm breakfasts for the wet, shivering crew, only flapjacks larded over with bacon grease and a muddy coffee made from beans placed in a piece of canvas and bruised between two rocks.

With winter setting in and their goods far behind them, they found themselves in the heart of the Rockies, sixty-five hundred feet above sea level, fifty miles still from their wintering place, "where no trail exists nor ever has existed . . . wholly unexplored . . . every mile to be contended with, swamps to be crossed, heavy timber to be hacked through, dense undergrowth to be levelled for our animals."

For weeks no scrap of news seeped through. Two thousand miles away a series of events not unconnected with their own toil was taking shape. Macdonald was in the midst of his futile negotiations with Macpherson. Allan was moving gingerly to dump his American associates. Rumours were beginning to reach Liberal ears of a damaging agreement signed by Cartier. But the men in the Athabasca Pass were cut off from the world. At last, on October 19, a pack train arrived and Rylatt was handed a slip of paper on which was scribbled the message he had been dreading:

"Dear Rylatt — The papers state your wife has passed beyond the stream of time. Don't be too cut up, dear old fellow."

There were no particulars. Three days later, while brooding in his tent, he was startled by a strange cry. His dog Nip, a faithful companion during all his hardships, who shared his blankets and his food, had broken through the shore ice and was struggling vainly in the river. Rylatt did his best to save him but failed. " 'Oh, God,' I cried in my distress, 'must everything be taken from me?' "

By the following April, near the Fiddle River, Rylatt was nearly dead himself of scurvy:

"My mouth is in a dreadful state, the gums being black, the teeth loose, and when pressed against any substance they prick at the roots like needles. At times the gums swell, almost covering the teeth. To chew food is out of the question and so have to bolt it without mastication. My legs also becoming black below the knee. . . . My breath is somewhat offensive and I am troubled with a dry cough. In fact I feel like an old man. . . ."

At length, Rylatt persuaded the reluctant Moberly to allow him to quit the service and go home. He said his good-byes on the evening of May 13, 1873, and this leave-taking was warm and fervent. Suddenly he "felt a pang of regret at having to turn my back on such comrades." They crowded around him with warm hand-shakes and

clumsy words of Godspeed. The cook appeared with some dough-
nuts, especially made for the occasion. In the two years together
these men had come to know one another as men can only under
conditions of hardship and stress. Rylatt and a burly Scots companion, Henry Baird, took three horses and set off south towards Kamloops through unknown country, trudging through soaking moss "so
deep that an animal could be buried overhead and suffocate," swimming and re-swimming the ice-cold rivers — packs, horses and all —
crawling on their hands and knees over the fallen timber, stamping
out a trail through the crust of the melting snow-fields, foundering
in the rapids of the treacherous watercourses, slashing away at the
impeding underbrush, flogging their animals unmercifully as they
struggled on in search of feed.

A month later they were still on the trail, provisions lost, matches
almost gone, sugar used up, a single sack of flour between them and
starvation. About one hundred and fifty miles out of Kamloops, they
happened upon a meadow where the horses could graze. They made
a fire, dried their clothing and cooked some flapjacks in a pan. Then,
stretched before the blaze, in the closest thing to comfort they had
known for many weeks, the two exhausted and weather-beaten men
fell to "cogitating on the possibilities and probabilities of the
Canadian Pacific Railroad."

"In the mind's eye we pictured a train of cars sweeping along
over this flat, over the fierce streams we had passed, puffing and
snorting up the mountains in gentle curves and windings, shrieking
wildly as some denizen of the forest, scared at the strange monster . . . is hurrying off. . . ."

They talked about "the weary looks in the eyes of the passengers,
longing for the end of the route." They could almost see them settle
back in their corners, yawn, complain of fatigue and "doze away the
terrible hours of idleness." Then their thoughts turned to the dining
car and, with watering mouths, the two men began to enumerate the
kind of dinner that might be served on such a train in the future:
". . . hot joints, mealy potatoes, pies, cheese, etc., and wine to be
had for the paying for."

The fantasy grew more graphic. The two began to conjecture that
the imaginary passengers on the imaginary train were gazing out on
them and remarking: "Those two fellows yonder seem to have it
pretty much to themselves, as they toast their skins . . . and are
doubtless happier and more at freedom than we. . . ."

At length, the train of imagination rolled on beyond the forested
horizon. Rylatt and Baird roused themselves and counted their

matches: there would not be many more hot meals. They still had a long way to go but the end of that long sentence on the Canadian Pacific Survey was at last in sight. They cooked some more flapjacks on what was left of the fire to eat cold on the morrow. They saved what little tea and tobacco was left for an emergency. Then, wearily, they shouldered their loads, gathered up their grazing horses and, with that strange vision of the future still fresh in their minds, set off once again into reality.

Winter Journey
Jon Whyte

In 1875 the Jarvis Expedition explored the region to the north of the Fraser and Athabaska Rivers, to determine if a route north of the Yellowhead Pass held promise for a railroad line. Edward W. Jarvis, the leader, wrote an account for the CPR. Charles Frank Hanington wrote letters to his brother, carrying them with him. The party set out from Fort George, British Columbia, proceeding to Quesnel before heading into the Rockies.

1)   January sets in very cold.
      We redouble our exertions to prepare everything.
      Thermometer down among the forties,
      one six a.m. marked fifty-three below.

2)   Alec appearing from the darkness, overdue,
January   moving slowly, weary, livid, drawn,
8th   face, flesh, clothing, hair, parka trim
      a frosty bristling, a silvery pallor;
      winter in every pace
      in his near-dead trudging.

      Seeing him, ourselves foresaw;
      the season getting on, we must be on our way.

3)   The sled dogs fossick warmth,
January   curling into each other and the snow.
14th
      No wind;
      all still.

4)   The largest, most roaring fire
little more than burns the side toward it;
the other, spitted to darkness, freezes.

5)   Were it anything except this cold, this glimmering,
we might retreat to sleep to dream of warmth,
mutter, "This is the maddest madness," and turn back.
Obliged to thrust on,
to measure how far, how near, how deep, how clear
Death's soft step sounds,
we won't turn back.

6)   In cold's depth
January the fire steams and spits; it does not smoke,
15th   the driest wood we find.

           Frost quills bare flesh.

7)   Alec suddenly and silently appears,
epiphany in frost,
knew his route, where he was going, fell into streams.

           We cannot tell in cold precision whither we go.

8)   Days so short we rise in darkness to revive the fire,
melt snow for tea;
while we drink it, fold our blankets,
take down the fly, harness the dogs;
in dawn's deep indigo strap snowshoes on,
move out to meet it.

9)   "I can't imagine a quicker way to harden a man's heart
January than to put him driving dogs."
16th
           Expected not so early on our way,
Death seized old Marquis
who limped all morning our third day,
at noontime wagged, then rolled to darkness,

           Jarvis reports, the official version,
noting the day forty-six below,
echoing involvement and discretion.
They buried Marquis in a grave of snow.

Marquis — leader — then Cabree, Sam, Buster,
dogs lively "as crickets" *at feeding time,*
writes Hanington. Marquis lacklustre,
iced, frozen to shoulders, thick in rime,

had to be shot;
Jarvis did the deed.
Whichever: we left the good old brute
more at ease than since he froze his feet.

10)
January
20th

The snow lies deeper as we near the mountains,
turn up the Fraser's north branch
to where we hope our Smoky River Pass shall be.

11)

The fellows in Quesnelle expressed
exalted notions of the pleasures we'd derive
from our winter journey through the mountains:
"God bless you old fellows — goodbye," they said.
"This is the last time we will see you."

12)
January
29th

We reload, relash sleds, four in number,
twenty-four dogs, eight of us,
mend moccasins and harness, glum in our
prospect of retreat; forward we must.

In blue and silver dusky light
hearing distinctly a chopping axe
on the far shore as we turn in, the bite
of blade, the wrench away: a fact

none will leave the fire or into cold dash
to solve: the mystery of our axeman company.
It deepens when we hear a large tree crash
branch-shatteringly. We sit, accepting and denying.

Morning, we see no fallen tree,
no notching blaze, no fallen branch, no print
explaining the sullen mystery.
Imaginations, spurred by nothing, will not rest.

13)

Hard work, breaking track;
anything to think of is pleasanter;

walking all day, thinking of nothing but "1, 2, 3, . . ."
is monotonous for anything.

14)   Tiger: shot, the 29th.
His lameness prevented his doing anything
except eat grub.

15)   February 4th: a heavy snowstorm
just to make things lively.

16)
February
8th
     Provisions for another month, no more;
no notion of how far we have to go.

One goes ahead setting the track,
flailing down the snow,
creating a trough
where the dogs can pull our sleds.
Where the canyon walls lean in on us
we abandon the stream to portage,
clamber up the walls
haul dogs and sleds too,
two men hauling, two men pushing.
Where the descent begins, returning to the stream,
the sled invariably tips,
pulling the dogs down with it.
Poor beggars: we cannot rest them or ourselves.

Each step an agony, snow sucking under,
caving beneath our feet which crave solidity;
we haul one up, the other steadying itself
on soft, collapsing crust.
One by one the river's branches we explore,
preferring none.
Mountains conceal their passages and passes
behind the steepest walls, the deepest canyons,
the most impenetrable portages, the thickest hollows
where snow piles up in deep soft sift
the wind has borne down watercourse.

We lack days to waste traversing an unknown,
apparently unlimited distance on a known
shrinking store of dry-flake salmon.

Plunging into the snow, our feet each step
create small avalanches from the toe.

Our feet are blistering;
nausea swims in our heads.

A mile more: walls of rock we cannot climb
confine the river's and our course.

We seize on any coign of vantage,
narrow ledges, banks of ice,
frost bridges from one boulder to the next,
black water boiling, foaming at our feet,
about to snap up, swallow any who slip.

Canyon succeeds canyon;
river bed so full of boulders,
our progress treacle slow.

The weather stormy,
snowfalls frequent, snowshoeing laborious,
our spirits sink.

In camp we shovel down to moss,
the snow so deep
we cannot peer from out the pit we dig.

17)   In stillness is beauty.
        In beauty is death.

18)   The blades of the mountains sharpen distinctly
        in the bright peach-golden light dancing to day,
        the sky pale blue;
        when shadows stretch to night: a spangled place.

        Great glittering blue
        glaciers ride the ridgewalls far above us.
        Jarvis thinks it would be beautiful
        to see it from the comfort of a Pullman.
        Each stream branch comes to this:
        an amphitheatre of high bare rocky peaks
        where slender clear-blue lines of glaciers menace.

        Hanington says:
        "We seem to have got to the back of the north wind."

19)   How many ways, how many branches,
February how many dead ends can streams flow from?
13th

Quaw said three days' travel, a fork to the left,
two days more, a fall high as a tree
we'd portage around;
five days, to a meadow,
three days' travel more,
a stream runs east, where we will see
the sun rise from the prairie.

Quaw's prediction: thirteen days, the height of land.
Eighteen days' travel back.

20)   In canyon's depth the gorge engulfs both sky and earth.
The rock leans in so doubtfully
Hanington creeps on it hands and knees toward a fall
"high-all-the-same one stick."
The snow collapses;
limpet-like he clings to rock
until we find a pole to support him.

21)   Retreating to a pyramid portage, ascending,
February we haul the dogs, whip, denounce, cajole,
15th   reach its summit, then descend and
cannot stop and in a melee roll.

A good man could disentangle them
without a whip and swearing.
We cannot be that sort of man,
nor keep a nerveless bearing.

At one hill's top the dogs surge up and disappear,
falling pellmell in their downward career,
till at a meagre sapling the sled shears
to one side, the dogs to the other veer,

dangling by traces in ludicrous plight,
swaying up and down, bobbing in the air,
like sleigh and reindeer caught in flight
by a chimney on a Christmas night.

22)   The day before the canyon
we sent back to Fort George
two Indians with seven dogs, one sled.
Sam and Chun escaped their keepers,
came back to us.

Our salmon running low,
Jarvis shoots them both.

23)
February
20th

To bed in all available clothing,
the thermometer at forty-two below,
we wake to rain pattering our faces;
within eight hours.

24)

Branches of possibility extend like arms of aspen:
from trunk to stems, from stems to branches,
branches to yet smaller branches,
filling out the tree of which one twig is one,
the branch seen from within.

The branching nerves of bodies form a tree;
from brain to trunk or branch
one touching nerve or point, the pass.

25)

"Give it up?"
"You know what I was thinking?"
"For God's sake, yes, we'll not go back."
"If we all come to grief, I am responsible."
"I'll take my own responsibility."

We'd sooner be found in the mountains.

26)
February
24th

Grand pyramids of peaks the entrance guard,
glacier most magnificent, transparent blue,
we fancy seeing rocks beneath and through it.

27)

Thunder rolls, our eyes peer high:
masses of ice and rock leap
point to point, spout from the sky,
a weird, gigantic fountain heaps

itself, burrows out anew, then falling;
a boulder plunges straight toward us where
we stand, wraith of nature so appalling
we did not make our camp near there.

28)

Cold exhilarating morning:
five paternoster lakes, highest in the mist.
Joyously we hail a tiny trickling stream,
the sweetest thing, running to the east.

101

We stop to wash our hands and faces,
the second time in our long journey,
to wash all B.C.'s grime and dust away.

29)   Eastward ho! Our spirits rising as we drop.

30)   The river bends sharply: an abyss yawns before us:
February   a fall two hundred feet.
26th   Had the day been misty, we'd have plunged with it.

31)   Scarcely a day passes when their dismal howl
does not announce to our unwilling ears
another dog has dropped.
A trivial incident like the death of a dog
(such mongrel curs as some of ours)
would not affect us in a civilized community.
Here it casts a gloom.
Even the dogs look at one another
as if to say, "It may be my turn next."

32)   Jarvis's face white, lips set.

A reeling, swirling, angering pain
rises in the wrinkling of the brain,
sways with each rough slouch forward
until our muscles knot, spine tears apart
in every jolt, then settles down relentlessly
while nerves their lacerations start anew
cold and numbness will not stanch,
a boring up the vaulted tendons of our feet,
a clawing up through our clenched calves,
whilst all the while our minds rebel,
call out to vomit, retch, heave up, to stop
the swarming and miasmal blurring of our way.
Mal de raquettes: the snowshoe torture.

33)   Knew we which river we proceed along
we could be happier.
It heads east, we think the Athabaska,
our hearts beat high.

It turns north, it is the Smoky,
Our spirits drop to zero.

34)   Nothing of the world remains:
        warmth went;
        familiarity;
        the places we might have known;
        shelter, time, and banter vanish;
        thoughts we might have had;
        all but the counting fades: "1, 2, 3, 4, 5 . . ."

35)   Dead reckoning,
        our course lies south and east;
        we proceed by north and east;
        holding our hope the river will turn east,
        we keep our course a few days more.
        It comes to nought.

        We turn south.

36)   A day of rest:
March   we cache our instruments,
6th   extra clothing we no longer need,
        mark our names, the date, upon a tree.
        Tomorrow we head south,
        depart this valley leading northward and away
        from any hope of meeting Indians who've wandered here
        in search of game.

37)   *Cultus copa nika; cultus copa mika.*
        What's bad for me is bad for you.

        To stay put too long is death.
        To slip and break a leg is death.
        In stillness: death.
        A silent axeman follows us,
        leaves no footprint in the snow.
        The silent man is following us.

        Hunger burdens our packs.

38)   Two hours before sunrise,
        our usual time to get going,

when we can see to put one foot before the other.

The frequent ups and downs wear on the dogs;
grown weak, they fall.
To cease their suffering
the stragglers receive the *coup de grace*.
Their bodies heap up on the sleds;
the others closing up, continuing,
at night howl requiems for dead companions.

39)
March
11th

Alec shoots a rabbit:
quite a feed for six men.

The Indians in mournful state weep bitterly,
declaring we are lost,
they'll never see their homes again.
Persuasive eloquence is difficult when we're uncertain
our reasoning is sound.

40)

Buster, a favourite among our dogs,
we cannot coax to leave the fire.
No one has the heart to shoot him.
We leave him to his fate.

41)

Thick mist shrouds everything:
we grope in darkness.

Times are hard when we eat dog to keep our strength
    up,
dog which has-starved, which we have worked to death.
Dog soup may not taste good, but it goes well.

42)
March
15th

The rising sun dispels the mist.
The snow has stopped.
Twenty miles away a high bold rock,
much like a photograph once seen: Roche à Miette.
If the Athabaska be not in that valley,
it lies beyond those mountains.
We lack both grub and strength to carry us across.

Alec, hoping we do not see him, steals from camp,
to assure himself by moonlight he's not mistaken.

43) Imagine our camp then:
opposite sit the Indians:
Johnny, silent and impassive,
the other two with their heads in their hands sobbing.
Jarvis, very thin, very white, very much subdued.
Alec chewing tobacco and looking about used up,
not sure if it be Roche à Miette or not.
In the centre I sit.
My looks I can't describe;
my feeling scarcely.
I don't believe the Athabaska lies in that valley.
I do believe we have not many days to live.
I have been thinking of "the dearest spot on earth to me,"
of our Mother and Father,
of all my brothers and sisters and friends,
of the happy days at home,
of all the good deeds I have left undone
and all the bad ones committed.
I wonder if our bones will ever be discovered,
when and by whom;
if our friends will mourn for us long,
or do as is often done,
forget us as soon as possible.
I have been looking death in the face
and have come to the conclusion
C. F. Hanington has been a hard case
and I would like to live a while longer to make up for it.

I am glad since we started
we didn't go back;
this has been a tough trip,
this evening the toughest.

44) Three miles from our camp
March the benches of our long-sought river.
16th The frail dogs stagger, barking feebly;
the effort too much for one, he drops in his traces.

On Lac à Brule, its snow blown off, the ice a glare,
we travel without snowshoes
our first time since Christmas
upstream to Jasper House

where, we hope, we can provision us.
The old fort leans most doubtfully.
It is abandoned, and we've come these twenty miles
for nought.

45)   Some Indians we meet sell us their last provisions:
        sixty pounds of dried deer meat.
        With one day's rest we start again.

46)   From McLeod Portage
March   our last view of the Rocky Mountains:
24th   few among us loath to turn their backs on where we
            toiled:
        bounded by lofty crests, the snowy peaks,
        more beautiful by rosy hues of rising sun,
        more and more interesting as we depart them,
        shaking the snow from off our feet against them.

47)   Tea now is everything;
        boiled over and over carefully,
        with one fresh grain each time.
        Tobacco in the evening improves on nothing.

48)   Numbness holds our limbs,
March   we cannot push one snowshoe before the other,
27th   as if we're marking time.
        No laughing matter,
        it could amuse a well-fed bystander.

49)   Despite our hunger and our weakness,
March   we stumble into Lake St. Anne.
30th   McGillivray sets a supper out for us,
        white fish and potatoes, milk and bread, sugar, tea.
        We eat a great deal more than can be good for us.
        For half an hour not a word;
        then we cannot mumble much.

        Five a.m.: we rise and steal some bread.
        At seven: breakfast.
        Then to a mission village where we buy butter, eggs,
        feed on grilled buffalo bones they serve us.
        With eggs, butter, cream, we return to the house

where we eat bread with cream and sugar up to noon.
At noon: another fill.
Afternoon and evening through we eat,
as hungry yet as ever.

Our great exploration at an end,
our hunger and great danger.

"It is altogether too large a country for six men."

50)
May
22nd

We had taken the sun's altitude each noon,
determining our latitude.
Using a compass, counting paces for dead reckoning;
sticks in our hands to knock the slush
from off our snowshoes every step, and counting:
at forty paces closing the left hand's little finger
— a hundred feet;
another forty paces, ring finger closing
— another hundred feet.
When we'd clasped closed our left hand's fingers and the
      thumb:
— five hundred feet;
shift the stick to the left hand,
start counting on the right.
When we'd clenched that fist,
we tallied on a thousand paces, notebook entry.

Somewhere on the plains,
when we and spring had both run out of snow,
we nailed our snowshoes to a tree,
appropriate inscriptions on them.

We reached Fort Garry, bathed and changed our clothes.
Walking on the hotel verandah:
"How far do you make it?"
My hand was clenched,
my fingers acting automatically,
closing automatically at every forty paces.
Funny, eh?

The Major's Bath
Tom Wilson

Major A.B. Rogers was the American surveyor in charge of preliminary route surveys for the Canadian Pacific Railway during the summer of 1881, and Tom Wilson was his special attendant.

It was a very hot day and the glaciers were pouring torrents into the streams. On reaching the creek we found it terribly swollen, and to make matters worse the current raced around numerous large boulders. All streams that run direct from glaciers begin to rise in the afternoon and subside in the early morning. Knowing this, I halted at the creek and suggested to the Major that it would be advisable to camp for the night and cross the stream when the water would be lower and less dangerous. He shot one of his famous "Blue————" oaths at me. "Afraid of it are you? Want the old man to show you how to ford it?" It all happened in half a minute; he spurred his horse in, the current took its legs from under it, the Major disappeared in the foaming, silt-laden water, and the horse rolled downstream.

I grabbed a long pole and managed to push it towards the Major; and he seized it and I hauled him ashore. The horse struggled to its feet and climbed out a little way below us. Once ashore, the old man, for so I had begun to think of him, gave me a funny look. "Blue————", he remarked, "Light a fire and then get that damned horse. Blue————, it's cold!" Needless to say we camped there that night and crossed the stream next morning.

This incident gave Bath Creek its name. The Bow River flows through Bow Lakes and there deposits its glacial silt in the flood season. Bath Creek flows direct from Daly Glacier, therefore there are many times when the Bow, before its junction with Bath Creek, is running clear; then the latter pours its torrent of silty water into the larger stream and discolours it for miles downstream. Whenever this occurred the men of our gang would remark, "Hello, the old man's taking another bath", hence the name.

Railway surveyor Major A. B. Rogers. Provincial Archives of British Columbia

Mr. Holt's Horse
Samuel B. Steele

Kicking Horse Valley, 1883.

The trail along the side of the mountains near Golden was only suitable for pack animals until the Tote road was constructed. It was very dangerous; at the highest part it was more than a thousand feet above the foaming torrent and bad enough anywhere. One of the most remarkable experiences on it was that of Mr. H. S. Holt, C.E., now of Montreal. He was making his trip over the pack trail from the head of the Kicking Horse to the Columbia. Mr. A. R. Hogg, a prominent engineer, two assistant engineers and two packers composed his party, and he was riding a spirited broncho which he had used on the plains, and which had no experience of mountain trails. When he got to the lower canyon of the Kicking Horse, being the leader of the party, he found the trail very bad; at one point his horse began slipping on a loose stone, but he managed to dismount and tried to make the brute back up, which she would have done had she been a trained mountain pony. Instead of backing up she started forward and hit Mr. Holt in the chest, knocking him over the side of the canyon, which at that point was perpendicular and about 75 feet from the trail to the river below. In falling he turned a complete somersault, landing on his stomach on the trunk of a dead tree which had been caught in the rocks on the side of the canyon. The distance was afterwards measured, and the tree was found to be 27½ feet below the trail. The horse and the stone on which she slipped, which must have weighed at least 800 pounds, also fell over the cliff, but fortunately fell clear of the tree in which Mr. Holt had lodged, and both fell to the bottom of the canyon.

When the rest of the party came up they lowered to Mr. Holt a lariat, which he tied under his arms, and they pulled him up to the trail. Looking down he saw the horse lying on the rocks below; thinking her leg was broken and being unable to get down the perpendicular wall of the canyon, he concluded that it was best to shoot her and proceeded to carry his idea into execution. He succeeded in putting five bullets of his revolver into the horse's head without touching a vital spot. The animal then struggled to her feet and fell into the river, which was at that season and all summer a raging torrent, and was carried down about half a mile to the opposite shore.

110

The next day Mr.Holt sent his packers back to try to recover the saddle and bridle and some papers which were in the saddle bags. They found the horse lying on the rocks with one eye shot out, three ribs broken and one leg almost cut off. As they knew that the animal was a favourite with its owner, they built a shelter of brush over the poor beast and made her as comfortable as possible. When it was reported to Mr. Holt, he sent them back with some oats and gave instructions to them to feed the poor animal and give her a chance to recover, which, wonderful to relate, she did. She was sent to Mr. Holt's ranch for a year, and when the Alberta Field Force was raised for the suppression of the rebellion I saw a man, who had been employed as a mail carrier in the Rockies, in the ranks of the Alberta Mounted Rifles, riding a one-eyed horse, which he informed me, and so did others, was the animal which went over the canyon with Mr. Holt.

End of Track
A. P. Coleman

The Bow Valley near Lake Louise, 1884.

The construction train, staggering along on no fixed schedule, gave plenty of time to look about before it stopped, for the last time, at "the End," near what is now the delightful tourist resort Laggan.

Whoever would advance beyond this must do so on foot or on horseback. It was evening, and my eyes turned from the mountains across the valley of Bow River to the "city," temporary and hideous, where night quarters must be found. The chief hotel seemed to be the "Sumit" House (Summit?), a low-browed log building with a floor of "puncheons" — slabs split with the axe — instead of boards.

When darkness fell I paid for my bed in advance, according to the cautious practice of the hostelry, and retired to the grey blankets of bunk No. 2, second tier, in the common guest-chamber, trying to shut out sights and sounds from the bar-room by turning my back. An hour or two later another man scrambled into the bunk, somewhat the worse for whisky, and tucked himself into the blankets beside me. It appeared that my half-dollar paid for only half the bed.

It was a relief to turn out before the sun and escape from the noisome air of the hotel into the stumps and half-burnt logs and general litter of the clearing outside, where one could take deep breaths of the keen morning breeze, fresh from the snow of the mountains.

The crude life of the city was not yet stirring, and the dusky peaks on each side dominated the pass, looking down coldly, perhaps scornfully, on the heaps of foulness and scars of fire that marred the beauty of the valley. Then the spell was broken, sunlight gleamed on the western peaks, smoke began to rise from camp fires and chimneys; there were voices and oaths, mules hee-hawed in the corral near by, and the valley once more yielded itself up to man's uses. . . .

That night, by the kind word of a high official, I had permission to join the railway contractors in their boarding-car, a shrewd and interesting set of men from everywhere — the logging camp, Old World Universities, the east, and the west. There were pious men from Scotland, impious ones from Montana, much-married ones from Utah, and prudish men from Ontario, chatting or sitting silent, all waiting for a signal. There was a clangour from a big tent near by; a brawny "cookee," with sleeves rolled up, vindictively hammered a crowbar bent into a triangle and hung in a tree; and each man moved toward the tent, for it was supper-time. The meals were rough but good, in so far as things can be good which come from a tin can. The advance of civilisation is marked by mounds of empty cans, and our age may some day be named the Age of Tin.

Later, after a look at the mountains, while the moon rose cautiously, and at last gleamed softly on a snowfield, I tried the new sleeping quarters in the box car, with the bunk-room up a little flight of stairs. A dim lamp showed two tiers of bunks already half filled with forms muffled in blankets. Soon I was joined to their number, and but for its unstable equilibrium, voted the boarding-car an immense improvement on the hotel. It was, unhappily, a sort of reversed pendulum on springs, that rocked for fully a minute when any late comer got on board; and we all shuddered in sympathy when any one turned over in his bunk.

The Railway Years

The Tourists and Settlers 1885–1918

Snow-draped peaks we passed by, and turquoise lakes set amidst the old pinewoods and ringed round by gaunt precipices, and above, the snow. Wonderful waterfalls that plunged sheer for hundreds of feet into rock-cut canyons where the wild waters raged in fierce tumult. Sometimes the whole undergrowth amidst the black stems of the burnt forest would be aglow with the many coloured 'painter's brush,' or a mass of gold orange daisies would have their colour set against the black satin stems of the charred trunks and a sapphire blue sky. The lure of the wilds always called us onward.

J. Norman Collie

By Car and by Cowcatcher
Susan Agnes Macdonald

In 1886, shortly after the completion of the Canadian Pacific Railway, Prime Minister Sir John A. Macdonald and his wife Lady Agnes rode the line to the west coast.

From Calgary to Laggan I had travelled in the car of the engine, accompanied by a victimized official. Perched on a little feather bench, well in front, and close to the small windows, I had enjoyed an excellent opportunity of seeing everything. Besides this, I had gained a great deal of useful information about engines, boilers, signals, &c., which may come in "handy" some day. During our stoppages the engineer and firemen had not failed to explain these things, and I had even ventured to whistle "caution" at a "crossing." The signal went very well for an amateur, but the Chief's quick ear had detected a falter, and at the next halt he sent a peremptory message, desiring me "not to play tricks," which, addressed to a discreet matron, was really quite insulting. I had even questioned the engineer as to the probable effect of a bad collision while I occupied this post. He promptly suggested, "most likely killed;" and added, reflectively, as he carefully oiled an already dripping valve, "which would be a bad job"!

When I announced my desire to travel on the cowcatcher, Mr. E——— seemed to think that a very bad job indeed. To a sensible, level-headed man as he is, such an innovation on all general rules of travelling decorum was no doubt very startling. He used many ineffectual persuasions to induce me to abandon the idea, and almost said I should not run so great a risk; but at last, being a man of few words, and seeing time was nearly up, he so far relented as to ask what I proposed using as a seat. Glancing round the station platform I beheld a small empty candle-box lying near, and at once declared

114

Laggan Station below Lake Louise circa 1890. Archives of the Canadian Rockies

that was "just the thing." Before Mr. E——— could expostulate further, I had asked a brakesman to place the candle-box on the buffer-beam, and was on my way to the "Jamaica" to ask the Chief's permission. The Chief, seated on a low chair on the rear platform of the car, with a rug over his knees and a magazine in his hand, looked very comfortable and content. Hearing my request, after a moment's thought, he pronounced the idea "rather ridiculous," then remembered it was dangerous as well, and finally asked if I was sure I could hold on. Before the words were well out of his lips, and taking permission for granted by the question, I was again standing by the cowcatcher, admiring the position of the candle-box, and anxiously asking to be helped on.

Before I take my seat, let me try, briefly, to describe the "Cowcatcher." Of course every one knows that the buffer-beam is that narrow, heavy iron platform, with the sides scooped out, as it were, on the very fore-front of the engine over which the headlight glares, and in the corner of which a little flag is generally placed. In English engines, I believe, the buffers proper project from the front of this beam. In Canadian engines another sort of attachment is arranged, immediately below the beam, by which the engine can draw trains backwards as well as forwards. The beam is about eight feet across, at the widest part, and about three feet deep. The description of a cowcatcher is less easy. To begin with, it is misnamed, for it catches no cows at all. Sometimes, I understand, it throws up on the buffer-beam whatever maimed or mangled animal it has struck, but in most cases it clears the line by shoving forward, or tossing aside, any

115

Prime Minister Sir John A. Macdonald and Lady Agnes (right) in British Columbia during their 1886 trip on the Canadian Pacific Railway. Canadian Railroad Historical Association

removable obstruction. It is best described as a sort of barred iron beak, about six feet long, projecting close over the track in a V shape, and attached to the buffer-beam by very strong bolts. It is sometimes sheathed with thin iron plates in winter, and acts then as a small snow-plough.

Behold me now, enthroned on the candle-box, with a soft felt hat well over my eyes, and a linen carriage-cover tucked round me from waist to foot. Mr. E——— had seated himself on the other side of the headlight. He had succumbed to the inevitable, ceased further expostulation, disclaimed all responsibility, and, like the jewel of a Superintendent he was, had decided on sharing my peril! I turn to him, peeping round the headlight, with my best smile, "This is *lovely*," I triumphantly announce, seeing that a word of comfort is necessary, *"quite lovely*; I shall travel on this cowcatcher from summit to sea!"

Mr. Superintendent, in his turn, peeps round the headlight and surveys me with solemn and resigned surprise. "I — suppose —

you — will," he says slowly, and I see that he is hoping, at any rate, that I shall live to do it!

With a mighty snort, a terribly big throb, and a shrieking whistle, No. 374 moves slowly forward. The very small population of Laggan have all come out to see. They stand in the hot sunshine, and shade their eyes as the stately engine moves on. "It is an awful thing to do!" I hear a voice say, as the little group lean forward; and for a moment I feel a thrill that is very like fear; but it is gone at once, and I can think of nothing but the novelty, the excitement, and the fun of this mad ride in glorious sunshine and intoxicating air, with magnificent mountains before and around me, their lofty peaks smiling down on us, and never a frown on their grand faces!

The pace quickens gradually, surely, swiftly, and then we are rushing up to the summit. We soon stand on the "Great Divide" — 5300 feet above sea-level — between the two great oceans. As we pass, Mr. E——— by a gesture, points out a small river (called Bath Creek, I think) which, issuing from a lake on the narrow summit-level, winds near the track. I look, and lo! the water, flowing *eastward* towards the Atlantic side, turns in a moment as the Divide is passed, and pours *westward* down the Pacific slope!

Another moment and a strange silence has fallen round us. With steam shut off and brakes down, the 60-ton engine, by its own weight and impetus alone, glides into the pass of the Kicking Horse River, and begins a descent of 2800 feet in twelve miles. We rush onward through the vast valley stretching before us, bristling with lofty forests, dark and deep, that, clinging to the mountain side, are reared up into the sky. The river, widening, grows white with dashing foam, and rushes downwards with tremendous force. Sunlight flashes on glaciers, into gorges, and athwart huge towering masses of rock crowned with magnificent tree crests that rise all round us of every size and shape. Breathless — almost awe-stricken — but with a wild triumph in my heart, I look from farthest mountain peak, lifted high before me, to the shining pebbles at my feet! Warm wind rushes past; a thousand sunshine colours dance in the air. With a firm right hand grasping the iron stanchion, and my feet planted on the buffer beam, there was not a yard of that descent in which I faltered for a moment. If I had, then assuredly in the wild valley of the Kicking Horse River, on the western slope of the Rocky Mountains, a life had gone out that day! I did not think of danger, or remember what a giddy post I had. I could only gaze at the glaciers that the mountains held so closely, 5000 feet above us, at the trace of snow avalanches which had left a space a hundred feet wide massed with torn and prostrate trees; on the shadows that played over the distant peaks; and on a hundred rainbows made by the foaming, dashing river, which swirls with tremendous rapidity down the gorge on its way to the Columbia in the valley below.

There is glory of brightness and beauty everywhere, and I laugh aloud on the cowcatcher, just because it is all so delightful!

Harassment at the Hot Springs
Edward Roper

Banff, 1886.

If I heard the remark once, I heard it five hundred times during our stay at Banff — "The miskitties *is* fierce to-day!" It was always that, with variations of grammar and pronunciation; but that was the usual formula.

It was a strange sight — everyone, walking, sitting, lying, had, every few seconds, to drive off or smash a mosquito.

The old hands, being used to it, regarding it as a natural thing in summer, professed not to mind. *But they did.* New-comers were made irritable, ill, with the annoyance. Up at the hot springs it was the same — worse. The patients sat on logs and rocks, whiling away the time squashing mosquitoes. Poor cripples on crutches would prop themselves against a tree or boulder whilst they slew those who were fast into them. How could they get their health benefited under such circumstances? That they did speaks greatly for the value of the treatment.

We went to church on Sunday in the Town Hall — a log shanty. The parson and the rest of us were hot and worried with these wretched insects. It was all we could do to keep our faces straight; it was such an absurdity — everyone flicking away or murdering the horrid things. An English lord and lady were staying there when we were. Mosquitoes evidently had no reverence for blue blood; perhaps its flavour may be better than the common puddle. Any way, his lordship wore low shoes — more foolish he — and the way those wretched "miskitties" worried round his ankles was a caution. His

118

lordship said to me, "They certainly are very bad, but really nothing to what they were at Harrison Lake and Sicamous"; so we were thankful that we took good advice, and did *not* stay there.

The men roofing the C.P.R. Hotel wore veils and gloves, and yet could hardly work.

A coloured man remarked, "They're big and bad enough in Manitoba; here they are like pigeons!"

It was next to impossible to sit still enough to draw.

They began operations about 10 a.m., and they kept steadily at work till 6 a.m. next day.

"How long is this kept going?" I asked a resident. He said, "*Oh, they don't trouble in cold weather.*"

The main street of Banff circa 1889. Archives of the Canadian Rockies

B.C., 1887
J. A. Lees and W. J. Clutterbuck

The Queen's Hotel has a fine ring about it, and in fact it is a fine place — so much so, that if it were much finer you could not see it at all. It consists of a low badly built log cabin, which hereabouts

Golden City, B.C., circa 1887. Archives of the Canadian Rockies

they call a "shack." It has a bar, a kitchen, a room with a bagatelle board in it, a feeding-room, and three tiny bedrooms with barely space for bed and wash-stand, but quite a number of draughts. It was, however, all very clean, and as far as such a place could be, comfortable, and Mrs. Green was an excellent cook. We found on the table in the sitting-room a sedately bound volume of considerable bulk, entitled "Reveries of a Bachelor," new edition. This implied a neatly veiled compliment to married men, for the book was nothing but an ingenious dodge for evading the N.W. drink regulations, a secret spring which was revealed to us by the landlord disclosing the neck of a whisky bottle most artfully concealed within the leaves. However, lots of books have worse things than this in them.

We wandered about the "suburbs" all day, and made divers discoveries. Item: That the waters of the Columbia, into which the Kicking Horse flows a couple of miles beyond the station, were too "riley" (British Columbian word meaning stained with snow) to allow of any fishing. Item: That the said suburbs consisted chiefly of brush and swamp, and were the lair of millions of mosquitoes. Item: That Golden City, or "Golden," as it is invariably called, contained one or two good fellows, but was on the whole one of the most pitiful places on the earth.

Since the early days of mining discoveries we imagine this city went steadily backwards, until the C.P.R. put life once more into its sinking frame. Now he would be a bold man who would deny that the future has great possibilities for it, for the Columbia valley above here is undoubtedly one of the favoured districts of the province, and is being rapidly settled. The river is navigable from its source down to Golden, but only a few miles below, and consequently any goods destined for the upper valley are brought here by the railway for transfer to the boats and two steamers which already ply on the river. The Provincial Government is also making a waggon-road along the valley to the lakes which form the headwaters, and on from there down the Kootenay, so that the settlers are not wholly dependent on the navigation, which of course is often interrupted by frost, floods, and low water; and it will not be very long before the iron horse will find his way across the beautiful parks which fringe the river bank, and destroy at one fell stroke the occupation of boats, pack-trains, and waggons, and to some extent even of the steamers.

There is a freedom and heartiness about these British Columbian folk (we shall in future adopt the custom of the country and use only the letters B.C.) which is very captivating to the sophisticated and conventional mind. The first friend we made was a little girl aged about five, who seemed to be living independently of her relations. She *said* her name was Miss Jenny Lorena Wells, which seems a good deal for one so young; and she imparted many details concerning the life and habits of her doll. Then our landlord was exceedingly hospitable and agreeable. We asked by way of conversation what was the name of the mountain straight opposite his door, a peak so striking in its rugged magnificence that in Switzerland they would have two railways and a dozen hotels planted on it. With princely generosity he replied, "You can call it what you darn like: every outfit that comes along gives it a new name, and I'll be shot if I can remember what the last one was." It was gratifying to reflect that we were now an "outfit," but we could not at that time think of an appropriate title for the mountain.

The east-bound train came in about 17 o'clock; and having nothing better to do, we strolled up to the station to see it pass, when to our astonishment we detected in a youth of fashionable exterior, surrounded by a bevy of sorrowing but high-born maidens, our longlost and little expected Cardie. It had taken him just a month of driving and training to get here from his eyrie in the Colorado mountains, and it was an extraordinary coincidence that after all the delays and minor calamities we had suffered, we should have thus managed to reach our goal on the same day.

Cardie soon put us right on several points of speech, *e.g.* we found that "truck" is the great and universal word for any emergency. "Is all that truck yours? What sort of truck have you got in it for cold weather? Yes, that 45.90 Winchester isn't bad truck to have around for a grizzly. Well, I should put it all on a truck and wheel it to the hotel." . . . The only other necessary piece of knowledge is "How to use 'What's the matter' in 500 different ways, by one who has been there." "What's the matter with some supper? What's the matter with the bread? (*i.e.* Please pass it). What's the matter with skipping out of this first thing in the morning?" Any one who will devote his mind to the study of these far-reaching productions of the Anglo-American tongue will find that the opportunities for their application are endless; in fact we now "have them in our houses and use no other."

With this newly acquired brilliancy there was no longer any difficulty in christening our mountain peak, and the world will be good enough to take notice that now and for all time it is to be known as the "What's-the-Matter-horn."

The canoes not having arrived, we decided to go for a ramble of three or four days to see what the country was like, and as there was no room in the Queen's for our "truck," we hired a small shack in which we stored all the more sumptuous portions of our apparel and various other things which we did not need to take with us. That finished, we lunched on the *Duchess* (the larger of the two Columbia steamers) with the captain, Mr. Armstrong, who was in all ways most obliging. His craft presented a somewhat decrepit appearance, as about a fortnight before our arrival she had been wrecked in the Columbia with a full cargo and some passengers. They had managed to fish her up again out of about fourteen feet of water, and she was now in steaming order, but all her fittings and former smartness had gone where other good things go. Her general aspect, in fact, was that of an old canal-boat into which a travelling gipsy's van had been hastily crammed without regard to its position or safety. One most valuable thing had, however, been saved from the general ruin, Sam, the Chinese cook: the best cook we "struck" (Anglicé — fell in with) on the mainland of B.C. Here we met also another of the N.W. Police officers, and altogether enjoyed ourselves, for the mosquito seemed unable to exist on the *Duchess*, though he flourished everywhere else.

The general good-fellowship and freedom from ceremony are not without their drawbacks. Within ten minutes of our arrival at Golden, half a dozen total strangers had pressed us to drink, and we thought

"What a nice place." We began to doubt the advantages of it when another total stranger adorned with two lovely black eyes dashed into the shack this evening while we were packing. In the same hearty and informal manner he immediately assailed Cardie and Jim with a selected assortment of the worst epithets yet coined, and challenged them both to mortal combat. We at last persuaded him to go and fight another man, who, we assured him, was thirsting for his blood, and at a late hour that evening were rejoiced to see him relieved of his lethal weapons by the community at large. This man, when sober, was a nice enough fellow, but the drink supplied in these western towns is as a rule bad enough to make even a dog behave disgracefully, let alone a man.

We discussed here with the authorities what it would be advisable to do whenever (and if ever) the canoes should turn up. We were uncertain whether to go down the Columbia northwards to what is called the Big Bend, or go up it to its source, and crossing the narrow strip of land, paddle down the Kootenay, our own inclination being for the former course. The experts said — "Oh yes, you can get round the Big Bend; one or two canoes have done it all right, but on an average they lose one man out of each party that goes down. You see the rapids are bad, and it is long odds against every one getting down safely." We talked it over, and made up our minds to go, as we all thought one man out of three would never be missed; but we soon found there was an irreconcilable difference of opinion between us as to which that one was, no less than three names being suggested. So we gave up the Big Bend, and finally decided to go up the river as soon as the canoes arrived, and in the meantime to try a little hunt.

On the morning of August 17th, we started in the *Duchess*, which was bound for the lake at the headwaters known as Lake Windermere, intending to get out of her at the first promising spot. Our progress was very slow at first, as this part of the river is rapid, and the old stern-wheeler did not make more than $1\frac{1}{2}$ miles an hour past the banks, though she was good for eight or nine through the water. The Columbia depends for its supply on the melting snow, and this was about coming to an end; the water therefore was falling rapidly, and leaving on either side huge marshy lagoons known as sloughs (pronounced sloo). These seemed to offer great attractions to enormous flocks of geese, ducks, and plover, while here and there the white wings of a swan might be seen reflected in the perfectly still waters. The banks of the river are for the most part densely wooded, except where one of these backwaters occurs, and in such places it is often impossible for the inexperienced to detect the true course, there being frequently so many different channels, and these so wide, that there is no perceptible stream in any of them. Skilfully steered, the *Duchess* found her way through the devious passages, every turn disclosing new beauties, as the two glorious ranges, the Rockies on our left hand (the east) and the Selkirks on the right, became visible above the high wooded bluffs which in many parts overhang the river. Forest fires were burning on all sides, but only making their existence known by a light blue haze, which filled the air and gave just that atmosphere to the view which in a dry mountain climate is so often wanting, and on this perfect day not one thing was lacking to complete our happiness.

Alas, earthly happiness seldom lasts long. We passed the place where the poor *Duchess* went down, and a little higher up, at a spot where the forest grew more densely than anywhere else, the steamer ran her nose into the bank, and we and our "truck" were bundled on shore. Five minutes later she was a mere puffing speck in the distance, while we were being literally eaten by the most awful mosquitoes it has ever been our lot to meet — or be meat for.

An Outing to Lake Louise
William Spotswood Green

1888.

A run of thirty miles brought us to Laggan, which is a place of more importance than Castle Mountain, for besides the inevitable water-tank, there are sheds in which the two monster locomotives, kept for working the steep gradients to the westward of the pass, find a home. Here also reside three troopers of the red-coated police, whose business it is to watch the pass, and prevent liquor being smuggled into the North-West territories from British Columbia. The station agent, who by the way is a first-rate entomologist, a contractor for cutting trees in the forest for the railway, two women and a child, with the section gang, made up the whole population, and to the boarding house where all these fed we made our way for breakfast.

124

The lakeshore at Lake Louise as it appeared in 1899. Archives of the Canadian Rockies

A most excellent breakfast we got, and while eating it we discussed our future plans. The contractor said that while prospecting for timber he had been up as far as Lake Louise, and advised us to follow the railway track for about two miles up the valley, and cross the Bow river by the railway bridge, and then strike up the mountain side through the forest. One of the railway men said he had a skow on the river, and though it was not very seaworthy, and the river was very swift, if we chose to take the risk of the passage we were welcome to it, and that by thus crossing the river we would save an hour's walking. We accepted his offer, and after breakfast took up our packs and went with him to the river, which is here a series of rapids, with one pool where the current being less swift offered a possibility for a ferry. The skow was just like a magnified pig-trough made of rough boards and square at both ends. At present it was sunk, and quite water soaked. We were not long, however, baling it out with the help of our kettle and frying-pan, and as the rapids commenced immediately below, we hauled it up along the bank as far as possible so as to make a good start. Putting our packs on the

125

one seat in the middle, H. took one paddle and I the other, and getting a good shove off from the owner, by paddling with might and main we reached the other shore in safety, but drifted down about 100 yards while making the passage. Here, making fast the skow to a tree, we shouldered our packs and struck up the mountain side for Lake Louise. We could see the valley occupied by the lake quite plainly from the railway, but every one had warned us that when we entered the dense forest it was quite possible for us to lose our way. The last word from the station agent was, "Be sure whatever happens you keep to the left, for then you will meet the creek from the lake."

At first our course lay up through the blackened poles of a young burnt-out forest. Then crossing some swamps we entered the living forest, and though much more open and composed of smaller trees than what we had been accustomed to in the Selkirks, we had to do a good deal of scrambling over fallen logs. Soon we were shut out from all view of the outside world and had to consider our direction with more care. The ground being uneven it was not always easy to judge our direction by the lie of the land. But keeping the station agent's last words before my mind, whenever alternative routes opened ahead I always took the one to the left. H. now considered that I was going too much to the left and preferred bearing away to the right, and as there was no third person to decide who had the best of the argument, and as the compass could not be appealed to owing to our not having mutually agreed upon bearings before entering the forest, he bore away to the right and I kept to the left. As long as possible we kept up communication by shouting to each other, and as we could not be far from the lake I felt certain that we must soon meet on its shore. In less than half an hour from hearing H.'s last shout I struck upon the stream coming from the lake, and in a few moments more stood upon its swampy shore.

I was quite unprepared for the full beauty of the scene. Nothing of the kind could possibly surpass it. I was somewhat reminded of the Oeschinen See in Switzerland, but Lake Louise is about twice as long; the forests surrounding it are far richer, and the grouping of the mountains is simply perfection. At the head of the lake the great precipice of Mount Lefroy stood up in noble grandeur, a glacier sweeping round its foot came right down to the head of the lake. Half way up the cliffs another glacier occupied a shelf, and from its margin, where the ice showed a thickness of about 300 feet, great avalanches were constantly falling to the glacier below. Above the upper glacier the peak rose in horizontal strata, the edges of which were outlined with thin wreaths of snow, to a gently sloping blunt peak crowned with a cap of ice. The mountains closing in on either side and falling precipitously to the lake formed a suitable frame to this magnificent picture.

The lake was of the deepest green-blue, like those in Switzerland, and the pine forest growing actually into the water, clad the mountain sides in dense masses wherever trees could find enough earth for their roots. All this was reflected in the lake, which was barely ruffled by little puffs of wind, now striking in one place now in another, and causing the water momentarily to sparkle in the sunshine.

There was a little too much smoke in the atmosphere to make photography a success, but I took a couple of views at once, for dark clouds heaving up from behind the peaks looked ominous, and I feared a break in the weather.

As shouting met with no response save the echo from the rocky walls, I lit a fire and piled on a quantity of green boughs, so as to make a good smoke. If H. was anywhere in the vicinity I felt sure he would turn up soon, so set to work hauling a few floating logs together, and when three were lashed side by side they made a famous raft, on which I thought we might paddle our camp to the head of the lake. Having paddled about a little to test its stability, I began to feel hungry, so opening the pack, I cut a few rashers of bacon, but had no bread or biscuit to eat with it, H. having all the biscuits in his pack; my pack consisted of the tent, one sleeping-bag, the bacon, kettle, frying-pan, and tea. His was made up of one sleeping-bag, a warm rug, the thin oiled sheet, biscuits, and a tin of beef.

Dinner over, and very heavy, threatening clouds pouring down from the mountain heights and filling the valley, I thought it better to pitch the tent, and had to break up my raft, for the rope stretched between two trees was needed for fixing it. I had this scarcely done when there came a blinding flash of lightning and a crash of thunder, which seemed almost as if all the mountains were tumbling about my ears. Then came a fierce storm of wind down the lake. The placid surface was lashed into spindrift in an instant, and the wild crashing of trees as they fell before the blast, rendered the scene almost terrifying. Then flash succeeded flash in quick succession, but the wind storm only lasted about five minutes.

All this time I was crouching in the tent, which I had pitched just inside the margin of the forest, and did my best to keep the sleeping-bag dry, but what with fluttering and banging about, a good deal of wet got in. In about half an hour the whole storm was over, the lake assumed a dull, leaden hue, the clouds hung low, and the wild cry of a loon swimming far out from the shore, was the only sound that broke the stillness. The vegetation was all dripping, and as night approached it felt very cold. Tea without milk, and bacon without bread was not luxurious, but I had to be satisfied, and wondering what had become of H., I turned into my sleeping-bag, but was too cold to sleep much. Avalanches, too, were constantly falling from the hanging glacier at the head of the lake. Between 2 and 5 A.M., the period of the greatest cold, they fell most frequently, at intervals of about twenty minutes, making the whole valley resound as with thunder. I was glad when day broke, and getting up, lit the fire and made breakfast — tea and bacon once more — then frying a number of pieces of bacon, I made them up in leaves, and with this provision for the day, started to walk round the lake and so reach the glacier.

Before leaving my camp I wrote a note for H. should he turn up, and nailed it with one of the spare boot nails I carried in my pocket to a tree close by. The clouds still hung low, and it began to rain. There was a kind of trail which I followed when possible, sometimes scrambling up into the woods and again wading in the water. The mountain-tops were cut off by clouds, but new views of strange castellated crags opened as I progressed. It was 6 A.M. when I started. In two hours I had reached a point not far from the glacier stream, above which the moraine rose in high piles of crags partly covered with vegetation. For more than an hour it had rained steadily, and between it and the reeking vegetation my clothes were as wet as if I had fallen into the lake. I now saw the utter hopelessness of further advance, the heavy rain clouds were coming lower and lower, so making a few hasty sketches I sat at the foot of a pine tree, and eating some bacon, attempted a last photograph, and then turned my back on Mount Lefroy whose cliffs were now quite invisible.

On regaining the tent I made no delay, but packing it up with the sleeping-bag inside, got the pack on my back. Owing to the wet it was about twice the weight it was before, and so disconsolately enough I started down through the forest to the Bow river. Not feeling certain that I should find the skow, I bore away to the left, and in due time reaching the railway bridge I crossed it, and arrived at Laggan about noon.

The police seeing that I was like a drowned rat took pity on me and lent me a change of clothes, so I turned out for dinner in riding breeches with broad yellow stripes down the legs, slippers, and an oilskin coat. I was a little anxious concerning H., and would have been more so only that the troopers had found evidence of his having returned to the skow, which was still fastened where we left it. There was a piece of white paper visible, fastened to a paddle, so H. must have returned so far, and then gone back up the mountain to look for me. I had left a note for him on the shore of the lake so it most probably was only a question of waiting.

About 3 P.M. a man came bringing information that H. was coming down to the skow, and all hands turned out in great excitement to see him attempt the passage single-handed. I came along too, as fast as the riding breeches would permit and brought the camera, so as to get a good photograph. One of the troopers ran off for his lasso, to catch H. if possible in mid-stream, and evidently to carry out the proverb concerning the "man that is born to be hanged," &c.

On H. reaching the skow the whole population of Laggan, including two women and one child, stood on the other side of the Bow. Carefully he placed his pack on board, then he began to haul the skow up stream and away from the rapids as far as possible; this was difficult and very tedious. All considered the odds decidedly against him. I shouted out to hold on till I could walk round by the railway bridge. But the roar of the waters drowned my voice. Then came the critical moment; he stepped on board, quickly coiled down the rope and shoved off — one frantic stroke of the paddle and the craft instead of going ahead, spun round like a top. It was now evident that all was up. The current made no delay, so I fixed the camera for one particular rock where the first wave of the rapids curled over. I felt sure that here the catastrophe would take place, but though I got a very fair instantaneous photograph, considering the weather it was a moment too soon. Passing over the first wave in safety the skow swept past the rock, but was swamped three seconds later. She did not roll over, but coming broadside on to a rock, filled and remained firmly jambed, with the river pouring over blankets and everything else.

The lasso was flung, but fell short. Then H. took to the water, and scrambling from boulder to boulder, the spray occasionally going over his head, he reached the shore. As soon as he regained breath, taking the end of some ropes we had tied together, he went into the rapids again, and making the end fast to the skow, he lifted the wet pack on to his back, out of which the water poured in a perfect stream. To carry the pack to land involved a real hard struggle with the seething water, but the beholders were much impressed, and one of the troopers remarked, "I guess that chap has got some sand in him," which I took to be no end of a compliment to H., and felt that whatever the "sand" might mean, it was well deserved. All hands hanging on to the rope, we hauled the skow to land, her symmetry being sadly marred by the process. H. now had to borrow a rig out, and we spent the rest of the evening in the police-hut playing whist and enjoying the good company of our kind hosts, while our clothes steamed away on a nearly red-hot stove.

How We Climbed Cascade
Ralph Connor

Just beyond the Gap lies Banff, the capital of the Canadian National Park, a park unexcelled in all the world for grandeur and diversified beauty of mountain scenery. The main street of Banff runs south to Sulphur mountain, modest, kindly and pine-clad, and north to Cascade, sheer, rocky and bare, its great base thrust into the pine forest, its head into the clouds. Day after day the Cascade gazed in steadfast calm upon the changing scenes of the valley below. The old grey face rudely scarred from its age-long conflict with the elements, looked down in silent challenge upon the pigmy ephemeral dwellers of the village at its feet. There was something overpoweringly majestic in the utter immobility of that ten thousand feet of ancient age-old rock; something almost irritating in its calm challenge to all else than its mighty self.

It was this calm challenge, too calm for contempt, that moved the Professor to utter himself somewhat impatiently one day, flinging the gauntlet, so to speak, into that stony, immovable face: "We'll stand on your head some day, old man." And so we did, and after the following manner.

We were the Professor, by virtue of his being pedagogue to the town, slight, wiry, with delicate taste for humor; the Lady from Montreal, who, slight as she was and dainty, had conquered Mt. Blanc not long before; the Lady from Winnipeg, literary in taste, artistic in temperament, invincible of spirit; the Man from California, strong, solid and steady; the Lady from Banff, wholesome, kindly,

An early climbing party camped on Cascade Mountain near Banff. Archives
of the Canadian Rockies

cheery, worthy to be the mother of the three most beautiful babes in
all the Park and far beyond it; and the Missionary.

It was a Thursday afternoon in early September of '91, golden and
glowing in smoky purple hues, a day for the open prairie or for the
shadowy woods, according to your choice. Into a democrat we
packed our stuff, provisions for a week, so it seemed, a tent with all
necessary camp appurtenances, and started up the valley of the little
Forty Mile creek that brawled its stony way from the back of the
Cascade. We were minded to go by the creek till we should get on
to the back of old Cascade, from which we could climb up upon his
head. Across the intervening stretch of prairie, then through the open
timber in the full golden glory of the September sun, and then into
the thicker pines, where we lost the sunlight, we made our way,
dodging trees, crashing through thickets, climbing over boulder
masses, till at last the Professor, our intrepid driver, declared that it
would be safer to take our team no further. And knowing him, we
concluded that advance must be absolutely impossible. We decided

to make this our camp. To me a camp anywhere and in any weather is good, so that it be on dry ground and within sight, and better within sound, of water. But this camp of ours possessed all the charms that delight the souls of all true campers. In the midst of trees, tall pines between whose points the stars looked down, within touch of the mountains and within sound of the brawling Forty Mile creek and the moaning pines. By the time the camp was pitched, the pine beds made and supper cooked, darkness had fallen. With appetites sharpened to the danger point, we fell upon the supper and then reclined upon couches of pine, the envy of the immortal gods. With no one to order us to bed, we yarned and sang, indifferent to the passing of the night or to the tasks of the morrow, while the stars slowly swung over our heads.

At last the camp was still. Down the canyon came the long-drawn howl of a wolf, once and again, and we were asleep; the long day and the soothing night proving too much for the shuddering delight of that long, weird, gruesome sound. We turned over in our sleep and woke. It was morning. The Professor had already "fixed" the horses and was lighting the breakfast fire. Unhappily, we possessed the remnants of conscience which refused to lie down, and though the sun had given as yet no hint of arriving, we persuaded ourselves that it was day. A solid breakfast, prayers, and we stood ready for the climb, greener at our work than the very greenest of the young pines that stood about us, but with fine jaunty courage of the young recruit marching to his first campaign.

An expert mountain-climber, glancing down the line, would have absolutely refused to move from the tent door. With the exception of the Lady from Montreal, who had done Mt. Blanc, not one of us had ever climbed anything more imposing than Little Tunnel, one thousand feet high. While as to equipment, we hadn't any, not even an alpenstock between the lot of us. As for the ladies, they appeared to carry their full quota of flimsy skirts and petticoats, while on their feet they wore their second-best kid boots. It was truly a case of fools rushing in where angels pause. Without trail, without guide, but knowing that the top was up there somewhere, we set out, water-bottles and brandy-flasks — in case of accident — and lunch baskets slung at the belts of the male members of the party, the sole shred of mountaineering outfit being the trunk of a sapling in the hand of each ambitious climber.

As we struck out from camp, the sun was tipping the highest

pines far up on the mountain side to the west. Cascade mountain has a sheer face, but a long, sloping back. It was our purpose to get upon that back with all speed. So, for a mile or more, we followed the main direction of the valley, gradually bearing to our right and thus emerging from the thicker forest into the open. When we considered that we had gone far enough up the valley, we turned sharply to our right and began to climb, finding the slope quite easy and the going fairly good. We had all day before us, and we had no intention of making our excursion anything but an enjoyment. Therefore, any ambition to force the pace on the part of any member was sternly frowned down.

By 10 o'clock we had got clear of the trees and had begun to see more clearly our direction. But more, we began to realize somewhat more clearly the magnitude of our enterprise. The back of this old Cascade proved to be longer than that bestowed upon most things that have backs, and the lack of equipment was beginning to tell. The ladies of our party were already a grotesquely solemn warning that petticoats and flimsy skirts are not for mountain climbers. And it was with some considerable concern that we made the further discovery that kid boots are better for drawing-rooms. But in spite of shredded skirts and fraying boots, our ladies faced the slope with not even the faintest sign of fainting hearts.

An hour more, and we began to get views; views so wonderful as to make even the ladies forget their fluttering skirts and clogging petticoats and fast disintegrating boots. But now we began to have a choice of directions. We had never imagined there could be so many paths apparently all leading to the mountain top, but we discovered that what had appeared to be an unbroken slope, was gashed by numerous deep gorges that forbade passage, and ever and again we were forced to double on our course and make long detours about these gulches. In the presence of one unusually long, we determined that it was time for our second breakfast, to which we sat down, wondering whether there had ever been a first. A short rest, and we found ourselves with our stock of water sadly diminished, but our stock of courage and enthusiasm high as ever, and once more we set out for the peak whose location we began to guess at, but of whose distance away we could form no idea.

By noon the Professor announced, after a careful estimate of distances, that we were more than half way there, and that in an hour's time we should halt for lunch, which double announcement spurred those of the party who had been showing signs of weariness to a last heroic spurt. It was difficult to persuade any member of the party as we sat waiting for the baskets to be opened, that we had had one breakfast that morning, not to speak of two. After lunch the Professor declared that, having been brought up on a farm, he had been accustomed to a noon spell, and must have one. Being the least fatigued, or the most unwilling to acknowledge fatigue, this suggestion of a noon spell he could afford to make. So, stretched upon the broken rocks, we lay disposed at various angles, snuggled down into the soft spots of the old bony back. We slept for a full half-hour, and woke, so wonderful is this upper air, fresh and vigorous as in the morning. We packed our stuff, passed around our water-bottles, now, alas! almost empty, tied up the bleeding right foot of the Lady from Winnipeg with a portion of the fluttering skirt-remnants of the Lady from Montreal, seized our saplings and once more faced the summit.

Far off a slight ledge appeared directly across our path. Should we make a detour to avoid it? Or was it surmountable? The Professor, supported by the majority of the party, decided for a detour to the left. The Missionary, supported by the Lady from Winnipeg, decided that the frontal attack was possible. In half an hour, however, he found himself hanging to that ledge by his toe-nails and finger-tips, looking down into a gully full of what appeared to be stone, in alpine vocabulary *scree*, and sliding out into space at an angle of forty-five degrees or less, and the summit still far above him. Hanging there, there flashed across his mind for a moment the problem as to how the party could secure his mangled remains, and having secured them, how they could transport them down this mountain side. He decided that in the present situation his alpenstock added little to his safety and could well be dispensed with. As it clattered down upon the broken rocks far below, he found himself making a rapid calculation as to the depth of the drop and its effect upon the human frame. Before reaching a conclusion, he had begun edging his way backward, making the discovery that all mountain-climbers sooner or later make, that it is easier to follow your fingers with your toes, than your toes with your fingers. The descent accomplished, the Missionary with his loyal following reluctantly proceeded to follow the rest of the party, who had by this time gone round the head of the gulch, or the *couloir* in expert phrasing, and were some distance in advance. A stern chase is a long chase, and almost always disheartening. But in this case the advance guard were merciful, and, sitting down to enjoy the view, waited for the pursuing party to make up.

It is now late in the afternoon, and a council of war is held to decide whether, with all the return journey before us, it is safe to still attempt the peak. We have no experience in descending mountains, and, therefore, we cannot calculate the time required. The trail to the camp is quite unknown to us, and there is always the possibility of accident. Besides, while the climbing is not excessively steep, the going has become very difficult, for the slope is now one mass of *scree*, so that the whole face of the mountain moves with every step. Still, the peak is very perceptibly nearer, and the party has endured already so much that it is exceedingly loath to accept defeat. Then, too, the atmosphere has become so rare, that the climbing is hard on the wind, as the Professor says. The ladies, despite shredded skirts and torn shoes, however, are keen to advance, and without waiting for further parley, gallantly strike out for the peak. It is decided to climb for an hour. So up we go, slipping, scrambling, panting, straining ever toward the peak. We have no time for views, though they are entrancing enough to almost make us content with what we have achieved. For an hour and then for half an hour, the ladies still in advance, we struggle upward. The climbing is now over snow and often upon hands and knees, but the *scree* is gone and the rock, where there is no snow, is solid.

At length the Professor demands a halt. In spite of desperate attempts at concealment, various members of the party are flying flags of distress. We are still several hundred yards from the coveted summit, but the rose tints upon the great ranges that sweep around are deepening to purple and the shadows lie thick in the valleys. If we only knew about the descent, we might risk another three-quarters of an hour. The ladies begin to share the anxiety of the men, knowing full well that it is they who constitute the serious element in the situation. With bitter reluctance they finally decide that they will not ask the men to assume any greater responsibility than they already bear. It is agreed that the men shall make a half-hour dash for the summit, while the ladies await their return. Stripping themselves of all incumbrances, the Professor and the Missionary make a final attempt to achieve the peak, the Californian gallantly offering to remain with the ladies. After a breathless, strenuous half-hour, the Professor, with the Missionary at his side, has fulfilled his threat and accomplished his proud boast. Breathless but triumphant, we are standing upon the head of the old Cascade.

We dare only take a few minutes to gaze about us, but these are enough to make indelible the picture before us. Down at our feet the wide valley of the Bow with its winding river, then range on range of snow-streaked mountains, with here and there mighty peaks rising high and white against the deep blue. One giant, whose head towers far above all his fellows, arrests the eye. There he stands in solitary grandeur. Not till years after do we learn that this is the mighty Assiniboine. But there are no words to paint these peaks. They are worth climbing to see, and once seen they are worth remembering. I close my eyes any day, and before me is spread out the vision of these sweeping ranges jutting up into all sorts of angles, and above them, lonely and white, the solitary sentinel, Assiniboine.

Without a word, we look our fill and turn to the descent. A hundred yards or more and we come upon our party who, with a reckless ambition, have been climbing after us. But the whole back of the Cascade lies now in shadow, and, though half an hour will do it, we dare not encourage them to take the risk. The party has been successful, though individuals have failed. And with this comfort in our hearts and with no small anxiety as to what awaits us, we set off down the slope. It is much easier than we have anticipated until we strike the *scree*. Here, for the first few steps, we proceed with great caution, but after a short time, becoming accustomed to have the whole mountain slip with us, we abandon ourselves to the exhilaration of tobogganing upon the skidding masses of broken rock; and touching here and there the high spots, as the Professor says, we make the descent with seven-leagued boots till we reach the timber. It is here we meet our first accident for the day. The Lady from Winnipeg has the misfortune to turn her ankle. But there is no lack of bandages in the party. In fact, by this time the ladies' skirts consist chiefly of bandages, so that with foot well swathed, and stopping now and then for repairs to the ladies' boots, slipping, sliding, stumbling, leaping, we finally, in more or less battered condition, arrive at camp. The indomitable Professor, aided by the Missionary and the Man from California, set about supper. But long ere it is ready the rest of the party are sound asleep. They are mercilessly dragged forth, however, to the refreshment of tea, toast and bacon, for which they are none too grateful, and after which they drop back upon their pine beds into dreamless sleep.

It takes us a full week, the greater part of it spent in bed, to realize that mountain-climbing, *sans* guides, *sans* mountaineering boots, *plus* petticoats, is a pastime for angels perhaps, but not for fools.

On the upper part of the mountain, the Professor and I were

greatly excited over what appeared to be the fossil remains of a pre-historic monster, and if its jawbone had not weighed several hundred pounds — the backbone must have weighed several tons — we would have carried it down as a present to the Museum. We left them behind us, and they are there to this day for some anthropologist to see.

Some Memories of the Mountains
Elizabeth Parker

My first visit to the Rockies was a summer in Banff in the late eighties before it began to be a popular watering place. There were good roads to the Cave and Basin, to the Hot Springs and to the Spray River below the Falls; but enough of mountain wilderness remained to give our holiday an aspect of remoteness. The next visit covered all the seasons and included a climb through the snow to the top of the hill called Tunnel; also a guideless rock-climb with five other unequipped innocents up the long ridge of Cascade Mountain to within 200 feet of the summit, on a glorious day in September. We saw Mount Assiniboine, a white pyramid south, piercing the blue above, and wondered if it had a name. I forget the year, but by that time the village had two wooden churches, a good school-house and several attractive residences. The C.P.R. hotel had many guests, and one of the curious sights at the Hot Springs was an array of crutches and staffs hanging on trees nearby. You were liable to meet distinguished persons almost any day. The longest drive, barring that to Canmore outside the park, was over the long loop, down the valley behind Tunnel Mountain. Other roads gave a choice of several towards the Spray; one to Sun Dance Canyon and another around the face of Tunnel Mountain. Besides, many trails and footpaths ran through the woods.

Winter was a continual joy by day and night. Every snowfall was windless and snow mushrooms were everywhere; the "gathered intensity" brought to the blue and purple in the recesses of the mountains westward, and all the changing colors were a daily wonder. In early spring on the hither side of Tunnel was a great bed of pale mauve crocuses. In summer there were fields of bluebells along the prairies on the eastern slope of the Bow, and the yellow columbine on Sulphur Mountain opened our eyes to luxuriant bloom in all its wildness. Early and late Fall, even in November, the air was crystal-clear, and the sky a rejoicing blue, to use offhand a term of Cole-ridge's. The clearness and the blueness enhanced the beauty of forest in its rich green of fir and the yellow deciduous poplar. How long ago it was! And what haunts the memory yet, is that lovely mountain landscape in the changing seasons. It was those early days in Banff that gave me an understanding of Wordsworth when I came to read his poetry.

There were other visits to Banff, in summer or in autumn. I remember a borrowed fishing basket and a climb down the steep bank of the river to the pool below the Bow Falls one fine sunset. When I reached the angler's recess, there I found a workman named Hughie, who generously helped with hook and fly and gentle instruction. I caught nothing, and Hughie gallantly helped me up the long, steep bank. Then I said, "It's a beautiful evening." He straightened himself, looked towards the west and said, "It's a *beautiful world*." Wordsworth would have made a poem on that incident, for it bore out his philosophy of the Dalesmen.

Changes at Banff
Alice Huntington

August, 1897.

Here, Calgary faces greet one everywhere. It is as though our little city had moved up bodily and straight way betaken itself to boating and biking, to climbing and driving, to swimming, to singing, to building camp fires, great roaring red fires, that blaze and crackle right merrily as the streamers of light go dancing through the trees.

But even home faces cannot hide the changes in this dear old Banff. We don't like changes. We loved everything about the place, even the blacksmith, and the fact that another swings the hammer over the red iron on the anvil makes us almost sad.

The Cave and Basin at Banff circa 1900. Archives of the Canadian Rockies

What is it to us that the new smithy is obliging, or that his work is well done, or that he is picturesque with his open collar and great muscles? Our smithy was all these and he had held Peggy's foot and called Peggy a pleasant name so we loved him, as we did all Banff.

The cave and basin no longer boast the gay window boxes and neat hedges. They look as if the departing spirits had pulled all their beauty out by the roots and taken it with them.

The sanctity of your dip is invaded by a crowd of curious onlookers.

Time was when you had the cave or basin for you and yours and none beside, but they have changed all that.

The ocean, you know, is large enough to cover one, even our lakes can make you forget the short comings of a bathing skirt, but these little pools of warm water are quite too suggestive of the bath to admit of even a small audience.

Yesterday, no, the day before, when the "Christian Endeavorers" were in the place, I saw a poor unhappy woman gripping the rope that divides the deeps from the shallows in the cave, and making wild efforts to keep her pretty toes out of sight. She had frightened bashful eyes that looked pleadingly at those thoughtless men who stood calmly looking on, exactly where she must almost touch them if she left the water, for there is no royal way to the dressing room, just that long shuddering dripping tunnel.

There was no escape — there she must stay until her torturers pleased to go. In very pity we turned away hoping those stupid men would follow. . . .

The post office, too, is changed. You no longer walk through an avenue of biscuits and cowboy hats, of coal oil and crockery, of neckties and canned pumpkin to get your Calgary letter.

Now, there are moccasins and bear skins, very little pictures with very big prices, fur slippers, Indian beads, and war clubs, baskets, and bark match safes, napkin rings, and a hundred other curios to distract you while the clerk looks through the waiting pile of letters for the one that is to bring you the news from home.

Yet another change! Bruin-of-the-barracks has deserted for Medicine Hat, and his little friend "Jocko," the monkey, no longer jumps jauntily on one's shoulder as one crosses the bridge to the Sanitarium.

All these changes in the little homes among these great unchanging mountains. How good it is to be back among them, and what sights we have! What sunrises, sunsets, storms, sunshine!

The First Ascent of Mount Temple
Walter D. Wilcox

The ascent of Mount Temple near Lake Louise in August of 1894 by three young American mountaineers — Walter D. Wilcox, Samuel E. S. Allen, and Lewis Frissell — was the first of a peak above 11,000 feet in the Canadian Rockies.

Camp in Paradise Valley near Lake Louise just prior to the first ascent of Mount Temple by Walter Wilcox, Samuel Allen, and Lewis Frissell in August of 1894. Archives of the Canadian Rockies

The mountaineer has many discomforts mingled with the keen enjoyment of his rare experiences. None is more trying than the early hour at which he is compelled to rise from his couch of balsam boughs and set forth on his morning toil. At the chill hour before dawn, when all nature stagnates and animate creation is plunged in deepest sleep, the mountain climber must needs arouse himself from heavy slumber and, unwilling, compel his sluggish body into action.

This is the deadest hour of the twenty-four — the time just before dawn. The breezes of early night have died away into a cold and frosty calm; the thermometer sinks to its lowest point, and even the barometer, as though in sympathy, reaches one of its diurnal minima at this untimely hour. And if inanimate nature is thus greatly affected, much more are the creations of the vegetable and animal kingdoms. The plants are suffering from the cold and frost; the animals of daytime have not as yet aroused themselves from sleep, while the nocturnal prowlers have already ceased their quest of prey and

141

returned to their dens. Even man is affected, for at this dead hour the ebb and pulse of life beat slow and feeble, and the lingering spark of life in those wasted by disease comes at this time most near going out.

At such an unseasonable hour, or more accurately at four A.M., were we up, on the 17th of August preparing for our ascent of Mount Temple. There was no trace of dawn, and the waning moon, now in her last quarter, was riding low in the southern sky, just above the sharp triangular peak at the end of our valley.

At nine o'clock in the morning, we had gained the summit of the pass between Mount Temple and Pinnacle Mountain, where we were 9000 feet above sea-level. The ascent so far had not been of an encouraging nature, as we had encountered a long, loose slide where everything moved threateningly at each step. I have never seen a more unstable slope. The stones and boulders would slide, and begin to move at a distance of ten and fifteen feet above the place where we stood, and on every side also. F., who was one of the party, was terror-stricken, for he now had a horror of moving stones of any description.

The view from this pass was very extraordinary. To the east stood the rugged, saw-edged mountains of the Desolation Range, looming up in solemn grandeur through an atmosphere bluish and hazy with the smoke of forest fires. The air was perfectly calm and had the bracing coolness of early morning and high altitude, which the rising sun tempered most gently. The weather conditions for accomplishing our ascent were perfect, but there was little prospect of a fine view by reason of the smoke.

The outlook from the pass was indeed discouraging. Cliffs and ledges with broken stones and loose debris seemed to oppose all safe passage. Fortunately, as we progressed the difficulties vanished, and not till we reached an altitude of about 10,000 feet did we encounter any real obstacles. We found a passage through the great rock wall which had defeated us last year, by the aid of a little gully, which, however, entailed some rather difficult climbing. This arduous work continued throughout the next 1000 feet, when, at an altitude of 11,000 feet, we came to the great slope between the southwest and west *arêtes* and found an easy passage to the summit.

Many a hearty cheer rent the thin air as our little party of three reached the summit, for we were standing where no man had ever stood before, and, if I mistake not, at the highest altitude yet reached in North America north of the United States boundary. The summit was formed of hard bluish limestones, broken and piled up in blocks, as on all high mountain tops. The cliffs toward the east were stupendous and led the eye down to the valley more than a mile below. The air was almost calm and just above freezing, and the snow was melting quite fast in the sun. The thermometer at the Lake Louise chalet reached seventy-two degrees at the same time that we were on the summit of Mount Temple, which proves this to be almost the highest temperature that ever occurs on this lofty point. It would be safe to say that the temperature on the top of Mount Temple never rises higher than forty degrees. . . .

This was our last exploit in Paradise Valley, and a few days later the various members of our party, one by one, bade farewell to the beautiful region of Lake Louise with its many pleasant associations.

I remained there five or six weeks longer until winter commenced in earnest and drove every one away. During the first week of October I made a final visit to Paradise Valley with Mr. Astley, the manager of the chalet, in order to bring back our tent and the camping utensils. Snow covered the ground in the shady parts of the woods, even at the entrance of the valley. The stream had fallen so much that its rocky bed proved the best route up the valley, especially for the horse. . . .

A few days later I went up to Lake Agnes to hunt for mountain goats, which frequent this place in great numbers. The snow was two feet deep. The lake was already nearly covered with ice, and I was compelled to seek shelter behind a cliff against a bitterly cold wind, driving icy particles of hail and snow against my face.

It was useless to prolong the contest longer. Winter had resumed her iron sway in these boreal regions and high altitudes, and in a few weeks Lake Louise too would begin to freeze, and no longer present its endless change of ripple and calm, light and shadow, or the reflected images of rocks and trees and distant mountains.

Death on Mount Lefroy
Charles E. Fay

On the morning of August 3, 1896, four American alpinists —
Dr. Charles Fay, Charles S. Thompson, George T. Little, and Philip S.
Abbot — set out from the chalet at Lake Louise and climbed to the high
pass between Mounts Victoria and Lefroy where they plotted out a route to
the summit of the latter peak.

At 12.30 P.M., leaving behind us two of our rücksacks with the remainder of our food and whatever else seemed unnecessary for the hours that we were expecting to be absent, we again set forth to complete, as we fondly believed, the largest enterprise in the way of mountaineering that has ever been accomplished on Canadian peaks. Our record shows that in the first half-hour we made excellent progress, for at one o'clock our aneroid reading was 10,400, three hundred feet above our lunching-place. The point at which it was made is one that will never fade from our memory, — the top of a low cliff, beyond the brow of which and somewhat higher up lay a narrow plateau covered with scree.

Of the next four hours and a half the writer of this narrative has a very vague recollection. Did not our record exist as a corrective for deceitful memory, I should without question underestimate the period fully one-half, either because it actually passed so quickly, or because in reminiscence the monotonous affords few halting-points, and so falsifies time just as the plains and the open sea falsify distance. These hours were spent either in cutting steps in our zigzag course up ice-slopes, or in wary advance up the unreliable slopes of rock, the effect of a slip upon which would differ slightly in ultimate results from a slip on the ice itself. Usually one moved at a time, the others maintaining meanwhile as secure an anchorage as possible. Caution governed every movement, as indeed it always did when Abbot was at the fore. On this day we were all deeply impressed with its needfulness. Even our leader smiled at the enormous size of the steps that were left in the wake of the party after each one had contributed his vigorous chipping to their enlargement. Some one, thinking of the possible lateness of the return and consequent necessity for speed, suggested that we might need all the advantage their size would offer when we came to descend. So indeed it proved!

At 5.30 we drew up under an immense bastion possibly seventy-five feet in height, behind which lay the summit, of which as yet, owing to foreshortening, we had had no satisfactory view. This frowning face rose sheer from a narrow margin of tolerably stable scree that lay tilted between its base and the upper edge of the sloping ice that we had just left behind us. Looking past it on the right we saw, a few hundred feet beyond, the tawny southern arête, so shattered as to be utterly impassable. In one place a great aperture, perhaps forty feet high and five or six in width, revealed the blue sky beyond. Evidently our course did not lie in that direction. On the left the dusky northern arête rose with an easy gradient possibly an eighth of a mile away, but across an ice slope similar to that up which we had so long been toiling, and in truth a continuation of the same. To cross it was perfectly feasible, but it would take so long to cut the necessary steps that a descent of the peak before dark would have been out of the question.

But now Mr. Abbot, who had moved forward along the rock-wall to the limit of the rope, cheerfully announced an alternative. His view beyond an angle in the bastion revealed a vertical cleft up which it was possible to climb by such holds as offered themselves. Bidding Thompson and me to unrope and keep under cover from falling stones, he clambered some thirty feet up the rift, secured a good anchorage, and called upon Professor Little to follow. This the latter proceeded to do, but while standing at the bottom of the cleft preparing to climb, he received a tingling blow from a small stone dislodged by the rope. A moment later a larger one falling upon the rope half severed it, so as to require a knot. As danger from this source seemed likely to continue, our leader had Little also free himself from the rope and come up to where he stood. From here a shelf led around to the left, along which Abbot now proceeded a few yards and discovered a gully leading upward, unseen from the point first attained, and this also he began to ascend. To Mr. Little's question, whether it might not be better to try and turn the bastion on the shelf itself, he replied: "I think not. I have a good lead here."

These were the last words he ever uttered. A moment later Little, whose attention was for the moment diverted to another portion of the crag, was conscious that something had fallen swiftly past him, and knew only too well what it must be. Thompson and I, standing at the base of the cliff, saw our dear friend falling backward and head-foremost, saw him strike the upper margin of the ice slope within fifteen feet of us, turn completely over and instantly begin rolling down its steep incline. After him trailed our two lengths of English rope — all we had brought with us — which we had spliced together in our ascent over the last rock slope, in order to gain time by having less frequent anchorages than were necessitated by the short intervals of one sixty-foot line. As the limp body rolled downward in a line curving slightly towards the left, the rope coiled upon it as on a spool, — a happy circumstance amid so much of horror, — for not only did this increase of friction sensibly affect the velocity of the descent of nine hundred feet to the narrow plateau of scree above mentioned, but doubtless the rope by catching in the scree itself prevented the unconscious form from crossing the narrow level and falling over the low cliff beyond. Had it passed this, nothing, apparently, could have stopped it short of the bottom of the gorge leading up to the pass from the western side of the Divide, — a far more fearful fall than that already made.

You would not pardon me if I could find words to describe our feelings. A single instant of supreme emotion may equal hours of grief or joy less intense. A single instant only was ours to yield to it. Mr. Little was still in a critical position, particularly if his nerves were unstrung. To ascend such a cleft is far easier than to descend, and he had had the aid of the rope in going up. He must forgive me if I mention here the self-forgetfulness with which he called down to us: "Never mind me. Hurry to help Abbot." "Our help is for the living. To reach Abbot will require hours. Everything must be forgotten save care for the present moment. Come down as far as you can with safe holds, and, Heaven helping, we will do our part." Happily the footholds lasted until he was far enough down to reach with his hobnailed shoe an ice-axe held braced against a projection by one of us who had crowded himself for a purchase into the base of the cleft. Another axe under his thigh and such handholds as he could grasp aided the remainder of the perilous descent. It was 6.30 as we stood together with grateful hearts at the base of the fatal bastion.

A brief gaze to where Abbot lay so still, a mutual promise of self-command and unremitting caution, and we began our descent with ice-axes only, each responsible for his own safety. Our ample footsteps were now a priceless safeguard. On the treacherous rock slopes we could indeed secure a tolerable substitute for seven feet of rope by attaching two ice-axes together by their straps, a wholly inadequate resource for this dangerous passage. Thus for three hours and until the beautiful sunset glow had faded on the high arête of Lefroy, we worked our slow way downward, and at length stood beside the motionless form that all this time had lain in full view. To our surprise life was not yet extinct. The fatal wound in the back of the head, evidently received in the short initial fall of perhaps twenty feet, was the only grievous outward mark, and the autopsy proved that not a limb was broken. A faint murmur, that my imagination interpreted as a recognition of our presence and an expression of gratitude that we at least had escaped from peril, alone broke the silence for a brief moment, and then we three bared our heads in the twilight, believing that his generous spirit was already passing. But a moment later the faint breathing was resumed.

If living, then of course we would bear him down with us, difficult

*Tom Wilson, George Little, Willoughby Astley, and Charles Fay rest beneath
Mount Lefroy on their way to recover the body of Philip Abbot, August 1896.*
Archives of the Canadian Rockies

as the labor would be. We now at least had the ropes, and with their
aid such a task did not seem impossible. To tarry in this spot was at
all events out of the question. With tender hands, having first disen-
tangled the ropes, we raised him, and began the dreary descent; but
we had scarcely reached the brink of the little cliff when he again
ceased to breathe. Not satisfied with this evidence, we tested pulse
and heart. That all was over in the mortal life of our loved companion
was subject to no manner of doubt.

The seriousness of the task we had assumed as a matter of course
at once became evident. To lower even the lifeless body down this
short precipice was a labor involving a large risk for three persons.
Only with competent aid and by long daylight could it be brought
from its lofty resting-place to the chalet we had left so hopefully that
morning. Twilight was deepening into dusk as we decided to leave
it here and descend as far as possible before darkness should prevent
further advance. By the dim reflection from the sky and the snow we
could faintly discern our upward footsteps in certain places; in others
merely divine them. The general course avoiding dangerous precipices on our left we could make out without difficulty. We reached
without mishap the top of the rock-strewn promontory, but by a
strange misfortune all three of us forgot that it was near this point,
and not in the pass itself, that we had left our rücksacks with food

147

and our only stimulant (excepting the flask that Abbot had carried, and which had been shattered into fragments in his first fall), together with an extra sweater — an oversight we had occasion bitterly to repent. Not until we reached the col and failed to find our belongings did the truth dawn upon us, and a return in the darkness failed to bring the seeker to the desired spot.

Assembled again at the pass — it was now 10.30 P.M. — we accepted the decree that we should here spend the remainder of the night. . . .

The bare rock of the lowest point of the pass, upon which we now found ourselves, was at least preferable to the snow for a couch, so we lay down upon it face downward. Soon, however, the rising breeze drawing freshly over the col from the north made us long for some shelter from its chill. The cairn would offer a slight defence, and up to it we hastened. Seating ourselves in its lee one close before the other, each held the one in front of him in a close embrace to utilize, so far as possible, our bodily warmth. Often we would lightly pound ourselves, or one another, to increase the sluggish circulation. Now and then Little would rise to stop some chink in the cairn, or even build an extension to our stony wind-break. I should not say that we suffered physically in any very serious sense of the term; we were simply decidedly uncomfortable. Our condition became somewhat the worse toward morning, when the sky became overcast and flakes of fine snow began to sift over us, the forerunners of a storm, the severity of which was fortunately delayed for some hours. The night wore on but slowly. Occasionally one or another would doze for a quarter or half hour, then, waking, consult the watch and congratulate himself on his happy fortune. By 4.15 it was light enough, despite the cloudiness, for one to move about, and only too gladly I proceeded to overcome my numbness by recovering the rücksacks. Strengthened for the descent by the welcome food — we had eaten nothing since noon of the day before — we set out at five o'clock, and reached the chalet at 9.30 A.M. in the midst of a rainstorm.

Misadventures on the Glacier
Hugh E. M. Stutfield and
J. Norman Collie

Wap#tik Icefield, 1897.

I: was near the top of the second peak that Thompson very nearly ended his mountaineering experiences. Not far from this second summit a huge crevasse partially covered with snow had to be crossed. All the party had passed over but Thompson, who unfortunately broke through and at once disappeared headlong into the great crack that ran perpendicularly down into the depths of the glacier. Those of the party who were still on the first peak saw their friends gesticulating in the far distance, but did not take much notice until Sarbach drew their attention to the fact that there were only four people instead of five to be seen: some one therefore, must have fallen down a crevasse. A race across the almost level snow then took place, Sarbach being easily first. Although Thompson was too far down to be seen, yet he could be heard calling for help and saying that, although he was not hurt, he would be extremely grateful to us if we would make haste and extricate him from the awkward position he was in, for he could not move and was almost upside down, jammed between the two opposing sides of the crevasse.

It was obvious that every second was of importance; a stirrup was made in a rope, and Collie, being the lightest member of the party — and, withal, unmarried — was told to put his foot into it, whilst he was also carefully roped round the waist as well. Then he was pushed over the edge of the abyss, and swung in mid-air. To quote his description: "I was then lowered into the gaping hole. On one side the ice fell sheer, on the other it was rather undercut, but again bulged outwards about eighteen feet below the surface, making the crevasse at that point not much more than two feet wide. Then it widened again, and went down into dim twilight. It was not till I had descended sixty feet, almost the whole available length of an eighty foot rope, that at last I became tightly wedged between the two walls of the crevasse, and was absolutely incapable of moving my body. My feet were close to Thompson's, but his head was further away, and about three feet lower than his heels. Face downwards,

149

and covered with fallen snow, he could not see me. But, after he had explained that it was entirely his own fault that he was there, I told him we would have him out in no time. At the moment I must say I hardly expected to be able to accomplish anything. For, jammed between two slippery walls of ice, and only able to move my arms, cudgel my brains as I would, I could not think what was to be done. I shouted for another rope. When it came down I managed to throw one end to Thompson's left hand, which was waved about, till he caught it. But, when pulled, it merely dragged out of his hand. Then with some difficulty I managed to tie a noose on the rope by putting both my hands above my head. With this I lassoed that poor pathetic arm which was the only part of Thompson that could be seen. Then came the tug-of-war. If he refused to move, I could do nothing more to help him; moreover I was afraid that at any moment he might faint. If that had occurred I do not believe he could have been got out at all, for the force of the fall had jammed him further down than it was possible to follow. Slowly the rope tightened, as it was cautiously pulled by those above. I could hear my heart thumping in the ghastly stillness of the place, but at last Thompson began to shift, and after some short time he was pulled into an upright position by my side. To get a rope round his body was of course hopeless. Partly by wriggling and pulling on my own rope I so shifted that by straining one arm over my head I could get my two hands together, and then tied the best and tightest jamming knot I could think of round his arm, just above the elbow. A shout to the rest of the party, and Thompson went rapidly upwards till he disappeared round the bulge of ice forty feet or more above. I can well remember the feeling of dread that came over me lest the rope should slip or his arm give way under the strain, and he should come thundering down on the top of me; but he got out all right, and a moment later I followed. Most marvellously no bones had been broken, but how any one could have fallen as he did without being instantaneously killed will always remain a mystery. He must have partially jammed some considerable distance higher up than the point where I found him, for he had a rück-sack on his back, and this perhaps acted as a brake, as the walls of the crevasse closed in lower down. We were both of us nearly frozen and wet to the skin, for ice-cold water was slowly dripping the whole time on to us; and in my desire to be as little encumbered as possible, I had gone down into the crevasse very scantily clad in a flannel shirt and knickerbockers."

A rapid descent to the head of the ice-fall quickly restored circulation, and that night over the camp fire the whole experience was gone over again, Thompson emphatically giving it as his opinion that, whatever scientific exploration or observation in future migh: be necessary on the summits of the Rocky Mountains, investigations made alone, sixty feet below the surface of the ice, in an inverted position, were extremely dangerous and even unworthy of record.

Bill Peyto
Walter D. Wilcox

Perhaps no more interesting character has ever appeared in this region than my old packer, Bill Peyto. I made my first excursion to Assiniboine with him and have travelled several hundred miles under his guidance. Bill is very quiet in civilisation, but becomes more communicative around an evening camp-fire, when he delights to tell his adventures. His has been a roving life. The story of his battle with the world, his escapades and sufferings of hunger and exposure, not to mention the dreams and ambitions of a keen imagination with their consequent disappointments, has served to entertain many an evening hour. Peyto assumes a wild and picturesque though some-what tattered attire. A sombrero, with a rakish tilt to one side, a blue shirt set off by a white kerchief (which may have served civilisation for a napkin), and a buckskin coat with fringed border, add to his cowboy appearance. A heavy belt containing a row of cartridges, hunting-knife and six-shooter, as well as the restless activity of his wicked blue eyes, give him an air of bravado. He usually wears two pairs of trousers, one over the other, the outer pair about six months older. This was shown by their dilapidated and faded state, hanging, after a week of rough work in burnt timber, in a tattered fringe knee-high. Every once in a while Peyto would give one or two nervous yanks at the fringe and tear off the longer pieces, so that his outer trousers disappeared day by day from below upwards. Part of this was affectation, to impress the tenderfoot, or the "dude," as he calls everyone who wears a collar. But in spite of this Peyto is one of the most conscientious and experienced men with horses that I have ever known.

In camp, Peyto always goes down to see his horses once or twice

Bill Peyto

a day even if they are several miles distant, and I have even known him to look after them in the depths of night when he thought they might be in trouble. When the order to march has been given the night before, our horses are in camp at dawn. Quick and cool in time of real danger, he has too much anxiety about trouble ahead, and worries himself terribly about imaginary evils. He sleeps with a loaded rifle and hunting-knife by his side. "Bill," said I, one night, upon noticing a row of formidable instruments of death near me, "why in the mischief do you have all of those shooting-irons and things here?" "I tell you," said he, with an anxious look, "I believe this country is full of grizzlies; I heard a terrible noise in the woods this afternoon, and besides that, they say the Kootenay Indians have risen. They may come into the valley any night."

Bill Peyto Alone
Gordon Burles

"It's time to go; I've had enough!
Damn this town, all those
pettifogging shopkeepers and
piddling government men — especially
that interfering muddler, Jennings.
There are too many of them, and
you never know what they're up to.
I fought in their wars — I guess
I had to do that; but they're not
going to make a hero of me for it.
It was tough enough; but, by God,
we're men aren't we?
But I don't care. As long as
they do as they're told
when they're out here around
Healy Creek. They're such greenhorns!
Someone's got to help them,
doesn't he? And those damned police!
They'd better leave my guns to me.
A man needs his gun: there are dangers
you can't always predict, you know.
No bear's going to take me before
my time, either; when he comes
stealing my grub he'll learn
about it from this gun barrel.
Anyhow, I've been around and had fun;
I'm let alone when I want it.
Soon I'll be back up in the larches.
There's snow on the ground now
and I'll see who's been bothering
my cabin. It's mighty pretty there
when no one's around; we'd better
like it while we can, because
we're not going to be around long!
Damnation, I s'pose that wife's
going to cry. By God, that's God's
affair, or somebody's, I don't know.
Whoever made the mountains made me
and I'm not waiting: I'm going."

Edward Whymper
Robert E. Campbell

Edward Whymper was the British mountaineer who made the first ascent of the Matterhorn in 1865. When he came to the Rockies in 1901, he was sixty-one years old.

In the winter of 1901, Whymper announced that he proposed to visit Canada. The Canadian papers were full of stories about him. This great man would put Canada on the map. It became fashionable to write about him. Reporters rushed to libraries for material. You could hardly pick up a paper that did not have something about Whymper. But there was one class of Canadians who did not enthuse over his coming. It consisted of the men who made their living by conducting mountain climbers into the mountains. We knew from experience that once a mountain was climbed it became, as it were, a dead duck.

Contiguous to the C.P.R. there were four peaks yet unmastered that were of sufficient importance to confer honour on any professional climber — Assiniboine, Deltaform, Hungabee and Goodsir. In the region of the North Saskatchewan there still remained the giants Lyell, Forbes, Athabaska, Columbia and, still farther north, Robson. Now the magic wand of Whymper and his four great guides, the best Switzerland could produce, would wave over the Rockies, leaving nothing but a trail of climbing desolation.

For a man who had travelled so much, Whymper was strangely ignorant of people. To him North Americans were of the lesser breeds, and he proceeded to act accordingly. Arriving in Banff in the early morning, he succeeded in antagonizing the dining-room help before finishing his breakfast. His manner of addressing them was obnoxious. By the time he had finished his name was anathema. Then he went in search of the manager.

"You know this chap Wilson?" he said curtly.

"Do you mean Tom Wilson?"

"I do not know what he is called. The chap that has the horses for transporting people into the mountains."

"Oh yes, I know him quite well."

"You will have him at my rooms at three this afternoon."

With that the great man turned on his heel and went off.

Mr. Matthews was not used to such brusqueness. He looked at

British mountaineer Edward Whymper (right) meeting Dr. James Hector at Glacier House in 1903.
Archives of the Canadian Rockies

his office staff. His clerks smiled. There was no telephone in Banff except to the station. So Mr. Matthews had to send a boy down town to find Tom and tell him that Mr. Whymper wanted to see him at 3 p.m. The message was delivered.

Tom Wilson was the type who never owned, or needed to own, a watch. A squint over his shoulder, and he would hit the time within fifteen minutes. Minutes were inconsequential to him. He counted time by days and months. Only when catching a train did minutes count, but he was never late. So early that afternoon he walked up to the hotel, where he stood chatting with the guests till he thought it was time to report. A bell-boy escorted him to Whymper's room and announced him. On the table stood a small clock showing the time was 2:55. The great man was walking up and down the room, a long-stemmed pipe in one hand and a glass of Scotch and soda in the other. Without any preliminaries he said his instructions were for 3. Tom was thunderstruck. He was a man slow to wrath, but in all his years in dealing with tourists he had never met with such peremptory usage. He turned to leave the room, but was stopped by Whymper telling him he would show him his luggage. Tom's only thought was to find some reasonable excuse for telling the old boy where to go.

Arriving at the baggage room, Tom saw a stack of boxes, all stamped E.W. There were twenty-nine pieces, each 40 x 16 x 16 inches, and put together with three-inch nails countersunk in the wood. Did Mr. Whymper propose to take all these boxes into the mountains? "What do you think I brought them here for? I do not propose to have my goods pillaged."

That was the opening Tom was looking for. The Irish blood of his ancestors boiled over. Pillage! He wanted Mr. Whymper, and anybody like him, to know that neither he or his men were thieves. For years he had been taking guests into the hills and never in all those years had any one ever hinted at dishonesty on the part of him or his men. As far as he was concerned, Whymper could go plumb to hell and get someone else to outfit him.

Mr. Whymper had been used to dealing with people who would knuckle down to him. Here it was different. Never in all his life had anyone ever told him to go to hell. Now it was his turn to be amazed. What was he to do when the only man who was in the outfitting business had walked out on him?

Tom strode down the hall to the rotunda. Never had the office staff seen him in an evident temper. Mr. Matthews asked him to come in to his office.

"What's the matter, Tom?"

Tom lost no time in telling him about Whymper having cast reflections on his honesty.

"But Tom, you are the only one here to outfit him."

Tom was adamant. Under no circumstances would he have anything to do with anyone who would treat his men as thieves. But there might be others who would. Peyto had returned, and was contemplating going into the business. That made a difference.

Bill Peyto had returned from the Boer War. He had worked for years with Tom. Everyone knew Bill was a top-notch man, who always had earned the good opinion of his guests. Matthews knew Bill, and as Tom would have nothing further to do with Whymper, perhaps Bill would like to start in business with such a noted customer.

Tom had left when the celebrity arrived in Matthews' office. What was Matthews to do? The C.P.R. had told Whymper that Wilson was the only outfitter, and had highly recommended him. Now Wilson had not only refused to outfit him, but had used insulting language. Inviting the guest to sit down, Mr. Matthews proceeded to give him some advice on the proper manner of dealing with Canadians. They were not lackeys, but employees, and if they were not treated properly he would soon find himself without any help. Then he told him about Peyto. Mr. Whymper was quick to learn, and instead of ordering the manager to find Peyto, he asked him in a gentlemanly way. Peyto came to the hotel, and they arranged for the trip. But Bill had to have some time to get an outfit ready. That was mutually agreeable. It was the custom for the outfitter to supply everything except liquor, guns and such personal stuff, and Bill's prices were based on that. But to his surprise, Whymper insisted on supplying the food. That was so much gravy to Bill, whose instructions were to report at Field. The baggage would go there by train. Whymper's plans were never disclosed until the last minute.

The following morning Tom came to Field to see me and report on what had taken place. The burning question was, how long would Bill get along with the old bird? We knew Bill's temper. It was good until his toes were trampled on, and then!! Tom thought about a week, but I figured what I would do under like circumstances. We knew Bill would not have the money to buy an outfit, but we knew his credit was good and he was honest. I thought it probable he would stand the gaff till he earned enough to make a good payment.

Peyto was a hustler, and lost no time in getting things together and coming to Field. When we heard that he was ordered to Field, it was quite obvious that dangerous Goodsir was the first quarry. We were wrong. Whymper's first area of operation was to be the Upper Yoho. Why? We couldn't guess. There was no mountain there worthy of his reputation. They had all been climbed.

Peyto and his friend Jack Sinclair pulled out early one morning going via Emerald Lake. Later the same day Whymper and his guides left, but were to travel via the Burgess Pass. The usual procedure for pack train work was to eat a hearty breakfast, travel for approximately seven hours, and then make camp, have a snack, and then have a big dinner. We seldom bothered packing a lunch with us, and to stop and make fire only delayed things; it was hard to keep the horses from rolling on their packs. But Whymper and his guides took a lunch prepared for them at the hotel.

Bill and Jack expected their guests to arrive if not before them, surely soon after. But they were disappointed. They pitched camp and then waited. But their guests failed to appear. Night came on, and the boys lit a great fire to guide their party. They fired their rifles, they yelled themselves hoarse; still no arrival. They sat up all night trying in every way to help their friends, for it seemed evident they had lost their way. It was all in vain. Morning came and they switched the bright fire to a smokey one, piling on wet and green wood.

Meanwhile they were very hungry. What were they to do? They must have food, and the food was packed in those big boxes. They had no screwdrivers. They tried to determine which of them contained the food. Imagination then played them tricks. They tried smelling for the ones with the bacon. They were sure they had the right ones. They tried using their axe for a screwdriver, but the screws were countersunk. Bill tried a beautiful camp knife he had brought from South Africa, and broke the end off it. Jack tried the same stunt, with the same result. They were thinking so much about their hunger that it made things worse. Bill got desperate and made the air blue with his language. He tried prying the lid off. It split. Now he was in trouble, the box instead of holding the bacon had scores of two ounce bottles with large mouths, packed in like eggs in an egg case. He might as well be hung for a sheep as a lamb, so he selected another box, only to find it had other stuff than bacon. A third was broken into, and now they had food.

Meanwhile the mountaineers had started to climb Mt. Field, and had found a bed of fossils with which they loaded their ruck sacks. Hours were spent in pursuit of trilobites, etc. While there, why not climb Mt. Wapta? They did. But after travelling the length of that mountain they ran into a precipice that even the Swiss could not navigate. They had to turn back. Strangers in a strange land, without any trails to follow, and in a thick forest to which they were unaccustomed, hungry and without a knowledge of where they were, they made a fire and spent the night bemoaning their fate, with Whymper railing at them for getting lost. Morning came. Two of them climbed a mountain to try and ascertain their whereabouts, and far in the distance spied smoke, but their pals were in a thick bush with no way to see them. They descended to rejoin their party. Now hungry and very tired, they had to climb the mountain again and travel to the camp miles away.

You would think that any man so tired and hungry would have some sympathy with his packers; but not Whymper. When he arrived, he flew at the boys, accusing them of pillage. It seems he could think of no other word. Peyto went wild. Wigs were on the green. It was all Jack could do to keep him from attacking his client. From that minute, hatred burned between them. Only Jack's constant reminders about the money they owed kept Bill from pulling out.

Then the Rev. James Outram came to camp as Whymper's guest. Outram was a most enthusiastic climber as well as a very skilful one. He was given the use of the guides and treated royally. Bill and he became very friendly, and when Outram mentioned how much he would like to have a go at Mt. Assiniboine, Bill made a deal with him and pulled out, leaving Whymper in the lurch.

Now the latter found himself in Field without any pack train. What was he to do? He consulted with Miss Mollison who managed the C.P.R. hotel. Things looked black for him. His Canadian trip had gone awry. She advised him to see me.

"But that is Wilson's outfit, and he has already said he would not take me out."

"I don't know why it is but Wilson never questions anything Campbell does. If Bob says he will do your packing he will do it."

From where she stood behind her counter she could look across and see me and some of our men getting packs ready to take a party of Philadelphians out for another try at Goodsir. She phoned me to say Whymper wanted to see me. Now I was a Hobson's choice. O.K. I would be just that. I answered that from where she stood she could see that I was busy getting things ready to start the Scattergood party out in the morning. I was busy, and I thought that Mr. Whymper had more time to come and see me than I to see him. So as the mountain was a very stable concern, Mohammed had to toddle across the Kicking Horse. I could easily have talked to him then and there, but I thought it might do him good to realize he was not the only pebble. I let him stand for about twenty minutes, and then announced I was at liberty to see him.

Could I arrange to take him out? Sure, nothing could be easier, but first we must have a very definite arrangement. He had made a most disparaging remark about our honesty, and had repeated the same accusation to Peyto. It was his fault, not Peyto's, that caused Peyto to pull out. He had agreed to furnish food and had not kept that arrangement. It was not Bill's fault that he and his guides got lost. That must not happen again. Under no condition was he ever to say or insinuate that our men were not honest. When travelling with the packs, he and his guides were to take orders from the Canadians. Why? We knew more about travel in the Rockies than he did. Heavy streams had to be negotiated, and to avoid any mishaps our men must be in command. He admitted that was reasonable. And further to avoid any interference on the part of our men his guides were to look after his camp duties, such as cooking. We would pack his food in saddle packs, as he saw us doing outside. I refused to pack his great boxes.

"But my men have never done any cookin'."

I explained that I had travelled with the Swiss guide in the employ of the C.P.R. and had always found him very adaptable. He wasn't pleased with that idea, but realized that I was in the saddle. And so it was arranged that I should take him out the following day.

I had intended sending my brother Dan and Tom Martin out with the Scattergoods, but I switched them around and sent two other men with them. I could count on Dan and Tom to take care of Mr. Whymper if need arose. I had to take a trip out to the same locality to see about obtaining timbers for a bridge over the Twin Falls creek, and decided I might as well go along with them. Along the trail I knocked over several fool hens (they are a special kind of grouse) with a pistol I carried for that purpose. When we arrived at where he wanted to camp, Dan and I caught the ponies carrying his goods and unpacked them where he desired. Meanwhile Tom had unpacked those carrying the cook boxes for their camp.

Not being used to camping duties, the Swiss guides were unprepared, and the result was confusion. Everybody tried to help at each bit of work. They started a fire and each contributed his share. Soon they had a bonfire rather than a small cook fire. Klukker, the oldest of the guides, was to do the cooking. He cut a panful of bacon and in trying to fry it let it drop in the flames. Then he tried to make a wooden handle by tying a piece of green willow to the handle with a bit of cord. The flames burnt the cord and that panful ended up in the fire. By this time Tom had our afternoon lunch ready, and we three were sitting eating and listening to our new friends talking in German. We did not know a word of that tongue nor did we need to. From the tone of their conversation we knew they were not having a prayer meeting. Suddenly Whymper's right flew out, connecting with Klukker's jaw, and the Swiss hit the dust. In a jiffy it looked as if the whole four of them were going to take a hand in the fray. We yelled at them to stop, and they did. I told Whymper he shouldn't do that. He glared at me and reminded me that I had insisted he run his own camp, and he would thank me to mind my own affairs and he would mind his. When you know you have the upper hand you can afford to be cool.

"That is just what I propose to do," I said. "I presume that you know something of the authority and duties of a Justice of the Peace in England?"

"Quite," he retorted. "What has that got to do with it?"

"Quite a lot. You have committed an assault. I am a J.P."

His face went blank. Used to seeing all the trappings of a court in England, it was hard for him to realize that before him stood a young fellow still in his twenties, his feet covered with moccasins, pants much the worse for wear, a buckskin shirt thrown open and an old black hat containing sundry holes, his thumbs shoved under a belt from which hung a gun on one side and from the other a sheath knife — embodying all the majesty of British Law. His face not only betokened surprise but doubt. It was Tom who broke the silence. "That's right, Mr. Whymper, Bob is a J.P.," he said. Whymper was flabbergasted. After a moment's silence he asked, "Well, what do you propose to do?" I replied that I hoped that I would not have to do anything more than to suggest he apologize to his guide for hitting him. Loss of face before one of his servants was a bitter pill. But he might be treated to a more bitter one if he refused. Walking over to his guide, he reached out his hand and made some remark in German. The four Swiss smiled. I gathered that the apology was not only ample but accepted. I waved the Swiss to go to our camp and told Tom to give them something to eat. Turning to Whymper I told him I would bring him his afternoon tea. That done I returned to the job of cleaning the fool hens. Dan helped the Swiss to get their camp in shape, Tom busied himself building bannocks, and the conqueror of the Matterhorn took a walk, no doubt communing with himself on the mentality of Canadians.

We had a good dinner that night, fried chicken with Swift's bacon, hot buns, jam and tea. The guides and we boys ate together, while Whymper ate his half chicken in his own tent. We found that one of the Swiss, Christian Kaufmann, spoke some English, and that helped some. After dinner Whymper came to our fire and asked to speak with me. We walked out of hearing. He asked me if there was not some way to make some changes in the set-up. I then spoke freely to him, telling him of our procedure with our tourist clients, and that I would be pleased to make arrangements with him if he would conform to our way of doing things, particularly as to his manner of treating the help. I went on to tell him that many of our help were medical students, and that the tall man who had been helping when he came over to our camp was a practising dentist, who had left with the Scattergood party as their cook. He was astonished, and confessed that he had no idea that men of that class would be found working in Canada. The upshot of the conversation was that I took over the management of affairs. The Swiss were delighted and did everything possible to help around camp.

From then on, Whymper's attitude changed, and during the seven summers I outfitted him there was never an unpleasant word between him and my boys. We grew to be great friends and I became his Canadian *fidus Achates*. After two weeks in the Upper Yoho the party returned to Field. He sent his guides back to their homes, and henceforth was looked after on his mountain travels by Canadians. With Dan and Tom he went to the Ice River for a ten-week trip. That part of the Rockies he found most interesting. Tom had taken a course in an American school of mineralogy. Dan was a very good botanist. They both had clambered among the rocks enough to be of assistance in that work. The three of them got along swimmingly.

I have often been amused when I read about our police and magistrates smelling the breath of those whom they suspect of being under the influence of liquor, and wonder if perhaps they got a kickback from their own breaths. What would they have done about Whymper? Never have I known such a man. When out on the trail his daily allowance was a bottle of House of Commons Scotch and ten pints of ale. And don't forget that the whiskey was pre-war stuff, when Scotch was Scotch, not the anaemic stuff you now pay up to $6.00 for. Yet I have never seen him under the influence of liquor. Many think that is impossible, nevertheless it is true. What he drank around the hotel no one can guess. I have never been in his rooms when I saw him farther from a Scotch and soda than the length of his arm. His dinners were well set. He ate at a table by himself and always had the same waiter, who knew exactly what drinks he wanted. With his fish and soup it was a pint of sauterne. His meats were washed down by a pint of St. Julien. His dessert was always MacLaren's cheese and soda biscuits, and with this he sipped a pint of Mumm's. He invariably spent two hours at dinner. Often after that he would send for his drinking pal, the C.P.R. trainmaster, and they would each have a pint of champagne. Then he would escort his friend down the three flights of steps to the railroad platform and conduct him to his home, and return to the hotel as brisk as a teenager going on a date. His room was on the third floor, and there was no elevator. Up those stairs he would go, and never a hand laid on the bannister, and often he would finish the day by writing a scientific treatise for the English journals. But he never drank his whiskey neat!; it was always either diluted with water or soda water, preferably the latter.

After his ten weeks on Ice River he had an imposing array of empties. The next summer I took a friend out to that locality. Dan and Tom had kept the camp respectable by caching the empties in a hole made by an upturned tree. My friend Mr. H. W. Du Bois of Philadelphia gathered them up. Placing the cases in the form of a pyramid, placing the empty bottles on the shoulder of the pyramid. Using a soft, black lead pencil he lettered in the legend 'Whymper Explorations in the Canadian Rockies and Ryes.' Then he took a photo. On his way home he showed the picture to a prominent C.P.R. official, who kidded Whymper about it. Was the old boy riled! Never again had he a kind word for the Yankee "rottas."

My Grizzly-Bear Day
William T. Hornaday

In September of 1905, William Hornaday, one of North America's leading wildlife conservationists, led an expedition to the Elk Valley in the southern Canadian Rockies for the purpose of collecting big game specimens.

When one can start out from camp, and in a walk of two hours find at least a dozen rubbing-trees of grizzly bears, each one with bear hair clinging to its bark, then may one say, "This is bear country!" That was what we found in the green timber of Avalanche Valley, between our camp and Roth Mountain, six miles below. All the rubbing-trees we saw were from eight to twelve inches in diameter, as if small ones had been specially chosen. I suppose this is because there are no large spur roots to interfere with the standing bear; besides which, a small tree offers a sharper edge.

On those trees we saw where several of the rubbing bears had bitten the trunk, high up, tearing the bark open crosswise. We also found, on some, raking claw-marks across the bark. Charlie Smith said that the tooth-marks are always made by grizzlies and the claw-marks by black bears.

163

As before remarked, Mr. Phillips and Charlie Smith were very desirous that I should find and kill a grizzly, but for several reasons I had little hope that it would come to pass. September is not a good month in which to find a bear of any species on those summits; nor is a short hunting-trip conducive to the development of bear-episodes, anywhere. In spite of Charlie's hopefulness, I did not take the prospect seriously, even though in the Michel store Mack had called for twine with which to stretch bear-hides! But in bear-hunting, "it is better to be born lucky than rich."

When Charlie came in on the evening of the 19th of September and reported a bear at the carcass of my first goat, it really seemed time to hope for at least a distant view of Old Ephraim. Believing that one good way to reveal certain phases of wild-animal life is in showing how animals are actually found in their haunts, I am tempted to set forth a statement of the events of September 20th. It may be that others wonder, as I often have, just how it *feels* to hunt a grizzly bear — the most dangerous American animal — and find him, at timberline. The really bold hunters may scoff at the courage and ferocity of the grizzly as he is to-day; but Charlie Smith openly declares that the one particular thing which he never does, and never will do, is to fire his last cartridge when away from camp.

It was the third day of Mr. Phillips's hunt for mountain sheep, and he was still absent. Charlie and I took two saddle-horses and set out before sunrise, intending to visit all the goat carcasses before returning. We pushed briskly up to the head of Avalanche Creek, climbed to the top of the pass, then dropped down into the basin on the north. I dreaded a long climb on foot from that point up to our old camp on Goat Pass, but was happily disappointed. Thanks to the good engineering of some Indian trail-maker, the trail led from the head of the basin, on an easy gradient, up through the green timber of the mountain side, quite to our old camp.

We found fresh grizzly-bear tracks within fifty feet of the ashes of our camp-fire; but our goat skins in the big spruce, and our cache of provisions near it, had not been touched. . . .

With only a few minutes delay, we mounted once more and rode on northward toward the scene of the first goat-kill. As we rode up the ridge of Bald Mountain, a biting cold wind, blowing sixty miles an hour, struck us with its full force. It went through our clothing like cold water, and penetrated to the marrow in our bones. At one point it seemed determined to blow the hair off Kaiser's back. While struggling to hold myself together, I saw the dog suddenly whirl head on to the fierce blast, crouch low, and fiercely grip the turf with his claws, to keep from being blown away. It was all that our horses could do to hold a straight course, and keep from drifting down to the very edge of the precipice that yawned only twenty-five feet to leeward. We were glad to get under the lee of Bald Mountain, where the fierce blast that concentrated on that bleak pass could not strike us with its full force.

At last we reached the lake we named in honor of Kaiser. Dismounting in a grassy hollow that was sheltered from the wind, we quickly stripped the saddles from our horses and picketed the animals so that they could graze. Then, catching up our rifles, cameras, and a very slim parcel of luncheon, we set out past the lake for the ridge that rises beyond it.

The timber on the ridge was very thin, and we could see through it for a hundred yards or more. As we climbed, we looked sharply all about, for it seemed very probable that a grizzly might be lying beside a log in the fitful sunshine that struck the southern face of the hill. Of course, as prudent hunters, we were prepared to see a grizzly that was above us, and big, and dangerous, — three conditions that guarantee an interesting session whenever they come together. . . .

We reached the crest of the ridge, without having seen a bear, and with the utmost caution stalked on down the northern side, toward the spot where the two goat carcasses lay on the slide-rock. The noise we made was reduced to an irreducible minimum.

We trod and straddled like men burglarizing Nature's sky-parlor. We broke no dead twigs, we scraped against no dead branches, we slid over no fallen logs. Step by step we stole down the hillside, as cautiously as if we had known that a bear was really at the foot of it. At no time would it have surprised us to have seen Old Ephraim spring up from behind a bush or a fallen log, within twenty feet of us.

At last the gray slide-rock began to rise into view. At last we paused, breathing softly and seldom, behind a little clump of spruces. Charlie, who was a step in advance, stretched his neck to its limit, and looked on beyond the edge of the hill, to the very spot where lay the remains of my first mountain goat. My view was cut off by green branches and Charlie.

He turned to me, and whispered in a perfectly colorless way,

"He's lying right on the carcass!"

"What? Do you mean to say that a *bear* is *really there?*" I asked, in astonishment.

"Yes! Stand here, and you can see him, — just over the edge."

I stepped forward and looked. Far down, fully one hundred and fifty yards from where we were, there lay a silvery-gray animal, head up, front paws outstretched. It was indeed a silver-tip; but it looked awfully small and far away. He was out on the clean, light-gray stipple of slide-rock, beside the scanty remains of my goat.

Even as I took my first look, the animal rose on his haunches, and for a moment looked intently toward the north, away from us. The wind waved his long hair, one wave after another. It was a fine chance for a line shot at the spinal column; and at once I made ready to fire.

"Do you think you can kill him from *here*?" asked Charlie, anxiously. "You can get nearer to him if you like."

"Yes; I think I can hit him from here all right." (I had carefully fixed the sights of my rifle, several days previously.)

"Well, if you don't hit him, I'll kick you down this ridge!" said Charlie, solemn as a church owl, with an on-your-head-be-it air. To me, it was clearly a moment of great peril.

I greatly desired to watch that animal for half an hour; but when a bear-hunter finds a grizzly bear, the thing for him to do is to kill it first, and watch it afterward. I realized that no amount of bear observations ever could explain to John Phillips the loss of that bear.

As I raised my .303 Savage, the grizzly rose in a business-like way, and started to walk up the slide-rock, due south, and a little quartering from us. This was not half so good for me as when he was sitting down. Aiming to hit his heart and lungs, close behind his foreleg, and allowing a foot for his walking, I let go.

A second or two after the "whang" the bear reared slightly, and sharply wheeled toward his right, away from us; and just then Charlie's rifle roared, — close beside my ear! Without losing an instant, the grizzly started on a mad gallop, down the slide-rock and down the canyon, running squarely across our front.

"*Heavens!*" I thought, aghast. "*Have I missed him?*"

Quickly I threw in another cartridge, and fired again; and "whang" went Charlie, as before. The bear fairly flew, reaching far out with its front feet, its long hair rolling in great waves from head to tail. Even at that distance, its silver-tipped fur proclaimed the species.

Bushes now hid my view, and I ran down a few yards, to get a fair show. At last my chance came. As the bear raced across an opening in my view, I aimed three feet ahead of his nose, and fired my third shot.

Instantly the animal pitched forward on his head, like a stricken rabbit, and lay very still.

"Ye fetched him that time!" yelled Charlie, triumphantly. "He's down! He's down! Go for him, Kaiser! Go for him!"

The dog was ready to burst with superheated eagerness. With two or three whining yelps he dashed away down the ridge and out of sight. By this time Charlie was well below me, and I ran down to where he stood, beaming up.

"You've fixed him, Director! He's down for keeps."

"Where is he?"

"Lying right on that patch of yellow grass, and dead as a wedge. Shake!"

The Exploration of Maligne Lake
Mary Schäffer

The first recorded visit to Maligne Lake was made by a railway surveyor in 1875, but the lake wasn't thoroughly explored until the summer of 1908 when two lady adventurers organized a pack trip to rediscover it. Following a crude map drawn by a Stoney Indian trapper, their party rode north from the CPR line at Lake Louise and into the ranges between the Athabasca and Brazeau Rivers. On July 7th the lake was spotted from a high peak, and the following day this unlikely party reached the shore and began the exploration of one of the Rockies' largest lakes. The members were Mary Schäffer of Philadelphia, Mary "Mollie" Adams ("M") of Boston, Stewardson Brown ("The Botanist") of Philadelphia, Banff guide Billy Warren ("Chief"), his assistant Sid Unwin ("K"), and camp cook Reggie Holmes ("Chef").

With the lake now found, fresh food for conversation developed. A high double-peaked mountain, with a very large glacier on its north face, could be seen above the tree-tops about thirty miles distant. It seemed a little too much to the north-east to be Mount Brazeau, while the one that "K." reached in his climb seemed too far to the south-west. Both were in splendid view and kept us guessing.

The Botanist quickly grew busy; he had struck a botanical haven, very rare specimens of other sections of the mountains were there in

167

Mary Schäffer at the Kootenay Plains. Archives of the Canadian Rockies

masses, and other plants he had not seen at all were there also. Dinner passed off with the exciting intelligence that "to-morrow will be devoted to building a raft, as the shores, as far as can be seen, are impassable for horses, and it must be fully three miles to the head of the lake. We will then take tents, blankets and food for three days, and you enthusiastic climbers can fight it out from the top as to which is Mount Brazeau."

Our part of the raft-making next morning was the uncommon permission to wash up the breakfast dishes, and the three men were soon swallowed up in the trees as they went down to the lake, each with his axe over his shoulder. With things snugged up and a huge pot of pork and beans set to simmer over the fire, I too strolled down. It *was* a stroll, too, that took about a half hour to do the job, as the fallen timber made it hard travelling and the sloughs near the lake boot-high. But we didn't make rafts every day or even reach a spandy-new lake, so the exertions seemed well worth the cause. As I came quietly out to the water's edge, there were two of the men out in the lake busily lashing two logs together, and "K." was just rounding a point gracefully riding a dead tree, which, at that moment, as gracefully rolled over and landed him in the water. He was, however, already so wet that he couldn't be much wetter, so he shook himself amidst a momentary smile all round, and shoved his old tree into place.

I found a dry spot and sat watching them come and go for an hour. "Chef," who was an accomplished axeman, wielded his axe with an artistic ability interesting to see; and as I looked at them all, working almost in silence, my mind went back to the first carpenters who had cut logs in those waters, — the busy little beavers whose work was still visible, but whose pelts had been the cause of their extermination.

At six o'clock the three men walked into camp, soaked, of course, but jubilant over results, and announced that H.M.S. *Chaba* would sail for the upper end of the lake to-morrow morning at nine.

A short pow-wow after supper resulted in learning that we were to go in style regardless of our plea that we were willing to rough it for a few days; air-beds, tents, and food for three days were to be taken on that raft.

Personally my sensations towards large bodies of water are similar to those of a cat, and though I begged to rough it, it was not so much to do something uncomfortable as to keep from drowning on an overtaxed raft. With qualms and misgivings next morning, I watched bags, boxes, and bundles carried out and deposited on the upper deck of the *Chaba*, the last two packages being "M." and myself, who were dumped unceremoniously on with the rest of the cargo. The Botanist waded out for himself, as did Muggins, the rowers climbed aboard, and we set sail. Now that she was loaded, the lower deck looked alarmingly under water, and "M." and I were seated high on a bag of flour, a slab of bacon, and bundles of blankets. To the novice in rafting, nothing could have looked more insecure or unreliable; wide gaps in the logs showed unmeasured depths of green water below, and it seemed as though, with a sudden lurch or sharp turn, we must be shot from our perch into the cold, unfathomed waters.

Determined to put up a brave fight, I clutched my log and awaited a spill. It never came; she rode as steady as a little ship and as slow as a snail. She was propelled by two sweeps twelve feet long; the men took twenty-minute turns at her, the rest of us looking on and silently wondering at the fearful task and lack of complaint. At noon she was paddled as near shore as possible and all hands landed for lunch; Muggins, who sat at the tip end of the landing-log voted the performance a terrible bore, and nearly jumped out of his skin when once he reached terra firma.

Back once more on the raft after an hour's rest, the men slowly pulled the clumsy little craft, foot by foot, past exquisite bays and inlets, the mountains closed more and more about us, and at six-thirty, as we seemed within a mile of our goal — the head of the lake, — we hove to, and camped by a stream which came from the double-peaked mountain. Landing, we found our new home was a garden of crimson vetches. As the warm winds swept across them, the odour brought a little homesick thought of the sweet clover-fields of the east in July.

Opposite our camp rose a fine snow-capped mountain down whose side swept a splendid glacier. As we paddled slowly in sight of it, "K." suddenly looked up and said, "That is the mountain from which I first saw the lake." So we promptly named it "Mount Unwin." Though the breath of the vetches remained with us all night, the thought of home fled with the crash of avalanches from Mount Unwin's sides, and the distant yapping of coyotes in the valley behind us. With the coming of morning, our plans were quickly laid to paddle the intervening mile to the end of the lake, take a light lunch, then climb for the keynote of the situation, — Lake Brazeau.

On one point we had found Sampson's map very much at fault: he had both drawn and mentioned "narrows" about two thirds of the way up the lake. These had never materialised and we commented on the fact of finding Sampson seriously at fault. The raft was growing to be so homey and reliable a vehicle that even the timid now stepped gaily aboard, all but Muggins; he hated that raft, and came aboard sighing and dejected as though he had been whipped, but of course had no intention of being left behind, and away we sailed with a pack-mantle hoisted to catch any passing breeze.

In about an hour, as we were rounding what we supposed to be our debarking point, there burst upon us that which, all in our little company agreed, was the finest view any of us had ever beheld in the Rockies. This was a tremendous assertion, for, of that band of six of us, we all knew many valleys in that country, and each counted his miles of travel through them by thousands. Yet there it lay, for the time being all ours, — those miles and miles of lake, the un-named peaks rising above us, one following the other, each more beautiful than the last. We had reached, not the end of the lake, but the narrows of which Sampson had told us. On our left stood a curiously shaped mountain toward which we had worked our way for two days. We called it "The Thumb"; next rose a magnificent double-headed pile of rock, whose perpendicular cliffs reached almost to the shore. Its height? I've no idea. It was its massiveness, its simple dignity, which appealed to us so strongly, and we named it "Mount Warren," in honour of Chief, through whose grit and determination we were able to behold this splendour.

As we slowly advanced beneath the shadow of "The Thumb," a large fissure, at least 1000 feet above us, became visible, and from it there burst a fine waterfall. So great was its drop that it became spray, waving back and forth in the wind, long before it touched the rocks below, then gathering itself in a little stream, tumbled headlong into the lake, losing itself in a continuous series of ringlets.

After four hours of tough rowing, we reached the head of the lake, and landed for lunch on an old alluvial fan. None of the higher peaks were here visible, the supposed Mount Brazeau south of us, the uncertain Mount Maligne east of us, or even Mount Unwin; they were all hidden by lower shoulders of themselves.

Like feudal lords (and ladies) we sat at our mid-day meal of tinned-meat and bannock that day. Our table, the clean sweet earth itself, was garnished with flowers, with vetches crimson, yellow, and pink. They spread away in every direction from us as far as the eye could see, and, the warm winds blowing down upon us from the southern valleys, swept across their faces and bore their clover-laden breath to the first white guests of that wonderful region.

With lunch over, we wandered about to drink it all in. How pure and undefiled it was! We searched for some sign that others had been there, — not a tepee-pole, not a charred stick, not even tracks of game, just masses of flowers, the lap-lap of the waters on the shore, the occasional reverberating roar of an avalanche, and our own voices, stilled by a nameless Presence.

We wanted a week in that heaven of the hills, yet back at "Camp Unwin" was only one more day's grub, so, scolding at Fate, we turned toward H.M.S. *Chaba* as she lay indifferently swashing her cumbersome form against an old beached log, whose momentary duty it was to prevent her from drifting off across the lake.

As we came up, Chief had just chopped out a smooth surface on the side of a small tree, and there, for the first time and only in all our wanderings, so far as I can remember, we inscribed our initials and the date of our visit.

Even then I think we all apologised to ourselves, for, next to a mussy camp-ground, there is nothing much more unsightly to the *true camper* than to see the trees around a favourite camping site disfigured with personal names and personal remarks, which never fail to remind one of the old adage taught the small boy in his early youth when he receives his first knife.

And one more name we left behind, not carved upon a tree but in our memories. All day the thought of one who loved the hills as we did ourselves was in my mind, and though she could not be with us, yet did I long to share our treasures with her. On the lake's west shore rose a fine symmetrical peak, and as we stepped cautiously aboard our craft (I never could get over the idea that she would go over with a sneeze), I said: "With every one's sanction I call that peak Mount Mary Vaux." There was no dissenting voice.

Foot by foot we left it all behind — the flowers, the tumbling avalanches, the great rock masses we had named, the untraversed valleys, and the beautiful falls.

The day was dying fast; as we glided by the tempting coves, and swept through the narrows, — now "Sampson's Narrows," — the setting sun touched a symmetrical snow-tipped peak on the eastern shore of the lake, the dark waters before us caught up the picture, threw back to us an inverted rosy summit, and we named it "Sampson's Peak" for him who had sketched us the little map. The heavy rhythmic breathing of the rowers and Muggins's occasional sighs were the only drawbacks to absolute and perfect enjoyment; but for the tense faces before us and the tenser muscles, we could have looked ahead and aloft and said, — "This is Paradise."

As we came into port under the shadow of Mount Unwin, the sweet odour of the vetches came out to greet us, the sun sank behind the hills, the winds died away, every ripple of the lake disappeared, even the mosquitoes ceased to bother us; The Thumb, Mounts Warren, Unwin, Sampson, and many other unnamed peaks were dyed in crimson, which changed to purple, to violet, then night with its cloak of darkness fell. As the evening's camp-fire was lighted, there came across the water the distant bark of a coyote, overhead passed a few belated duck; except for these there seemed no other life than that of our little family hidden there in the wilderness where "home" had never been before.

Camping in the Rockies
Mary Vaux

From the Canadian Alpine Journal, 1907.

To begin with, a good tent is required, plenty of warm blankets, and a canvas sheet to spread under and over the blankets on the bough-bed, to prevent dampness from above and below; then, a small pillow is a great luxury, and takes but little room in the pack. Of course, it is presupposed that the women of the party wear rational clothes: knickerbockers, a flannel shirtwaist, and knotted kerchief at the neck; stout boots, with hobnails, laced to the knee, or arranged for puttees; woollen stockings, a felt hat with moderate brim, and a sweater or short coat completing the outfit. A light waterproof coat, opened well behind, to allow it to part over the horse's back, and which may be fastened to the saddle, is very necessary in a region where storms must be expected frequently. Each person should be provided with a canvas bag, which can be securely buttoned, wherein to place the necessary toilet articles. An extra pair of light shoes, a short skirt to wear in camp and a golf cape with hood, add greatly to the comfort of the camper; also a good-sized piece of mosquito netting, to keep off intruding bulldogs, if you wish to rest in the tent in the heat of the mid-day sun; while a hot water bottle and a box of mustard may be tucked in along with a few simple medicines in case of emergency. On two occasions I would have given a great deal for a mustard plaster, and on a third occasion it was of great value.

The food taken is largely a matter for personal selection. We have eliminated canned things very largely, and find the change to dried foods not at all distasteful — of course, with the proviso that they are properly cooked. Bacon, ham, tea, coffee, evaporated cream, butter, oatmeal, rice, beans, flour, canned tomatoes, canned soup, onions, potatoes, pickles, marmalade, cheese and dried fruits can be so prepared that, with hunger sauce, there is nothing left to be desired in the way of a larger bill of fare. Trout and game are always a welcome addition to the larder. Cakes of chocolate and raisins may be added to the list, when it is desirable to have something in the pocket on a day's climb, and the return to camp is uncertain. In all preparations it must be remembered that the altitude at which we camp is considerable, and that a necessary attribute towards a good time is to be warm and comfortable at night, when the thermometer may probably fall to 28°, and there will be ice along the brook-sides, in the morning. Then, do not forget the cold dip in the mountain stream, as the crowning luxury of all.

Hip-Hip-Hurrah!
Conrad Kain

The Canadian Alpine Club's 1909 camp was held at Lake O'Hara, and club president A. O. Wheeler imported a young Austrian guide named Conrad Kain to lead the camp participants up the area's peaks.

Again a group for Mt. Huber. Fifty-five people all told. It was a frosty morning, and when we, climbing through a gully from Lake O'Hara, reached the pass between Wiwaxy Peaks and Mt. Huber, it began to storm and to snow. Everyone turned back. Only Mr. Fynn, who also led a party, and I with three women and a man, waited in the shelter of the rocks for better weather.

I promised sunshine, and told amusing little stories of climbing and from experiences as guide, so that the people would not lose their courage and desire for the ascent. We waited in the cold, and at last, at last, a blue patch appeared in the sky! For a few minutes the sun even appeared through the fog. Right above the pass some easy climbing begins. But the rocks were very cold and progress was slow. Mr. Fynn had to turn back with his party, as one of the ladies had almost frozen her fingers. I would have had to do the same thing if I had not fortunately brought several extra pairs of gloves for my women. Now we came to the glacier, which we ascended diagonally, then over a short ice-ridge to a wall of rock, a step which interrupts the glacier. Then over the glacier again to the col between Mt. Victoria and our peak.

The weather changed in the meantime, but as the ladies knew that we were the only ones out of fifty-five people who had not given up the tour they were full of joy and desire to reach the summit, despite the obstacle presented by the unfavorable weather. I promised to bring them safely back to camp, and told them they should

Alpine Club of Canada members leaving the Lake O'Hara camp for a climb, 1909. Archives of the Canadian Rockies

not be dismayed by the fog, and that if only a wind did not arise we would attain the peak without trouble. In this fashion I kept up their confidence and courage.

The man had nothing much to say (as is usual when ladies are in the majority) and without difficulty we reached the ice-slope, now covered with fresh snow, where there are the only really dangerous places of the whole excursion. I was obliged to improve the old steps, which Mr. Fynn and I had made several days before, as they had melted out considerably, but without especial incident we reached the summit of Mt. Huber. For the few minutes of our halt we had a good view down to camp.

While descending the risky spots on the ice-slope a wind sprang up, and away went our good steps in the snow. That was not pleasant for me, for, as guide, I could not go first in descending and my tourists were all beginners. I put the strongest woman in front. Slowly and with great care we went down step by step. A single misstep would have been fatal, for I could not anchor myself. I breathed easier when the last woman descended over the little bergschrund.

As we approached camp I announced our approach by a loud yell. Everyone came toward us, more than a hundred people with the Club President at their head. Mr. Wheeler offered me his hand and said: "I thank you, Conrad. Now you have your witnesses, and I see that it is just as Dr. P. wrote to me about you, that Conrad never stops until he has completed his task." As he finished his speech, the young men lifted me on their shoulders and carried me to the camp-fire, with a fearful shouting of "Hip-Hip-Hurrah," and singing "He is a jolly good fellow!" Naturally the ladies were also given a thunderous Hurrah.

To the Top of Mount Robson
George Kinney

Distressed to hear that a group of foreign alpinists was on its way to climb the Rockies' highest summit, 12,972-foot Mount Robson, the Reverend George Kinney made his way west across country from Edmonton in the spring of 1909, hoping that he might somehow beat them to it. Along the way he met a fledgling packtrain guide named Donald "Curlie" Phillips. Phillips had never climbed a mountain of any description before, but he agreed to join Kinney for an attempt on the Rockies' most difficult peak. After a long overland trek; they reached the base of Mount Robson on July 24th and waited for a break in the weather.

At last the weather began to clear up, and Monday, August 9th, we again climbed the rugged north shoulder. Crossing the difficult shale slope, we passed the camp spots of our former trips, and with our heavy fifty-pound packs, struggled up those fearful cliffs till we reached an altitude of nearly ten thousand five hundred feet. We would soon have reached the top of the west shoulder, when the storm caught us. For a couple of hours we had watched the storm-clouds gather, then gradually obliterate the peaks; yet we pushed on, hoping they were only squally. We were climbing in a narrow couloir when it began to snow. We did not mind it at first but in a few minutes it had snowed three inches, and slides began to come down. Realizing at once our danger, we hastily cached our packs under a sheltering rock and hurried down the cliffs. But we had a bad half-hour before we got out of danger and glissaded the draw down the long shale slope. We got to Camp Robson at the foot of the mountain in a discouraged frame of mind, for we were hundreds of miles from civilization, with scarcely any provisions and the mountain was still unscaled.

For three days it stormed, and we lived on birds and marmot (a kind of mountain ground-hog). Then Thursday, August 12th, dawned fine and clear. As we had lots of time to make our "Highest Up" Camp that day, we spent most of the morning repairing our boots and clothes and making ready for our final climb. After an early dinner we climbed the several thousand feet of cliff to where we had cached our packs the Monday the storm caught us. Shouldering the packs, we climbed more cliffs, and finally worked our way to the top of the west shoulder, 10,500 feet above the sea. Here, at an altitude equal to that of Mt. Stephen, we chopped away a couple of feet of snow and ice, and feathered our bed with dry slate stones. We shivered over the little fire that warmed our stew and then, amid earth's grandest scenes, we went to bed with the sun and shivered through a wretched night.

Friday, August 13th, dawned cold and clear, but with the clouds gathering in the south. Using our blankets for a wind-brake we made a fire with a handful of sticks, and nearly froze as we ate out of the pot of boiling stew on the little fire. Then we laid rocks on our blankets so they would not blow away, and facing the icy wind from the south, started up the west side of the upper part of the peak. The snow was in the finest climbing condition, and the rock-work though steep offered good going. Rapidly working our way to the south, and crossing several ridges, we had reached, in an hour, the first of two long cliffs that formed horizontal ramparts all around the peak. We lost half an hour getting up this cliff, but finally found an easy way up it.

The clouds that came up with a strong south wind, had gradually obscured the peak, till by the time we reached the cliff, they were swirling by us on our level, and at the top of the cliff it began to snow. For a moment I stood silent, and then turning to my companion said: "Curlie! my heart is broken." For a storm on the peak meant avalanches on that fearful slope, and there would be no escaping them, so I thought that we would have to turn back, and our provisions were now so low that we would not have enough to make another two-day trip up the mountain. It meant that this was our last chance; but, to my surprise, it did not snow much, the clouds being mostly a dense mist. In a few minutes I said, "Let us make a rush for the little peak," meaning the north edge of the peak which was directly above us. "All right," says Curlie, from whom I never heard a word of discouragement, and away we started, keeping to the hard snow slopes. Though these were extremely steep, the snow was in such splendid condition that we could just stick our toes in and climb right up hand over hand.

By the time we had conquered the second of the long ramparts of cliffs, that form black threads across the white of the peak, we concluded that it was not going to snow very hard, as the clouds were mostly mist and sleet. Swinging again toward the south, we headed directly for the highest point of the mountain, which we could see now and then through the clouds. Small traverse cliffs of rock were constantly encountered, but they were so broken that we could easily get up them, by keeping to the snow of the little draws. For hours we steadily climbed those dreadful slopes. So fearfully steep were they that we climbed for hundreds of feet, where standing erect in our foot-holds, the surface of the slopes were not more than a foot and a half from our faces; while the average angle must have been over sixty degrees. There were no places where we could rest. Every few minutes we would make foot-holds in the snow large enough to enable us to stand on our heels as well as our toes, or we would distribute our weight on toe and hand-holds and rest by lying up against the wall of snow. On all that upper climb we did nearly the whole work on our toes and hands only. The clouds were a blessing in a way, for they shut out the view of the fearful depths below. A single slip any time during that day meant a slide to death. At times the storm was so thick that we could see but a few yards, and the sleet would cut our faces and nearly blind us. Our clothes and hair were one frozen mass of snow and ice.

When within five hundred feet of the top, we encountered a number of cliffs, covered with overhanging masses of snow, that were almost impossible to negotiate, and the snow at that altitude was so dry that it would crumble to powder and offer poor footing. We got in several difficult places that were hard to overcome, and we fought our way up the last cliffs, only to find an almost insurmountable difficulty. The prevailing winds being from the west and south, the snow, driven by the fierce gales had built out against the wind in fantastic masses of crystal, forming huge cornices all along the crest of the peak that can easily be distinguished from the mouth of the

Grand Forks, some ten miles away. We finally floundered through these treacherous masses and stood, at last, on the very summit of Mt. Robson.

I was astonished to find myself looking into a gulf right before me. Telling Phillips to anchor himself well, for he was still below me, I struck the edge of the snow with the staff of my ice axe and it cut in to my very feet, and through that little gap, that I had made in the cornice, I was looking down a sheer wall of precipice that reached to the glacier at the foot of Berg Lake, thousands of feet below. I was on a needle peak that rose so abruptly that even cornices cannot build out very far on it. Baring my head I said, "In the name of Almighty God, by whose strength I have climbed here, I capture this peak, Mt. Robson, for my own country, and for the Alpine Club of Canada." Then, just as Phillips and I congratulated each other, the sun came out for a minute or two, and through the rifts in the clouds, the valleys about us showed their fearful depths. The Fraser lay a thread of silver, over eleven thousand feet below. Before I could take any photos the clouds shut in again thicker than ever. We were nearly frozen, so could not remain at the top till the clouds should break. We could not build a cairn there, in which to cache the Canadian flag, that Mrs. Dr. Geo. Anderson, of Calgary, had donated, and our records; for if we left them in the snow they would have been lost, so we cached them on our return, in a splendid natural cairn, a few hundred feet below the peak.

On three different little cliffs near the summit, we met with great difficulty in descending, but we finally managed. After caching our records and getting down near the twelve thousand foot level, we found a new danger that nearly finished us. The storm had increased, but the temperature had risen. In fact a chinook was melting the lower snows. We found our trail nearly melted away. To make the matter worse, the slopes were so steep that the snow never could lie very deep, even in the couloirs; and we frequently had to make detours around places where the ice or rock beneath the thin snow would allow of no footholds whatever.

It was so cold and stormy at the summit, we did not get anything out of our packs to eat. While I fixed the cairn Phillips ate some Peter's chocolate, and later on I snatched a moment to eat some, paper and all. But during the twelve hours climbing and returning on that slope, there was no time to do anything but get to the summit and then to safety. So very dangerous did the snow get, that our return trip cost us seven hours of distressing work, while the climb to the summit was made from our "Highest Up" Camp, at 10,500 feet, in five hours. We had to use the rope all the way down, and only one of us could move at a time, while the other got as good an anchorage as possible. But finally we reached the lower of the two bands of cliffs where we unroped, and then rapidly got down to camp "Higher Up," where we soon devoured everything edible in sight. The storm was raging fiercely above us, night was gathering, and we had thousands of feet of cliff still to descend before reaching Camp Robson that night, yet we lingered on the west shoulder, eating and resting, and oh, so glad that the peak had, at last, really been won.

It was a long three-hour struggle with our packs down those cliffs. We had half a mile or more of ledges to follow, to the north there were several deep gorges with ice steps to cross, then a long glissade and more cliffs. So it was long after dark before we reached Camp Robson and finished the big return trip from base to summit in twenty hours. We were so tired we could hardly eat or rest and our feet were very sore from making toe-holds in the hard snow. But we had stood on the crown of Mt. Robson, and the struggle had been a desperate one. Three times we had made two-day climbs, spending ninety-six hours in all above ten thousand feet altitude, so far north. During the twenty days we were at Camp Robson we captured five virgin peaks, including Mt. Robson, and made twenty-three big climbs.

Others will doubtless some day stand on Mt. Robson's lonely peak, but they who conquer its rugged crags will ever after cherish in their hearts a due respect and veneration for its mighty solitudes.

Mount Robson Reprise
Conrad Kain (translated by P. A. W. Wallace)

During the Canadian Alpine Club camp of 1913, the guide Conrad Kain and two club members, Albert MacCarthy and William Foster, climbed the Rockies' highest mountain. As was later disclosed, theirs was actually the first ascent of the mountain since Kinney and Phillips stopped just short of the true summit. But reaching the summit of Mount Robson is one thing

and getting back down in one piece quite another, as Kain and his Herren
discovered.

On the crest of the king of the Rockies, there was not much room to
stand. We descended a few meters and stamped down a good space.
It was half-past five o'clock. Our barometer showed exactly 13,000
feet.

The view was glorious in all directions. One could compare the
sea of glaciers and mountains with a stormy ocean. Mt. Robson is
about 2,000 feet higher than all the other mountains in the neighborhood. Indescribably beautiful was the vertical view towards Berg
Lake and the camp below. . . . Unfortunately only fifteen minutes
were allowed us on the summit, ten of pure pleasure and five of
teeth chattering. The rope and our damp clothes were frozen as hard
as bone. And so we had to think of the long descent — 5.45 o'clock.

As far as the steep couloir, all went well. The descent over this
piece was difficult. All the steps were covered with snow. Except for
this, we had no difficulties till the shoulder. As it was late, I proposed
to descend by the glacier on the south side, for greater safety. Besides
the question of time, it seemed to me too dangerous to make our
descent over the route of ascent. As a guide with two *Herren,* one

*Conrad Kain (left) with Albert H. MacCarthy and William W. Foster
following their ascent of Mount Robson in 1913.* Archives of the Canadian
Rockies

has to take such dangers more into account than do amateurs, for upon one's shoulders rests the responsibility for men's lives. Also as a guide one must consider his calling and the sharp tongues that set going on all sides like clockwork when a guide with his party gets into a dangerous situation. It was clear to me that we must spend a night on the mountain. The descent was not quite clear to me. I was convinced that on this side we could get farther down than by the way we came up. My bivouac motto is: "A night out is hardly ever agreeable, and above 3,000 meters always a lottery."

After the shoulder, we had a steep snow-slope to the glacier. I made about 120 steps. Once on the glacier, we went down rapidly for a few hundred meters until a sheer precipice barred the way. So far and no farther. Vain was my search for a way down. We had to go back uphill, which was naturally no pleasure. Between rocks and glacier was a very steep icy trench which offered us the only descent. I examined the icy trench for a few minutes, and the ice cliffs over-hanging us. I saw the opportunity and, of course, the dangers too. Mr. Foster asked me what my opinion was, whether we could go on or not. I answered, quite truly: "We can; it is practicable but dangerous." Captain MacCarthy said: "Conrad, if it is not too dangerous for you, cutting steps, then don't worry about us. We'll trust to you and fortune."

That made matters easier for me, as I could see that both *Herren* had no fear. I lengthened the rope and left the *Herren* in a sheltered spot. I made the steps just as carefully and quickly as I could. When I had reached a good place I let both *Herren* follow. Mr. MacCarthy went last, and I was astonished at his surefootedness. This dangerous trench took a whole hour to negotiate. The rock was frozen, but the consciousness that we had such terrible danger behind us, helped us over the rocks. In greater safety we rested beneath the rocks.

Below us was the glacier which, seen from above, promised a good descent almost to timber-line. I remembered that the glacier had still another break-off and knew that we must camp out. However, I said nothing of this to my *Herren*, but the opposite. I pointed with my axe to the woods with the words: "It will be a fine night down there in the woods beside a big fire." Both chimed in, for the word "fire" makes a very different impression when one is standing in soaking clothes upon ice and snow; from the word "fire" when one is aroused by it from a sound sleep.

We did not find the glacier as good as we expected. We searched our way through ice debris in an avalanche bed. Here on the glacier the sun bade us good night. The sunset was beautiful. It would have been more beautiful to us if the sun had been delayed one hour. It was a melancholy moment when the last glow of evening faded in the west. We rested and spoke on this theme. Mr. MacCarthy said: "It is as well that the law of nature cannot be changed by men. What a panic it would raise if we succeeded in delaying the sun for an hour! It is possible that somewhere some alpinists will to-morrow morning be in the same situation as we are, and will be waiting eagerly for the friendly sun."

Despite the approach of darkness we went on. About ten o'clock in the evening we reached the rocks. It was out of the question to go any further. Our feet felt the effects of the last seventeen hours on ice and rock, and so we were easily satisfied with a resting place. A ledge of rock two meters wide offered us a good place to bivouac. We made it as comfortable as we could. We built a little sheltering wall about us. Our provision bag still had plenty of sandwiches, and Mr. MacCarthy, to our surprise, brought a large packet of chocolate from his rucksack. We took our boots off. I gave Mr. Foster my dry pair of extra mitts for socks, so we all had dry feet, which is the important thing in camping out. The *Herren* had only one rucksack between them, into which they put their feet. Both *Herren* were roped up to a rock.

I gave a few hints on bivouacing, for there are some tricks in sleeping out on cold rocks that one can only learn by experience. Fortunately the night was a warm one, threatening rain. Clouds were hanging in the sky, which, however, the west wind swept away to the east. In the valley we saw flickering the campfire of the Alpine Club and of the construction camp of the Canadian Northern and Grand Trunk Railways. I was very tired and went to sleep without any trouble. A thundering avalanche woke me from a sound sleep. I heard Mr. Foster's teeth chatter as he lay beside me. I uttered no word of sympathy, but went to sleep again.

Later I was awakened by a dream. I dreamed that we were quite close to a forest. I saw wood close at hand, and dry branches ready for kindling. In the dream I reproached myself what the *Herren* would think of me, sleeping here in the forest with firewood, but without a fire and almost freezing. With these reproaches I awoke and sat up to convince myself whether the forest and firewood were really so near. But I saw only a few stars and in the east a few gray clouds lit up with the dawn. I could not get to sleep again, but lay quietly and listened to the thunder of the avalanches which broke the almost ghostly silence of nature. At daybreak it became considerably warmer, so my *Herren*, who had spent a cold and sleepless night, now fell sound asleep.

At six o'clock the friendly beams of the sun reached us. I wakened my *Herren*. Both sat up and described the pain in their eyes, which they could not open. The eyes of both were greatly swollen. It was not a pleasant sight. I thought both were snow-blind. Snow-blind, at a height of 9,000 feet, and in such a situation — that might have an unpleasant ending. After some cold poultices, the pain abated and both were able to keep their eyes open.

I told my dream. Both *Herren* had dreams of a similar nature, which had reference to the cold night. Mr. Foster dreamed that a number of his friends came with blankets and commiserated the barren camping ground, and no one covered him. Mr. MacCarthy, in his dream, implored his wife for more blankets, and his wife stopped him with the curt reply: "O no, dear, you can't have any blankets. Sleeping without any is good training if we want to go to the North Pole."

I searched for a descent over the rocks. After a quarter of an hour I came back.

"Yes, we can make it without further difficulty."

At 6.45 a.m. we left the bivouac, which will certainly remain in our memory. We did not get down so easily after all. We had to get around sheer walls. The climbing was difficult, and at some places the rock was very rotten. This was very unpleasant for my *Herren*. They could only see a few steps through their glasses and swollen eyes.

At last we had the most difficult part behind us, but not the most dangerous. We had to traverse a hanging glacier. For ten minutes we were exposed to the greatest danger. I certainly breathed freely when we lay down to rest under some overhanging rock. Our barometer showed 8,200 feet, time 10.15 a.m. That eight hundred feet had taken three hours to negotiate. I said to my *Herren*: "I am happy to be able to inform you that we have all dangers behind us. We shall reach the green grass in the valley safe and sound even to our swollen eyes."

We crossed loose stone to the southwest ridge. This ridge should be the easiest way up to the peak. From here we had a beautiful view of Lake Kinney below. Without further difficulty we descended through a wild, romantic gorge to the lake. In the gorge we had a slide over old snow. At eleven o'clock we took a long rest and devoured everything eatable we could find left in our provision bag. Then we followed the newly-built trail to camp.

About five o'clock in the afternoon we came, hungry and tired into camp, where we were hospitably received by our fellow campers with food and drink and congratulations.

From what Donald Phillips himself said, our ascent was really the first ascent of Mt. Robson. Phillips' words are as follows: "We reached, on our ascent (in mist and storm), an ice-dome fifty or sixty feet high, which we took for the peak. The danger was too great to ascend the dome."

Phillips and Kinney made the ascent over the west ridge. The west side is, as far as I could see, the most dangerous side that one can choose. Kinney undertook the journey from Edmonton alone with five horses. On the way he met Donald Phillips who was on a prospecting tour. Mr. Kinney persuaded Phillips to accompany him. Phillips had never before made this kind of a mountain trip and says himself that he had no suspicion of its dangers. They had between them one ice-axe and a bit of ordinary rope. They deserve more credit than we, even though they did not reach the highest point, for in 1909 they had many more obstacles to overcome than we; for at that time the railway, which brought us almost to the foot of the mountain, was then no less than 200 miles from their goal, and their way had to be made over rocks and brush, and we must not forget the dangerous river crossings.

Christmas Dinner
A. O. Wheeler and Tom Wilson

All who know anything about the Canadian Rockies will have heard of the oldest and most celebrated of its guides, Tom Wilson, of Banff, who was with Major Rogers during construction days of the Canadian Pacific Railway, and who discovered the famous Lake Louise and the Yoho Valley. Mr. Wilson's home is at Banff, but his business of horse-ranching takes him for a large part of the year to the Kootenai Plain, on the North Saskatchewan, where his ranche is situated. Some little time before last Christmas Day he started from his ranche

Pioneer guide and outfitter Tom Wilson lost part of his toes on each foot and nearly lost his life during a snowshoe trip from the Kootenay Plains to Lake Louise. He was on his way to have Christmas dinner with his family in Banff. Archives of the Canadian Rockies

to celebrate the annual festival with his family at Banff. It meant a snowshoe tramp alone of seventy miles through lonely tree-clad valleys, through rock-bound gorges and over wind-swept passes, where all nature lay stark and stiff in the icy grip of winter. The tale is best told in Mr. Wilson's own words, and those who know can easily read between the lines and can, perhaps, picture the terrible agony, the fierce despair, the grim determination, and the hardly-won fight against that overpowering desire to sleep which is the most deadly enemy in a case of this kind. The trip was made up the Siffleur River, over the Pipestone Pass and down the Pipestone to Laggan, and so by rail to Banff. Mr. Wilson writes me: —

"There is not much to tell of my trip over the Pipestone Pass. It was simply the case of a man starting on a seventy-mile snowshoe trip across the mountains to eat his Christmas dinner with his wife and family, and of getting there and eating the dinner, the pleasure being well worth the trip. I rode to within eight miles of the summit and started early the next morning on snowshoes to cross the pass

(8,300 feet alt.) It was snowing a little and very cold when I started, and when I got opposite the Clearwater Gap a blizzard came up, and I could not see more than six or eight feet ahead in that grey snow light that makes everything look level. I was on the trail along the mountain side, and was afraid of falling down one of those steep side collars (which you will remember on that side), and of breaking my snowshoes, so I turned and went down the mountain to the creek bottom. The snow was seven or eight feet deep and I fell through a snow bridge, getting both feet wet. It was below zero and a long way to timber whichever way I turned; a little nearer turning back, but I never like hitting the back trail. It was eight o'clock at night before I crossed the summit of the pass and reached the first timber. I got a fire started, but it was drifting and snowing so hard that the snow covered my sox and moccasins as fast as I could wring them dry, and, owing to the fierce wind, the flames leaped in every direction, making it impossible to get near the fire, so at half past nine I gave it up, put on my wet footgear and snowshoes and started down the valley. I could not see and felt the way with a stick. By daylight I had made three and a half miles; not much, but it kept the circulation going. In the heavy timber I made a fire and got dried out. My feet were beginning to pain as they had been thawed out twice already. I made three miles more that day and finished the last of my grub. The big snowshoes sank fifteen inches in the soft new snow and were a heavy drag on frozen toes. I saw it meant three or four more days tramping without grub to make Laggan. I made it in three, but the last day I could only make about fifty yards without resting, and my back tracks did not leave a very straight line. The chief trouble I had was to keep from going to sleep; it would have been so much easier to quit than to go on."

Mr. Wilson concludes his letter with the remark, "I think this is the longest letter I ever wrote."

Think for a moment what it really meant; that every time he put on his snowshoes his toes got frozen owing to the tight shoe straps; that every time he took them off his feet had to be thawed out; that every step had to raise a load of ten to fifteen pounds of soft snow; that wood had to be collected and cut to keep alive during the night; that fierce pain would drive away sleep; that he had no food, and always before him those interminable, slow, dragging miles of snowy wilderness. It must have required iron determination to make the end of that never-ending track, to eat his Christmas dinner with his wife and family.

Even such an awful experience could not dull Tom's keen native wit, and his remark to the doctor while examining his poor feet, "I hope I won't have to lose them, Doctor, I've had 'em a long time and I'm sort of used to 'em," shows the spirit of the man. We are happy to add that Mr. Wilson is now progressing well towards recovery. He has lost part of several toes on each foot, but as he says himself, the doctor has left him well balanced, by taking the same number of parts from each foot, and he can't complain.

Swift, the Frontiersman
F. A. Talbot

Lewis Swift's home was situated just a short distance down-valley from the present-day village of Jasper.

Swift, according to his own statement, squatted down in this district about five-and-twenty years ago. It was hard going at first, for he was pretty well all alone, save for a few Indians and one or two half-breeds in Jasper Park. He staked off some 2,000 acres on the hillside, which gradually slopes down from the feet of the mountains, hemming him in behind, to the river's bank, giving him a nice stretch of tolerably open flat near the water. The country was covered for the most part with poplar and cottonwood, with a few large Douglas firs here and there. In order to secure a constant supply of pure, fresh water, he pitched his shack beside a rushing creek rising amid the snows of Pyramid Mountain, the four-sided, pointed white peak of which just peeps over a mountain wall and keeps its eye on his back door from a height of 8,000 feet. His tools comprised an axe and hammer. With these he shaped some respectable logs and built his shack, chinking the interstices with moss, and crudely shingling the roof. At the front the roof projects, forming a stoep where he receives visitors, for no passer-by omits, under any pretence, to look up Swift, a rough welcome, the swopping of a few yarns, items of news and bush gossip serving to break the monotony of life in the wilderness.

As his personal requirements in regard to the necessities of life were few, he only cultivated about two acres of land. This is within a stone's throw of his home, and on practically level surface; the remainder was largely used for grazing purposes. But Swift practised no half-methods. When he had got a roof over his head and had broken his plot of ground, he trudged off to Edmonton, about 350 miles distant, for supplies. He bought provisions, seeds for his land, and a few head of cattle, which he drove home over the trail, making them swim the Athabaska. This in itself was an undertaking from which many men would have shrunk, and he paints vivid pictures of the difficulties he encountered with his stock during that tedious drive over the execrable, littered, narrow path.

On arriving home at last, he seeded his ground with vegetables and what not. Planting finished, he set to work upon improvements, and to-day uses the very tools he then contrived with so much effort, and at the expenditure of considerable inventiveness. He felled a huge fir having a solid cylindrical trunk. A section about 5 feet long and about 2 feet in diameter was cut out and turned into a roller, the shafts being crudely fashioned from small straight jack pine. His plough and harrow are likewise fashioned primitively from wood, as are also his other garden implements. He uses them to this day, regarding his handiwork with justifiable pride, and disclaiming the idea of resorting to modern tools.

Lewis Swift's cabin in the Athabasca Valley near present-day Jasper, 1911.
Archives of the Canadian Rockies

His greatest anxiety was in regard to his flour. This commodity is weighty for transport, and large quantities had to be brought in every time he made the trip to Edmonton — a journey which, owing to its trials, dangers, and laborious character, he only took about once a year. Even then it entailed his absence from home for a month or six weeks. At last he decided to attempt to solve this problem himself by building a mill. He secured a small corn grinder in Edmonton, and set to work to fashion a waterwheel. That waterwheel is Swift's greatest achievement. Bearing in mind the fact that the only tools at his command were an axe, adze, saw, hammer and nails, and that he was single-handed, his achievement is a striking *tour de force*.

"It war a tough job and no error," Swift remarked as he showed us his handiwork, "an' it took me more weeks 'n I can remember to rig it up, workin' from dawn to twilight. But I never felt so proud of meself as when I at last cried 'Done!' and threw down my tools. I war not long in seein' whether it would work or not. I fixed up th' corn mill, yanked on the belt, and opened the sluice. It war some little while 'fore the wheel gave any signs o' movin, and I war half afraid that summut had gone wrong somewhar, when thar war a creakin' and a grindin', and it began to move. I let in more water, and soon it war poundin' round steadily, an' the little pulley on the corn mill war whizzin' round to beat th' band. Then I didn't care a hang. When harvest time came round I got my wheat in, threshed it as best I could, and set th' box o' tricks to work. That flour was perfect. Sure that wheel war a pretty tough proposition, but it war the best summer's work I ever put in. What it has meant to me you cannot guess, but I've not had to go to Edmonton to fetch flour for ten years past, and that has lifted a pretty heavy load off my mind, I can tell yar."

Swift, however, did not rest on his oars. The summer sun is hot, and sometimes weeks will go by without a drop of rain falling, and that just at the period when the crops long for a drink. A failure of his crops would spell disaster. Swift saw that, and was resolved to take no chances. He drove a ditch from his tiny mill-pond right through his cultivated patch from one end to the other. On either side of this main channel he cut lateral shallow trenches. Every one is fitted with a primitive sluice gate at its junction with the main ditch, while the latter is similarly fitted at the pond. When the ground becomes somewhat parched, Swift just diverts a portion of the water from the stream, sends it surging down the main ditch, and then turns it on to the ground, flooding the farm just when, where, and to what extent he deems advisable.

When we arrived, his farm was a picture of flourishing fertility. The vegetables were healthy and well nourished, the potatoes of large size, and the corn in first-class condition. Swift never knows what a shortage is in his crops; irrigation, primitive though it may be, has saved them time after time. "After I got these jobs done," pointing to the improvements, "I only made that 700-mile trip to Edmonton and back once a year, travellin' light jes' to fetch letters like," he chuckled. Witnessing the many striking evidences of his enterprise and ingenuity, I suggested that he should go on, harness the creek a bit more, and generate his own electricity. "So I would," he rapped back, "but I don't understand th' blarmed thing. Th' juice beats me." As he accompanied these reflections with a ruminating scratch of his head, I went away with the half-smothered idea that, if he remained on his farm, he would set about electrically lighting his shack before long.

Along the New Transcontinental
J. Burgon Bickersteth

As Canada's second transcontinental railway, the Grand Trunk Pacific, pushed its tracks up the Athabasca Valley and over Yellowhead Pass in 1911 and 1912, a small village named Fitzhugh appeared near the confluence of the Athabasca and Miette rivers. In 1913, as it settled into its new role as headquarters for the national park, the town's name was changed to Jasper.

Fitzhugh is situated in Jasper Park Reserve, a large tract of country reserved by the Government for the nation. No game may be shot in it, and, as the Government have not yet surveyed the town-site, Fitzhugh is little more than a camp. The place consists of the depot, the round-house (for engines), and railway yards, a large restaurant and hotel, a hospital, a store kept by the doctor, and a few houses dotted about here and there in the bush.

The valley is not more than three-quarters of a mile broad, and on each side the hills rise steeply, the lower slopes covered with pines, which seem to find some root in the rocky crags. The mountains are not so much covered as heavily sprinkled with snow, and they take on every fantastic shape you can imagine. Fitzhugh is entirely surrounded by these immense castellated peaks. The country looked wild, unexplored, uninhabitable, and unkempt.

A curious assortment of men jumped from our train, and hurried up to Beecham's stopping-place to get accommodation for the night. Most of them were going on first thing next morning to the front. I stayed the night with most hospitable people called Hamilton. Mr. Hamilton is conductor on the train which runs every day from Fitzhugh to the end of steel and back, and I arranged to accompany him on his trip the following day.

After supper I went round to see the doctor, who keeps the only store in the place. He is the G.T.P. doctor, and has many curious cases to attend. The other night he was sent for to see a Galician labourer in a car some way down the track. The man did not seem very bad, and the doctor asked him if he had been eating anything which disagreed with him. The Galician shook his head, but a friend (?) lying close to him volunteered the information that he had eaten twenty-seven sausages for breakfast. I can quite believe this. I myself have seen a man eat eleven boiled eggs straight off, and follow them up with meat, vegetables and pudding.

The next morning I was down early to catch the train going west. To watch the crowd was an education in itself. If Canada can assimilate such a cosmopolitan collection as this, she will do well. Great fair-haired Swedes, sallow-faced Italians and Galicians, black swarthy-looking Russians, keen-featured Yankees and Canadians, and not a few strong-looking fellows "with the map of England written plain on their face." They wore all kinds of clothes and all kinds of headgear, and nearly every one carried a pack or a roll of blankets.

As the conductor backed his "mixed" train (*i.e.* passenger and freight combined) into the station, there was a general stampede for the two passenger coaches which were at the end, behind a long row of flat gravel cars. I found a seat at the far end, among a whole bunch of foreigners, who talked continuously and seemed excited about nothing. They behave very much like animals, and when they get a little drink in them they are far worse than animals. While we waited they began to eat, passing round huge hunks of bread out of which they each took a bite in turn, and then some awful pink concoction in a bowl into which they each stuck a dirty fork, or possibly their still dirtier fingers.

Not far from me was an English-speaking fellow, who was wearing an attractive costume, being completely dressed in a moose-hide suit, with beautifully embroidered facings. Some of the men were already drunk. One fellow in front of me fell down as he was climbing up into the car, but his friends bundled him in somehow, and he kept reeling up and down the train, making himself a great nuisance. The cars were of the rough colonist type, and showed signs of hard usage, which is not surprising when one saw the type of men who used them.

Not long after we started, the conductor made his way down the train and beckoned me to follow him. I was taken into the baggage car, where I made the acquaintance of the train crew, namely the two brakemen, the train agent, and the newsagent. The main passenger trains in this country are provided with a newsagent, a loquacious individual who continually walks from one end of the train to the other selling papers, tobacco, and candies. Here I made the whole trip, sitting on a packing-case before the big folding doors, which gave one a fine opportunity of seeing the country.

As the train was a mixed passenger and freight, we were constantly stopping at various places to take on or put off "flat-cars" full of gravel, or "dump-cars" full of "dirt" deposited there by the steam shovel, trucks loaded with rails or ties, "box-cars" full of provisions, coal or lumber — all the hundred and one things which were wanted up at the front by the camps.

Letters and packages were shovelled off in the most bewildering way at various points along the line. One of the brakemen would lean out as we passed some gang of men, and heave a big parcel into the middle of them.

On one occasion, having stopped alongside a dilapidated train, the moving home of a large gang of labourers, we were already starting again when the brakeman suddenly ejaculated, "Gee whiz, those two cases should have been put out here." "Quick, then," says the conductor; "dump 'em out right now." The two cases are seized, pushed through the wide doors, and fall with a crunching kind of thud on the grade below. Somebody puts his head out of the stationary train, and says in a very sarcastic voice, "With care, I guess, eh?" and sure enough, as the cases roll over, there, in big letters, are scrawled "With Care." But the train had taken us well out of hearing. . . .

We got back to Fitzhugh that night, and the next day or two I visited in and around Fitzhugh. On Sunday afternoon we had a service in Mr. Hamilton's house, at which quite a number were present, amongst others, the Methodist student who has been living in Fitzhugh for a time, and will shortly be returning to college.

I should have left next morning, had not the doctor asked me to stay and take the funeral of a Russian patient, who, he said, could not live many hours. The man had been sent down from Mile 28 with double pneumonia, and I had already seen him once or twice when visiting in the hospital. . . .

Nobody understood Russian, and he knew not a single word of any other language. I went over on Sunday and Monday to see him. He made signs for a pencil, but was really too weak to write. We could only discover that he came from Bessarabia, and the doctor was not certain that we even had his name right; so how can his parents be communicated with? He lay there hour after hour on the point of death. As he was evidently a member of the Greek Catholic Church, we cut him out a cross of blue paper, at which he gazed enraptured. During the afternoon we got a swarthy Russian, who had just come into Fitzhugh and could talk a little English, to come and see him. It was a curious scene — the little wooden room which served as a ward; the other beds occupied by this cosmopolitan crew wide-eyed in their curiosity; the sick man lying there gasping, his eyes so glassy and face so pallid that one would have thought him dead, had not one heard the quick uncertain breath; the doctor, myself, and a Galician boy standing round; and on his knees by the bedside, his lips quite near to the sick man's ear, the great black-bearded Russian. He did what he could, but it was of no avail. The man was too far gone to speak.

About 5 P.M. I returned to the hospital, and found the bed screened off with blankets, roughly rigged up with ropes. From the other side came dreadful sounds. I went in at once, and found Williams, the orderly, holding the poor man down by his arms, while another man was holding his legs. It was the most horrible death scene that I have ever witnessed. The man was absolutely yellow in colour, and was choking and fighting for breath. This fearful fight went on for nearly half an hour. The wooden hospital was very close, and behind the blankets it was almost unbearable. Two or three of the foreigners were peeping round to see the last. One would never believe that a man in his condition could have had the strength to fight for so long. Then suddenly, with a gurgle, he seemed to give it up, and sank back dead. I said the Commendatory Prayer, or as much of it as I could remember, as he passed away, and then we tied up his head and wrapped him in a blanket. The doctor had already ordered a rough wooden box from one of the men at the station, and, by the time he was washed and ready, they brought it

The town of Fitzhugh (later Jasper) as it appeared during the construction of the Grand Trunk Pacific Railway circa 1912. Archives of the Canadian Rockies

over to the hospital. He was put into it, nailed down, and put outside; there was nowhere else to put him.

Next day, after seeing the park ranger about the burial place, the doctor and I went down with four labourers on a hand-car to a place where there is a flat stretch of land near the Athabasca River. Here, where an Indian baby and a Finlander were already buried, we told the men to dig the grave for the Russian. A more beautiful place no one could desire for a last resting-place. Imagine a long stretch of short green grass, sloping down to the Athabasca, and all round young green pines; opposite, the hills rose steeply from the river, and away to the east shone the snow-covered peak of Mount Hardisty. Behind us, the forest-covered slopes ran right up to the rocky cliffs of Pyramid Mountain, and along the side of the hill went the great Transcontinental line, in the construction of which this man, like many another, had met his death.

The doctor and I went back and got a wagon, on which we placed the coffin. I jumped up with the driver, who had much difficulty in restraining his language, because his team of grey mules was obstreperous; but the gravity of the situation made him do his level best, and it really was humorous to see a sudden outburst hastily smothered with a furtive look at me. Williams rode with us, and sat on the coffin, the only place there was. Our curious funeral procession went bumping along over a vile trail, and when at last we reached the place we found the grave ready and the men sitting round smoking.

"Say, parson, we've dug it good and deep," said the foreman; "he won't be popping up again next spring as some of 'em do!"

We lowered the coffin into the grave at once, and then I put on cassock, surplice, and hood, and read the Burial Service. The men stood round with bare heads, and one of them threw earth on the coffin at the right moment. After the service was over, they did not take long to shovel back the sandy soil. Another fellow and I cut down some small spruce trees, put posts and rails round the grave, and made a cross. We wrote the date on the cross, but not his name, as we did not know it for certain. So there we left him, and another is added to the number of those who never return. It is a tragedy which is enacted over and over again out here. Pioneer work demands its toll; and nowhere a heavier one than in railway construction.

Tay John
Howard O'Hagan

All his years in the west, Jack Denham had lived in the midst of events. Yet they had somehow passed him by. He had not given them their shape, and they left him apparently only the man he had always been. He had gone into the Yellowhead country with a survey party scouting a route for the new railway, to swing an axe or handle the rod before the transit of the engineer. To the mountains he had returned to see the rails put down. Up there, he said, at one time only the width of a mountain stream kept him from the adventure of his life.

He would talk about it anywhere — in a pause during dinner at the hotel. He would allude to it suddenly at the bar among strangers over the second glass of whisky. Two tall pale glasses of whisky were his limit. One drink of whisky was good for you, two were too many, three were not enough. "I always take too many," he explained with a laugh and a wide gesture.

He might meet a friend at the street corner and follow him to his destination, talking, stretching his story the length of Edmonton. It became known as "Jackie's Tale." It was a faith — a gospel to be spread, that tale, and he was its only apostle. Men winked over it, smiled at it, yet listened to its measured voice, attentions caught, imaginations cradled in a web of words.

"I almost had an adventure there," Jack Denham would burst forth, referring to the mountain stream, drawing his chin down against his shoulder, jutting out his lower lip and running his fingers over his soft, fur-like beard.

Do you see what I mean? (the tale continued.) An adventure. A real one. Blood in it. It was a close call. I would have been in on it too, but there was the creek in the way . . . and a man besides.

It would have taken courage to cross that creek. I don't think it was possible to cross. I don't know now. Hard to tell. At the time, anyway, it was impossible. It wasn't wide. Twice as wide as a man, standing, might jump perhaps, but deep and swift. Boiling. There were rapids. That creek — it was white. It was jagged. It had teeth in it. I felt it would have cut me in two. I would have hesitated even with a horse . . . and I was afoot.

And what I saw was worth more than what I would have done. What would I have done had I been on the other side of the creek? That's what I don't know. That's what no man would know, unless he knew what he had always done and could see himself as clearly as I saw that other man across the water from me. But he knew. At least he had no doubts — this other man. No doubts about himself. And there was no doubt about what he saw before him, or, for that matter, about that river at his back. He could no more have forded the river than I, and he had no time. It was a matter of moments, I tell you; split seconds. It was the stuff of a nightmare come alive in broad daylight and throwing its shadow on the ground before you.

Do you see? No matter — for him, for this other man I mean, it must have seemed like a nightmare. Yet I doubt if he, a man of his type, would ever have had a nightmare in his life. No, his sleep would be sleep — just sleep — like a deep shadow between each of his days. Nothing more than that. No place of visions. No birth of creatures to stay with him when he woke and stand between him and the sun. With me it was different. I was an onlooker. I saw what he didn't see. I saw him, for instance. Still, he was aware, it appears to me now, long before I, that something waited for him, although his back was towards it.

You see, I had gone up that valley alone, on foot. It was Sunday, and I left the three of them in camp: Burstall, the boss; Hank, the horse wrangler — we had twelve head of horses with us — and Sam, the cook. We were well up into the mountains, and were on one of the rivers, the Snake Indian. It flows into the Athabaska. There were any number of passes there, and any number of unnamed streams. It is a good game country, too, and on the alplands I could see caribou and flocks of mountain sheep. I had my glasses with me, so that I could have a good look at the high country, also a revolver — only a twenty-two — on the chance of knocking over a few grouse. It was a busman's holiday for me, a walk. It was nothing unusual for us to walk twenty miles in a working day — but here was this valley, with no name, a clear flow of water, clear and cold as spring water, coming from it through a lane of spruce-trees by our camp, and I wanted to see where it led to. A new mountain valley leads a man on like that — like a woman he has never touched.

His experience tells him it will be much like others he knows — a canyon to go through, a meadowland or two, some forest, and its head up against a mountain wall or trickling from a grimy glacier. Yet still he goes up it hoping vaguely for some revelation, something he had never seen or felt before, and he rounds a point or pushes his head over a pass, feeling that a second before, that had he come a second earlier, he would have surprised the Creator at his work — for a country where no man has stepped before is new in the real sense of the word, as though it had just been made, and when you turn your back upon it you feel that it may drop back again into the dusk that gave it being. It is only your vision that holds it in the known and created world. It is physically exhausting to look on unnamed country. A name is the magic to keep it within the horizons. Put a name to it, put it on a map, and you've got it. The unnamed — it is the darkness unveiled. Up in those high places you even think you can *hear* the world being made. Anyway you can hear the silence, which is the sound of the earth's turning, or time going by.

At any rate I had gone up this river, or creek, or whatever you want to call it, and its valley had surprised me. It was tight and narrow all the way. A canyon at first where I had some pretty rock climbing to do. After that a long belt of forest. Near the end of this forest belt I found a dead tree that spanned the stream and crossed to the other side where the going appeared better. There was no sign of man up there at all — no old stumps, no blazes — nothing. Beside the caribou and sheep far above the timber I saw not a living thing —

not a squirrel, nor a mouse, nor a humming fly. I came almost to the headwaters where a great glacier moved down, when I turned around to reach camp before dark. It got on my nerves a bit, I guess, that river, being penned up with it all day long and having its roar in my head. It filled my head, my thoughts. It was enough to make me stagger. I crossed the river again on the dead tree, and about two miles below that tree and about the same distance above the canyon through which the river broke out into the main valley where we had our camp, I stopped to have a smoke and to look up a side valley coming down from the north. A stream came in from the north across from me and spread in shallows over a gravel flat. Tall green grass grew there on a sort of island, and behind was the forest leading up a narrow valley between two towering mountains. Somewhere up there I remember was a waterfall. I could see it, but though it was quite close, a long white line against the rock, the sound of its fall was drowned by the river before me. As I say, it wasn't wide, that river I was following. Twice as wide as a man might jump, perhaps, but it was swift, and I could hear the boulders rolling in the surge of its waters.

Then across from me, as though he had grown there while my eyes blinked, I saw a man. He was stripped to the waist, wearing only moccasins and a pair of moose-hide leggings. Behind him some little distance I saw his rifle stacked against a tree and beside it his pack with a shirt of caribou hide, the hair still upon it, tossed upon the ground. He had come down the creek opposite me. What he was doing there when I saw him, standing out on that flat among the grasses, I don't know. About to make his camp for the night perhaps.

Anyway, he saw me. He doubtless saw me before I saw him. He would have, that sort of fellow. He looked at me, yet gave no sign of recognition. He was tall, dark of skin as an Indian, yet his hair was full and thick and yellow, and fell low to his shoulders. His eyes were black, and I was so close to him that I could see their whites, and his nostrils flex ever so slightly and his white teeth showed when he breathed. From behind me the shadows of the trees were reaching across the water, but he stood full in the sun. His brown skin glowed, and his muscles were a pattern of shadows across his chest and belly. He had a build, that fellow. Still, there was something, it is hard to say, something of the abstract about him — as though he were a symbol of some sort or other. He seemed to stand for something. He stood there with his feet planted apart upon the ground, as though he owned it, as though he grasped it with them. When he moved I would not have been surprised to have seen clumps of earth adhere to the soles of his moccasins and the long shadows of his muscles across his body — they weren't strength in the usual sense of being able to lift weights and that kind of thing. They represented strength in the abstract. Endurance, solitude — qualities that men search for. It was in his face, too, long and keen as though shaped by the wind, and beardless as a boy's — those fellows — I could see he was of mixed blood — are often lightly bearded. I felt I was an intruder, and could I have spoken to him I believe I would have tried to excuse my presence there, along the lonely river.

But I couldn't speak to him. There was too much noise with that confounded water. I shouted. "Hallo!" I shouted; "Hallo!" I waved my arms and shouted again. It seemed absurd. I was so close to him that he should have been able to hear a whisper. He stood there across from me, too, with his head tilted a bit as though he were listening. Yet even then it seemed he wasn't listening to me at all, but to something else I couldn't hear. Had he been able to hear me, for all I knew then, he wouldn't have understood what I said. But, still, he wasn't all Indian. There was that yellow hair. It was long and heavy. A girl would have been proud of it, and he had it held with some sort of band around his forehead. A black band, like a strip of hide cut from some small fur-bearing animal. A piece of marten, say.

Yes, his hair shone. It seemed to shed a light about him. Then he looked directly at me. I was still gesturing, throwing my arms about, trying to draw attention to myself. In short, making a very vulgar display. He looked as though he thought so, anyway. My arms dropped to my side. I tell you, I was ashamed. I have no doubt he would have spoken to me had we met in the usual way. But here was this rushing torrent between us. We couldn't cross it. Our voices couldn't be heard above it. He accepted that for the impossibility it was, while I was making frantic efforts at evasion. When he looked at me I could see the reflected light of the sun burning deep down in his dark eyes. Then he turned slowly, as if in disgust at what he saw, and took a step back towards his rifle.

And in that moment, while his foot was lifted for his second step, and his back towards me, it happened. Suddenly it seeemed to me like a play being put on for my benefit, with the forest and mountains for backdrop, the gravel bar where this Yellowhead was for stage, and the deep river with its unceasing crescendo for the orchestra pit.

A bear was there above him, between him and his rifle. It may have been there for some time. Anyway it was there now, no question about it. A grizzly bear at that, a silver tip, with a great roll of muscle over its shoulders and the hair slowly rising in fear along the length of its backbone. For the bear was frightened, make no mistake about that. Later when it stood up I saw it was a she-bear. She probably had a cub cached somewhere close by. As a rule, of course, a bear won't attack a man — but this was a she-grizzly, and she was trapped. There was the pack behind her, you see, with its human smell. There was the man before her. Her cub was somewhere near by. If she hadn't been frightened or angered — and the cause and often the result of the one is much the same as the other — she would have turned around and left a situation she was unprepared to meet. But, no, she stood her ground.

And my Yellowhead across from me stood his. He slowly, ever so slowly, put his foot back upon the ground and waited. He stood, a bronze and golden statue planted among the grasses that rose up to his knees. This was the sort of thing I had sometimes dreamed of — of meeting a bear one day close up, hand to hand so to speak, and doing it in. An epic battle: man against the wilderness. And now I saw the battle taking form, but another man was in my place and with the river between us I could give no help. None at all. My revolver? I might have hit the man, but against the bear it was worth no more than shooting peas. I waited.

Something was going to happen. The grizzly opened her mouth. I saw her sharp white teeth. She flicked the grass with her long-nailed fore-paw. That paw seemed suddenly to sprout out from her body, then to be drawn back. She advanced a step. I saw the right hand of this Yellowhead fellow move gently to his waist and come out with the handle of a gleaming knife in its fist. The muscle along his shoulders rippled. His rifle was beyond his reach, past the bear. He glanced not once at the river nor at me behind him. His eyes I knew were on the bear. She swung her head low, from side to side, as though she cautioned him to be careful. Her mouth opened and she roared. I could hear that across the river. It came to me faintly, like a cough.

Then Yellowhead moved quickly. His left hand swiped the band off his head and threw it towards the grizzly, not directly at her, but just above her head. She reared up, and then I saw the hang of her laden teats. She stood so that she towered above Yellowhead. That's what I called him now. I found myself saying "Yellowhead," "Yellowhead." I had to give him a name so that I could help him —

morally, you know. I had to align him with the human race. Without a name no man is an individual, no individual wholly a man.

There she was above him, immense and unassailable as a mountain side. She clawed the air after this black thing that flew towards her. And when she swung he sprang beneath her arm. I saw his left hand grab the long fur around her neck, and I saw his right swing twice with the long-bladed knife, and the knife stayed there the second time, a flash of light embedded in her side, searching for the great, slow beat of her heart. It was a matter of moments. Then they were on the ground rolling over and over. I caught glimpses now and then of that yellow mass of hair, like a bundle the she-grizzly held with affection to her breast. It was his only chance. If he had stepped back from her those claws would have ripped his belly open, torn his head from off his shoulders. He did the one thing, the only thing he could have done, and did it well.

They rolled to the very edge of the stream on whose other bank I stood. They were quiet there. Yellowhead was beneath. "If he's not dead," I said, "he's drowned." The great mass of fur was quiescent before me, and from its side a stream of dark blood flowed into the hungry river.

Then the mass quivered. It heaved. A man's head appeared beside it, bloody, muddied, as though he were just being born, as though he were climbing out of the ground. Certainly man had been created anew before my eyes. Like birth itself it was a struggle against the powers of darkness, and Man had won. Like birth, too, it was a cry and a protest — his lips parted as though a cry, unheard by me, came from them. Death, now that is silence — an acceptance — but across this creek from me was life again. Man had won against the wilderness, the unknown, the strength that is not so much beyond our strength as it is capable of a fury and single passion beyond our understanding. He had won. *We* had won. That was how I felt. I shouted. I did a dance. Then I calmed down. I wanted more than anything I knew to go across and touch this man, this Yellowhead, to tell him, "Well done!" But I couldn't cross that river. I might have gone back to the foot log, but that would have taken more than an hour, and it would seem that I was leaving him in his moment of victory — when no man wishes to be alone. A victory is no victory until it has been shared. Defeat? Well, that is another matter.

But Yellowhead was damaged. Somehow the grizzly had clawed his face. One side of it streamed blood. It looked raw like meat. For a time he sat there on the ground, among the grasses, and the blood ran off his shoulder, down his arm, down between his very fingers. He didn't look at me. Seemed to have forgotten all about me. He stared with wonder, I think, at the body of the bear lying half in the river. He spat some of her fur out, caught between his teeth. Then he washed his face, found the band for his hair and bound it back. After that he took his knife, still caught between the she-grizzly's ribs, cut her head off, neatly severing the vertebrae at its base, climbed with it up a tree and left it there, caught in a crotch so that it gazed upon the scene of its dismay.

He came down to the side of the river, bathed his face again. It still bled. I shouted, but he didn't hear me, or didn't care to. He disdained me, that fellow, absolutely.

It was growing dusk now. He went back to the edge of the forest where his pack and rifle rested. He staggered once and leaned against a tree. Then he pulled on his caribou-hide shirt, hoisted his pack and shouldered it. He picked up his rifle and stepped, without one backward glance, behind the trees. He vanished, as though he were leaving one form of existence for another. For a moment or two I saw his yellow head, a gleam of light being carried away through the timber. He had come down from the high country to do his job, and having done it, left. Entering the forest his pack brushed against a branch of spruce. The branch moved there before my eyes, swayed gently, touched by an invisible hand after he had gone. It moved. The river flowed. The headless trunk of the she-grizzly swung out a bit from the bank, rolled over in the force of the current, as if in her deep sleep she dreamed. Night's shadow was on the valley. Trees creaked in a new wind blowing. An owl hooted somewhere close to me.

It was late when I got back to camp. It was dark, black as the inside of a bear. Night was about me like a covering from which I tried to escape. My hands wandered far from me feeling my way. My fingers touched branches, the harsh bark of trees. I pulled them back to me, held them against my sides. They were some company for me in the darkness.

Days passed before I told them in the camp of what I had seen on the banks of the river that streamed clear and fresh and nameless before our tents. It took me a time to find the words.

If there had been a glass of whisky — whisky, another victory of man against the powers of darkness, whatever they may be.

The Rockies
Rupert Brooke

I was advised by various people to "stop off" at Banff and at Lake Louise, in the Rockies. I did so. They are supposed to be equally the beauty spots of the mountains. How perplexing it is that advisers are always so kindly and willing to help, and always so undiscriminating. It is equally disastrous to be a sceptic and to be credulous. Banff is an ordinary little tourist resort in mountainous country, with hills and a stream and snow-peaks beyond. Beautiful enough, and invigorating. But Lake Louise — Lake Louise is of another world. Imagine a little round lake 6000 feet up, a mile across, closed in by great cliffs of brown rock, round the shoulders of which are thrown mantles of close dark pine. At one end the lake is fed by a vast glacier, and its milky tumbling stream; and the glacier climbs to snowfields of one of the highest and loveliest peaks in the Rockies, which keeps perpetual guard over the scene. To this place you go up three or four miles from the railway. There is the hotel at one end of the lake, facing the glacier; else no sign of humanity. From the windows you may watch the water and the peaks all day, and never see the same view twice. In the lake, ever-changing, is Beauty herself, as nearly visible to mortal eyes as she may ever be. The water, beyond the flowers, is green, always a different green. Sometimes it is tranquil, glassy, shot with blue, of a peacock tint. Then a little wind awakes in the distance, and ruffles the surface, yard by yard, covering it with a myriad tiny wrinkles, till half the lake is milky emerald, while the rest still sleeps. And, at length, the whole is astir, and the sun catches it, and Lake Louise is a web of laughter, the opal distillation of all the buds of all the spring. On either side go up the dark processional pines, mounting to the sacred peaks, devout, kneeling, motionless, in an ecstasy of homely adoration, like the donors and their families in a Flemish picture. Among these you may wander for hours by little rambling paths, over white and red and golden flowers, and, continually, you spy little lakes, hidden away, each a shy, soft jewel of a new strange tint of green or blue, mutable and lovely. . . . And beyond all is the glacier and the vast fields and peaks of eternal snow.

If you watch the great white cliff, from the foot of which the glacier flows — seven miles away, but it seems two — you will sometimes see a little puff of silvery smoke go up, thin, and vanish. A few seconds later comes the roar of terrific, distant thunder. The mountains tower and smile unregarding in the sun. It was an avalanche. And if you climb any of the ridges or peaks around, there are discovered other valleys and heights and ranges, wild and desert, stretching endlessly away. As day draws to an end the shadows on the snow turn bluer, the crying of innumerable waters hushes, and the immense, bare ramparts of westward-facing rock that guard the great valley win a rich, golden-brown radiance. Long after the sun has set they seem to give forth the splendour of the day, and the tranquility of their centuries, in undiminished fulness. They have that other-worldly serenity which a perfect old age possesses. And as with a perfect old age, so here, the colour and the light ebb so gradually out of things that you could swear nothing of the radiance and glory gone up to the very moment before the dark.

It was on such a height, and at some such hour as this, that I sat and considered the nature of the country in this continent. There was perceptible, even here, though less urgent than elsewhere, the strangeness I had noticed in woods by the St. Lawrence, and on the banks of the Delaware (where are red-haired girls who sing at dawn), and in British Columbia, and afterwards among the brown hills and colossal trees of California, but especially by that lonely golden beach in Manitoba, where the high-stepping little brown deer run down to drink, and the wild geese through the evening go flying and crying. It is an empty land. To love the country here — mountains are worshipped, not loved — is like embracing a wraith. A European can find nothing to satisfy the hunger of his heart. The air is too thin to breathe. He requires haunted woods, and the friendly presence of ghosts. The immaterial soil of England is heavy and fertile with the decaying stuff of past seasons and generations. Here is the floor of a new wood, yet uncumbered by one year's autumn fall. We Europeans find the Orient stale and get too luxuriantly fetid by reason of the multitude of bygone lives and thoughts, oppressive with the crowded presence of the dead, both men and gods. So, I imagine, a Canadian would feel our woods and fields heavy with the past and the invisible, and suffer claustrophobia in an English countryside beneath the dreadful pressure of immortals. For his own forests and wild places are windswept and empty. That is their charm, and their terror. You may lie awake all night and never feel the passing of evil presences, nor hear printless feet; . . .

Here one is perpetually a first-comer. The land is virginal, the wind cleaner than elsewhere, and every lake new-born, and each day is the first day. The flowers are less conscious than English flowers, the breezes have nothing to remember, and everything to promise. There walk, as yet, no ghosts of lovers in Canadian lanes. This is the essence of the grey freshness and brisk melancholy of this land. And for all the charm of those qualities, it is also the secret of a European's discontent. For it is possible, at a pinch, to do without gods. But one misses the dead.

Legends from a New Era

The Rockies Post-1918

We were not pioneers ourselves, but we
journeyed over old trails that were new to us,
and with hearts open. Who shall distinguish?
J. Monroe Thorington,
The Glittering Mountains of Canada

A Wonderful Delusion
Morley Roberts

As a young man working his way across North America in 1884, Morley Roberts was employed on a construction crew building the Canadian Pacific Railway down the rugged Kicking Horse Valley. In the mid-1920s he returned to the Canadian Rockies as a tourist and found the scene quite changed.

The truth is that I could not take beautiful Banff seriously. I dreamed it, and like so many dreams it was at once absurd and wonderful. On a pine-covered bank or bluff above the crystal foam of the Bow I came to a gigantic castle. It had no business to be there, for when I was thereabouts so long ago no one could have thought of it. It was full of most curious-looking people who seemed very busy about nothing at all but were as happy as grigs, whatever a grig may be. They wore all kinds of odd costumes. Some women, so greatly determined on being noticed as to defy ridicule, flaunted about in long shining boots and scarlet jackets and jockey caps, while others wore clothes "made in America" in the backwoods, which looked as if they had been cut out with an axe. This dream-castle hall was full of such people who all talked at once and I saw in a moment that they were not real. I, or someone else, had imagined them. If any of us workers of the old days had seen their like we should have thought we had delirium tremens at the least. As a matter of fact I dream a great deal, but, having at times a power of knowing it is a dream, sometimes say to myself, "very soon this will be a nightmare", especially if I seem to be in a badly lighted room with several sinister-looking men in it and others peeping in through half-open doors. This dream I present with my compliments to Dr. Freud. In my Banff dream there was nothing ominous. But assuredly I was utterly out of place, as he might be who had come into a drawing-room with a pick and shovel and railroad mud all over him. And then someone drew my attention to a man on the other side of the room. This was a real man, a live one, not a dream ghost in colour from Chicago, or a dream dowd from Dullopolis. He was so real that he had a name. Go to Banff and ask for Bill Potts and see if I do not speak the truth. He obviously belonged to the west and could almost to a dead certainty tell a cayuse from a cow, not always an easy piece of discrimination. And I am pretty sure that he looked across the hall and saw that I had been in the neighbourhood over forty years ago and also knew a cayuse from a cow. For men of the west know each other by a look in the eye which when once acquired is never quite lost. So when Bill Potts and I shook hands I said, after a look at him and a look round the hall, "I don't believe it". And people may believe it or not when I say that he replied at once, "No more do I". So we talked, and said there was no such place as Banff, but that it was all very wonderful and incredible and utterly out of place if it did exist. And the ghosts went on buzzing in this happy hall of Eblis. Naturally enough the railroad says there is such a place, but when an old pick-and-shovel man like myself, and Bill Potts, who must be a kind of relative of mine as he was born at Morley, a small but respectable and conservative cow-town some miles to the east, went on saying "there ain't no such place", there must be something in it.

Absurd as it may appear I found a real difficulty in ridding myself of the feeling that I had dreamed everything I saw at Banff but the mountains and the river. Still I haven't the least doubt that it all seemed natural enough to the crowd of ghosts who possibly had come up from the valley of the Ghost River which flows into the Bow lower down. But no one must run away with the belief that I have invented Mr. Potts. No one could walk through him. During our talk I assured him that I recognized him at once, though as a matter of fact he was not born when I first passed the unnamed Banff, and he owned that he recognized me as having been in the west long before he was thought of. And we shook hands again over the statement that Banff was a mere delusion, though wonderful.

The Birth of an Iceberg
Cora Johnstone Best

When Banff photographer Byron Harmon and mountain guide Conrad Kain travelled to the Lake of the Hanging Glacier in 1922, they plotted their own cinematic extravaganza.

There hadn't been much said about it but those thirty-six sticks of dynamite had been carried all the way from Windermere on one of the horses (not Old Bill) to assist Nature in the final act of bringing forth a natural phenomenon. The act was to be called "The Birth of an Iceberg," in case it was an iceberg. Of course, the title could be changed in case it happened to be a monstrosity. It seems that when Freeman's party went up to the lake they had the same idea. Whether Harmon had purloined the act, after the Freeman failure, or whether

An early attempt by Banff photographer Byron Harmon to film The Birth of an Iceberg *at the Lake of the Hanging Glaciers*. Archives of the Canadian Rockies

the idea was common property I don't know, but I heard Harmon and Conrad discussing the possibilities. "Now" said Harmon, "you remember that when they touched off the dynamite, it made a lot of noise but that was all there was to it; there wasn't a chunk of ice big enough to photograph. And you remember that whale of an avalanche that came down from the jar of the explosion? It came right off that peak there and I'm going to focus on that same peak and I'm sure to get what they missed." Harmon wagged his head and we all stood around with satisfied smiles on our faces.

The next morning broke just right. We were up early and in feverish haste to be off to the scene of action. Tom was sent for a horse and after a long while he came back with Old Bill, as he was the only one to be caught. The tripod, and camera boxes were loaded and we started for the lake. The exact spot for Harmon's moving picture camera had been picked out for days, also the exact spots for Mrs. Shippam's moving picture, and for each of their two still cameras. The whole scene had been gone over carefully so there would be nothing left undone that ought to be done.

Conrad went over and dug a hole in the ice and placed his dynamite, tamped it down and lighted the fuse. When he came back he remarked that something should come loose as there were seventeen sticks about to let go. Harmon took a last anxious look into the finder, — yes, the exact peak, and it was rounded high with new snow. He mopped his face and looked along the line to see if everything was ready. It was. This would be a grand success, undoubtedly. The earth shook; the air turned purple; Mother Earth agonized, and a few pounds of ice tinkled off into the water as the smoke drifted away. But, of course, that was understood. We were waiting for the aftermath, the mighty avalanche we were sure to get.

Now, when Old Bill had been unloaded he had strolled off to browse on some tufts of green and no one had given him a second thought. When the first report of the discharge took place, Old Bill started a little charge of his own. What mattered it to him if the cameras were in his line of advance? He came down the stretch hitting on all four, his mane flying, his nostrils dilated and flaming, his eyes holding the fire of battle. He hit Harmon first! Down went the camera and Old Bill walked up the spine of the vanquished photographer, hit the second, third and fourth cameras with sickening precision and careered off down the valley. And then it happened! The whole top of the mountain eased off a bit, toppled and crashed to the glacier below in the mightiest of the mighty avalanches.

Hollywood at Lake Louise
Walter D. Wilcox

In 1927 or thereabouts Ernst Lubitsch came to the lake from Hollywood with a large company of moving picture people to portray a play called "The King of the Mountains." Besides the mechanical force including recorders, stage setters, porters, and experts on photography, there were a number of actors including John Barrymore, Varconi and a lovely Alsatian blonde. The company remained six weeks at the lake and no expense was too much to preserve harmony, and make everyone happy, and the show a success. Guides and experts were sent out on the remote passes and hillsides in the neighboring valleys to study and approve scenes suitable to the forthcoming play. Moving picture shows, dinners and champagne suppers made the evenings glide by all too fast.

At the highest point to which horses could go, everything was unpacked and an hour or more was spent arranging loads for the porters and Swiss guides. Owing to the cumbersome cameras and heavy batteries some of the men had to struggle with loads up to 75 lbs. or more. Barrymore complained loudly, but the Alsatian in her high-heeled shoes climbed heroically over the rounded cobbles and rough stones. It was a wonder that the entire company reached the upper glacier without accident but they did.

Arrived on the pure white snow of the glacier, nearly two hours were spent arranging sets and practising preliminary scenes. The most important of all was where the villain, represented by John Barrymore, seizes the faithless wife, represented by the blonde, and dashes up the mountain side trying to escape from the angry mob. For this scene a snow slope more or less free of crevasses was selected, and all cameras pointed toward it, when a signal was given and Barrymore started on his 100 yd., up-hill dash. Now the snow was rather soft, the grade pretty steep and the altitude about 9000 feet. Barrymore was in no sense a mountain climber, but to all appearance the scene went off most successfully, except that the protagonist returned in a state of near collapse. But Lubitsch's brow was clouded. Something had gone wrong, yet he dared not tell Barrymore. Waiting a discreet interval he went over to Mr. Barrymore and said in a quiet voice, "Well, Mr. Barrymore, I am sorry to say that we have to do that last scene once more, again," to which the great actor replied that such an idea was the last in the world that he had in mind, though it was more tersely and shockingly expressed. Lubitsch, almost weeping, said that he was spending $10,000 a day on this enterprise, also that this was the principal scene of the play, and without it he would be ruined. In a word, Barrymore finally relented and did the scene over again.

Then followed a collation such as the snow-clad Rockies had never seen before and probably never will again. The pretty Alsatian put on a frock that would have graced a ball-room. Tarpaulins were spread out on the snow, cocktails were passed around, accompanied by sandwiches, chicken-à-la-King (which Lubitsch thought appropriate to the play) and ice cold champagne. Under a blue sky and bright sun, the helmet-shaped Mt. Lefroy and the inspiring slopes of Mt. Victoria on which avalanches were now thundering made a wonderful background for a group of people that was almost unique.

John Barrymore and Camilla Horn on Saddleback above Lake Louise during the filming of King of the Mountains *(later released as* Eternal Love) *in 1927. Archives of the Canadian Rockies*

The Grizzly
James Oliver Curwood

Of all the living creatures in this sleeping valley, Thor was the bus-
iest. He was a bear with individuality, you might say. Like some
people, he went to bed very early; he began to get sleepy in October,
and turned in for his long nap in November. He slept until April,
and usually was a week or ten days behind other bears in waking.
He was a sound sleeper, and when awake he was very wide awake.
During April and May he permitted himself to doze considerably in
the warmth of sunny rocks, but from the beginning of June until the
middle of September he closed his eyes in real sleep just about four
hours out of every twelve.

He was very busy as Langdon began his cautious climb up the
gully. He had succeeded in getting his gopher, a fat, aldermanic old
patriarch who had disappeared in one crunch and a gulp, and he
was now absorbed in finishing off his day's feast with an occasional
fat, white grub and a few sour ants captured from under stones which
he turned over with his paw.

In his search after these delicacies Thor used his right paw in
turning over the rocks. Ninety-nine out of every hundred bears —
probably a hundred and ninety-nine out of every two hundred —
are left-handed; Thor was right-handed. This gave him an advantage
in fighting, in fishing, and in stalking meat, for a grizzly's right arm
is longer than his left — so much longer that if he lost his sixth
sense of orientation he would be constantly travelling in a circle.

In his quest Thor was headed for a gully. His huge head hung
close to the ground. At short distances his vision was microscopic in
its keenness; his olfactory nerves were so sensitive that he could catch
one of the big rock-ants with his eyes shut.

He would choose the flat rocks mostly. His huge right paw, with
its long claws, was as clever as a human hand. The stone lifted, a
sniff or two, a lick of his hot, flat tongue, and he ambled on to the
next.

He took this work with tremendous seriousness, much like an
elephant hunting for peanuts hidden in a bale of hay. He saw no
humour in the operation. As a matter of fact, Nature had not
intended there should be any humour about it. Thor's time was more
or less valueless, and during the course of a summer he absorbed in
his system a good many hundred thousand sour ants, sweet grubs,

214

and juicy insects of various kinds, not to mention a host of gophers and still tinier rock-rabbits. These small things all added to the huge rolls of fat which it was necessary for him to store up for that "absorptive consumption" which kept him alive during his long winter sleep. This was why Nature had made his little greenish-brown eyes twin microscopes, infallible at distances of a few feet, and almost worthless at a thousand yards.

As he was about to turn over a fresh stone Thor paused in his operations. For a full minute he stood nearly motionless. Then his head swung slowly, his nose close to the ground. Very faintly he had caught an exceedingly pleasing odour. It was so faint that he was afraid of losing it if he moved. So he stood until he was sure of himself, then he swung his huge shoulders around and descended two yards down the slope, swinging his head slowly from right to left, and sniffing. The scent grew stronger. Another two yards down the slope he found it very strong under a rock. It was a big rock, and weighed probably two hundred pounds. Thor dragged it aside with his one right hand as if it were no more than a pebble.

Instantly there was a wild and protesting chatter and a tiny striped rock-rabbit, very much like a chipmunk, darted away just as Thor's left hand came down with a smash that would have broken the neck of a caribou.

It was not the scent of the rock-rabbit, but the savour of what the rock-rabbit had stored under the stone that had attracted Thor. And this booty still remained — a half-pint of ground-nuts piled carefully in a little hollow lined with moss. They were not really nuts. They were more like diminutive potatoes, about the size of cherries, and very much like potatoes in appearance. They were starchy and sweet, and fattening. Thor enjoyed them immensely, rumbling in that curious satisfied way deep down in his chest as he feasted. And then he resumed his quest.

He did not hear Langdon as the hunter came nearer and nearer up the broken gully. He did not smell him, for the wind was fatally wrong. He had forgotten the noxious man-smell that had disturbed and irritated him an hour before. He was quite happy; he was good-humoured; he was fat and sleek. An irritable, cross-grained, and quarrelsome bear is always thin. The true hunter knows him as soon as he sets eyes on him. He is like the rogue elephant.

Thor continued his food-seeking, edging still closer to the gully. He was within a hundred and fifty yards of it when a sound suddenly brought him alert. Langdon, in his effort to creep up the steep side

215

of the gully for a shot, had accidentally loosened a rock. It went crashing down the ravine, starting other stones that followed in a noisy clatter. At the foot of the coulee, six hundred yards down, Bruce swore softly under his breath. He saw Thor sit up. At that distance he was going to shoot if the bear made for the break.

For thirty seconds Thor sat on his haunches. Then he started for the ravine, ambling slowly and deliberately. Langdon, panting and inwardly cursing at his ill luck, struggled to make the last ten feet to the edge of the slope. He heard Bruce yell, but he could not make out the warning. Hands and feet he dug fiercely into shale and rock as he fought to make those last three or four yards as quickly as possible.

He was almost to the top when he paused for a moment and turned his eyes upward. His heart went into his throat, and he started. For ten seconds he could not move. Directly over him was a monster head and a huge hulk of shoulder. Thor was looking down on him, his jaws agape, his finger-long fangs snarling, his eyes burning with a greenish-red fire.

In that moment Thor saw his first of man. His great lungs were filled with the hot smell of him, and suddenly he turned away from that smell as if from a plague. With his rifle half under him Langdon had had no opportunity to shoot. Wildly he clambered up the remaining few feet. The shale and stones slipped and slid under him. It was a matter of sixty seconds before he pulled himself over the top.

Thor was a hundred yards away, speeding in a rolling, ball-like motion toward the break. From the foot of the coulee came the sharp crack of Otto's rifle. Langdon squatted quickly, raising his left knee for a rest, and at a hundred and fifty yards began firing.

Sometimes it happens that an hour — a minute — changes the destiny of man; and the ten seconds which followed swiftly after that first shot from the foot of the coulee changed Thor. He had got his fill of the man-smell. He had seen man. And now he *felt* him.

It was as if one of the lightning flashes he had often seen splitting the dark skies had descended upon him and had entered his flesh like a red-hot knife; and with that first burning agony of pain came the strange, echoing roar of the rifles. He had turned up the slope when the bullet struck him in the fore-shoulder, mushrooming its deadly soft point against his tough hide, and tearing a hole through his flesh — but without touching the bone. He was two hundred yards from the ravine when it hit; he was nearer three hundred when the stinging fire seared him again, this time in his flank.

Neither shot had staggered his huge bulk, twenty such shots would not have killed him. But the second stopped him, and he turned with a roar of rage that was like the bellowing of a mad bull — a snarling, thunderous cry of wrath that could have been heard a quarter of a mile down the valley.

Bruce heard it as he fired his sixth unavailing shot at seven hundred yards. Langdon was reloading. For fifteen seconds Thor offered himself openly, roaring his defiance, challenging the enemy he could no longer see; and then at Langdon's seventh shot, a whip-lash of fire raked his back, and in strange dread of this lightning which he could not fight, Thor continued up over the break. He heard other rifle shots, which were like a new kind of thunder. But he was not hit again. Painfully he began the descent into the next valley.

Thor knew that he was hurt, but he could not comprehend that hurt. Once in the descent he paused for a few moments, and a little pool of blood dripped upon the ground under his foreleg. He sniffed at it suspiciously and wonderingly.

He swung eastward, and a little later he caught a fresh taint of the man-smell in the air. The wind was bringing it to him now, and in spite of the fact that he wanted to lie down and nurse his wound he ambled on a little faster, for he had learned one thing that he would never forget: the man-smell and his hurt had come together.

He reached the bottoms, and buried himself in the thick timber; and then, crossing this timber, he came to a creek. Perhaps a hundred times he had travelled up and down this creek. It was the main trail that led from one half of his range to the other.

Instinctively he always took this trail when he was hurt or when he was sick, and also when he was ready to den up for the winter. There was one chief reason for this: he was born in the almost impen-etrable fastnesses at the head of the creek, and his cubhood had been spent amid its brambles of wild currants and soap berries and its rich red ground carpets of kinnikinic. It was home. In it he was alone. It was the one part of his domain that he held inviolate from all other bears. He tolerated other bears — blacks and grizzlies — on the wider and sunnier slopes of his range just so long as they moved on when he approached. They might seek food there, and nap in the sun-pools, and live in quiet and peace if they did not defy his suze-rainty.

Thor did not drive other bears from his range, except when it was necessary to demonstrate again that he was High Mogul. This hap-pened occasionally, and there was a fight. And always after a fight

Thor came into this valley and went up the creek to cure his wounds.

He made his way more slowly than usual to-day. There was a terrible pain in his fore-shoulder. Now and then it hurt him so that his leg doubled up, and he stumbled. Several times he waded shoulder-deep into pools and let the cold water run over his wounds. Gradually they stopped bleeding. But the pain grew worse.

Thor's best friend in such an emergency was a clay wallow. This was the second reason why he always took this trail when he was sick or hurt. It led to the clay wallow. And the clay wallow was his doctor.

The sun was setting before he reached the wallow. His jaws hung open a little. His great head drooped lower. He had lost a great deal of blood. He was tired, and his shoulder hurt him so badly that he wanted to tear with his teeth at the strange fire that was consuming it.

The clay wallow was twenty or thirty feet in diameter, and hollowed into a little shallow pool in the centre. It was a soft, cool, golden-coloured clay, and Thor waded into it to his armpits. Then he rolled over gently on his wounded side. The clay touched his hurt like a cooling salve. It sealed the cut, and Thor gave a great heaving gasp of relief. For a long time he lay in that soft bed of clay. The sun went down, darkness came, and the wonderful stars filled the sky. And still Thor lay there, nursing that first hurt of man.

David
Earle Birney

Written in 1940, "David" was one of the first of Birney's poems to be published and is still one of the most popular. It is loosely drawn from his own climbing experiences when he was working summers in Banff.

I

David and I that summer cut trails on the survey,
All week in the valley for wages, in air that was steeped

In the wail of mosquitoes, but over the sunalive week-ends
We climbed, to get from the ruck of the camp, the surly

Poker, the wrangling, the snoring under the fetid
Tents, and because we had joy in our lengthening coltish
Muscles, and mountains for David were made to see over,
Stairs from the valleys and steps to the sun's retreats.

II

Our first was Mount Gleam. We hiked in the long afternoon
To a curling lake and lost the lure of the faceted
Cone in the swell of its sprawling shoulders. Past
The inlet we grilled our bacon, the strips festooned

On a poplar prong, in the hurrying slant of the sunset.
Then the two of us rolled in the blanket while round us the cold
Pines thrust at the stars. The dawn was a floating
Of mists till we reached to the slopes above timber, and won

To snow like fire in the sunlight. The peak was upthrust
Like a fist in a frozen ocean of rock that swirled
Into valleys the moon could be rolled in. Remotely unfurling
Eastward the alien prairie glittered. Down through the dusty

Skree on the west we descended, and David showed me
How to use the give of shale for giant incredible
Strides. I remember, before the larches' edge,
That I jumped a long green surf of juniper flowing

Away from the wind, and landed in gentian and saxifrage
Spilled on the moss. Then the darkening firs
And the sudden whirring of water that knifed down a fern-hidden
Cliff and splashed unseen into mist in the shadows.

III

One Sunday on Rampart's arête a rainsquall caught us,
And passed, and we clung by our blueing fingers and bootnails
An endless hour in the sun, not daring to move
Till the ice had steamed from the slate. And David taught me

How time on a knife-edge can pass with the guessing of fragments
Remembered from poets, the naming of strata beside one,

David

And matching of stories from schooldays. . . . We crawled astride
The peak to feast on the marching ranges flagged

By the fading shreds of the shattered stormcloud. Lingering
There it was David who spied to the south, remote,
And unmapped, a sunlit spire on Sawback, an overhang
Crooked like a talon. David named it the Finger.

That day we chanced on the skull and the splayed white ribs
Of a mountain goat underneath a cliff-face, caught
On a rock. Around were the silken feathers of hawks.
And that was the first I knew that a goat could slip.

IV

And then Inglismaldie. Now I remember only
The long ascent of the lonely valley, the live
Pine spirally scarred by lightning, the slicing pipe
Of invisible pika, and great prints, by the lowest

Snow, of a grizzly. There it was too that David
Taught me to read the scroll of coral in limestone
And the beetle-seal in the shale of ghostly trilobites,
Letters delivered to man from the Cambrian waves.

V

On Sundance we tried from the col and the going was hard.
The air howled from our feet to the smudged rocks
And the papery lake below. At an outthrust we balked
Till David clung with his left to a dint in the scarp,

Lobbed the iceaxe over the rocky lip,
Slipped from his holds and hung by the quivering pick,
Twisted his long legs up into space and kicked
To the crest. Then grinning, he reached with his freckled wrist

And drew me up after. We set a new time for that climb.
That day returning we found a robin gyrating
In grass, wing-broken. I caught it to tame but David
Took and killed it, and said, "Could you teach it to fly?"

VI

In August, the second attempt, we ascended The Fortress,
By the forks of the Spray we caught five trout and fried them
Over a balsam fire. The woods were alive

With the vaulting of mule-deer and drenched with clouds all the
  morning,

Till we burst at noon to the flashing and floating round
Of the peaks. Coming down we picked in our hats the bright
And sunhot raspberries, eating them under a mighty
Spruce, while a marten moving like quicksilver scouted us.

VII

But always we talked of the Finger on Sawback, unknown
And hooked, till the first afternoon in September we slogged
Through the musky woods, past a swamp that quivered with
  frog-song,
And camped by a bottle-green lake. But under the cold

Breath of the glacier sleep would not come, the moon-light
Etching the Finger. We rose and trod past the feathery
Larch, while the stars went out, and the quiet heather
Flushed, and the skyline pulsed with the surging bloom

Of incredible dawn in the Rockies. David spotted
Bighorns across the moraine and sent them leaping
With yodels the ramparts redoubled and rolled to the peaks,
And the peaks to the sun. The ice in the morning thaw

Was a gurgling world of crystal and cold blue chasms,
And seracs that shone like frozen saltgreen waves.
At the base of the Finger we tried once and failed. Then David
Edged to the west and discovered the chimney; the last

Hundred feet we fought the rock and shouldered and kneed
Our way for an hour and made it. Unroping we formed
A cairn on the rotting tip. Then I turned to look north
At the glistening wedge of giant Assiniboine, heedless

Of handhold. And one foot gave. I swayed and shouted.
David turned sharp and reached out his arm and steadied me,
Turning again with a grin and his lips ready
To jest. But the strain crumbled his foothold. Without

A gasp he was gone. I froze to the sound of grating
Edge-nails and fingers, the slither of stones, the lone
Second of silence, the nightmare thud. Then only
the wind and the muted beat of unknowing cascades.

David

Somehow I worked down the fifty impossible feet
To the ledge, calling and getting no answer but echoes
Released in the cirque, and trying not to reflect
What an answer would mean. He lay still, with his lean

Young face upturned and strangely unmarred, but his legs
Splayed beneath him, beside the final drop,
Six hundred feet sheer to the ice. My throat stopped
When I reached him, for he was alive. He opened his grey

Straight eyes and brokenly murmured, "Over . . . over."
And I, feeling beneath him a cruel fang
Of the ledge thrust in his back, but not understanding,
Mumbled stupidly, "Best not to move," and spoke

Of his pain. But he said, "I can't move . . . . If only I felt
Some pain." Then my shame stung the tears to my eyes
As I crouched, and I cursed myself, but he cried,
Louder, "No, Bobbie! Don't ever blame yourself.

I didn't test my foothold." He shut the lids
Of his eyes to the stare of the sky, while I moistened his lips
From our water flask and tearing my shirt into strips
I swabbed the shredded hands. But the blood slid

From his side and stained the stone and the thirsting lichens,
And yet I dared not lift him up from the gore
Of the rock. Then he whispered, "Bob, I want to go over!"
This time I knew what he meant and I grasped for a lie

And said, "I'll be back here by midnight with ropes
And men from the camp and we'll cradle you out." But I knew
That the day and the night must pass and the cold dews
Of another morning before such men unknowing

The ways of mountains could win to the chimney's top.
And then, how long? And he knew . . . and the hell of hours
After that, if he lived till we came, roping him out.
But I curled beside him and whispered, "The bleeding will stop.
You can last." He said only, "Perhaps. . . . For what? A wheelchair,
Bob?" His eyes brightening with fever upbraided me.
I could not look at him more and said, "Then I'll stay
With you." But he did not speak, for the clouding fever.

I lay dazed and stared at the long valley,
The glistening hair of a creek on the rug stretched
By the firs, while the sun leaned round and flooded the ledge,
The moss, and David still as a broken doll.

I hunched to my knees to leave, but he called and his voice
Now was sharpened with fear. "For Christ's sake push me over!
If I could move . . . or die. . . ." The sweat ran from his forehead,
But only his eyes moved. A hawk was buoying

Blackly its wings over the wrinkled ice.
The purr of a waterfall rose and sank with the wind.
Above us climbed the last joint of the Finger
Beckoning bleakly the wide indifferent sky.

Even then in the sun it grew cold lying there. . . . And I knew
He had tested his holds. It was I who had not. . . . I looked
At the blood on the ledge, and the far valley. I looked
At last in his eyes. He breathed, "I'd do it for you, Bob."

> IX

I will not remember how nor why I could twist
Up the wind-devilled peak, and down through the chimney's empty
Horror, and over the traverse alone. I remember
Only the pounding fear I would stumble on It

When I came to the grave-cold maw of the bergschrund . . . reeling
Over the sun-cankered snowbridge, shying the caves
In the névé . . . the fear, and the need to make sure It was there
On the ice, the running and falling and running, leaping

Of gaping greenthroated crevasses, alone and pursued
By the Finger's lengthening shadow. At last through the fanged
And blinding seracs I slid to the milky wrangling
Falls at the glacier's snout, through the rocks piled huge

On the humped moraine, and into the spectral larches,
Alone. By the glooming lake I sank and chilled
My mouth but I could not rest and stumbled still
To the valley, losing my way in the ragged marsh.

I was glad of the mire that covered the stains, on my ripped
Boots, of his blood, but panic was on me, the reek

Of the bog, the purple glimmer of toadstools obscene
In the twilight. I staggered clear to a firewaste, tripped

And fell with a shriek on my shoulder. It somehow eased
My heart to know I was hurt, but I did not faint
And I could not stop while over me hung the range
Of the Sawback. In blackness I searched for the trail by the creek

And found it. . . . My feet squelched a slug and horror
Rose again in my nostrils. I hurled myself
Down the path. In the woods behind some animal yelped.
Then I saw the glimmer of tents and babbled my story.

I said that he fell straight to the ice where they found him.
And none but the sun and incurious clouds have lingered
Around the marks of that day on the ledge of the Finger,
That day, the last of my youth, on the last of our mountains.

Toronto 1940

Memories of a Mountain Guide
Edward Feuz, Jr.
(as told to Imbert Orchard)

I came out in 1903. I was nineteen. I was here as a porter, at the old Glacier House Hotel. We had the [Illecillewaet] glacier coming down right behind the hotel, almost into the trees. We had to go up there whenever people wanted to go, sometimes twice a day. We had to chop a few steps going up with the ice axe and rope the people on and go up with them.

I stayed two winters [at Glacier House] to learn English. Two long winters I put in there. They were horrible. So much snow, and the only live thing we had was the train, two trains a day, one from the east and one from the west and they would stop half an hour to eat. In those days they had no dining cars through the mountains. So they stopped there to eat, and sometimes people were tired from riding on the train, and they would stop over.

Edward Feuz, Jr., was one of a number of guides brought from Switzerland by the Canadian Pacific Railway to lead climbs in the Canadian Rockies and the Selkirk Range. Archives of the Canadian Rockies

After the two winters, I went home. I was twenty-one, I was then of age. You see, you can't be a guide until you get of age. I just had a porter's license. A porter's license means you can go along with a party, but you must carry the rucksack. There's lots of guides that will carry only a few pounds, you see, and they have to hire a porter to carry the rope and the provisions. So I got my papers, I got my book, and then I came out here again.

We climbed with a lot of important people. My father climbed with Lord Minto. And we climbed with an Indian prince up Mount Sir Donald. Both of us went with him to be sure he was safe. And I climbed with that big man, Amery — Viceroy of India, you know. They named a big mountain after him on the Jasper highway. Mount Amery.

Amery came out on political matters [in 1929]. He had to give a lecture in Edmonton, but in the meantime, he wanted to climb these mountains. He was quite a climber in his young days; he was out with Mummery and all kinds of climbers. So I got orders from [CPR] headquarters in Montreal to be ready for Colonel Amery.

Amery was a lovely person, a small, little man, didn't talk very much, very nice to travel with. We were out a whole month together. Mr. A. O. Wheeler, the organizer of the Canadian Alpine Club was there too. He was trying to be the boss like he always had. We were on the way to the mountain and Wheeler wanted to camp — I don't know how far away. So I had a row with Mr. Wheeler. I said, "Do you have to climb the mountain with Colonel Amery or do I have to climb the mountain with Colonel Amery? I'm going to camp where I want to camp." I had been there before, and I knew exactly where to camp you see. So we went up there, and we climbed the mountain. But that's some story.

We started up 3 o'clock in the morning with the lantern on the Alexandra River. Going up through the trees, we could see the weather was threatening. The clouds were down and the weather was going to be bad. But I kept on going. I thought, "Well, we're still in the trees. If it comes on bad, we can still go back." So, I kept going, kept going. The weather didn't improve. We got above timber line and I looked up at the mountain and I said, "Well, Colonel, it doesn't look to be a very nice day. I think we should go back. We should have a nice day going up there on the first ascent. You can't see very well, and it's not much pleasure."

But the Colonel, he turned around and said, "Edward, yes, but we don't turn around in Switzerland, when we climb the mountains, do we?" he said, in a nice English way. I said, "Yes, we don't turn around. We go there. But in Switzerland you see signs ahead of you all the time where you should climb the mountains. I've never been up this mountain before. I've got to find it first. It's a different thing, Colonel, but if you insist to go, I can stand as much as you, Colonel, so say yes or no." He said, "Let's go."

So I went. And do you know it got so bad we finally had to crawl on top on our hands and knees. The snow came down so fast in your face it stuck right to the eyelashes, and you couldn't see more than ten or fifteen feet ahead. I said, "Well, we come to the top, Colonel." I made a stoneman. And the Colonel was lying stomach down, out of the storm, to rest his face.

Down in the valley, it was all black. Off we went, down, down and down, slow in that storm. When you're up that high, you can't go very fast. You've got to make sure of your handholds and your footholds, so that nothing happens. But everything is slippery. We went down, and when we got into the first trees, it was pitch dark. So I took my little folding lantern that I always have and I shoved a candle in. I kept it at the back for the Colonel, so he could see where he stepped in the trees. He was so tired, the poor chap, that he could hardly lift his feet any more. So we walked in the trees for an hour. I said, "Colonel, I think a good idea would be to stop here for the night and make a fire and then go home in the morning. You're tired and it's very slow going. We'll never get there tonight. We'll have to walk all night. I've been out lots of times in worse places than this — right up in the rocks, and tied on to the rocks all night. Here we can make a little fire and be comfortable."

Amery turned around and says, "Oh, no. We don't do that in Switzerland. We go right down to the hut." I said, "Yes, but in Switzerland, you have a trail to go right up to the hut. You can see your little trail where people walked before. Here we have nothing. I can't see where I'm going, and you're so tired you can't move." "Oh, I think we'll go on, Edward," he says. I said, "All right, Colonel, we go on."

It wasn't fifteen minutes after he says, "Edward, I think your idea is a splendid idea." "All right, Colonel. When we get down a little further and I hear some water, we'll stop there and I'll make a fire and I'll make you a lovely cup of tea, and I'll make you comfortable and we'll stay there for the night." "Very nice," the Colonel said.

So I went down there and started the fire quick. I made him a bough bed next to the fire with branches, and by that time the kettle was boiling, so I gave him a cup of nice tea. And before five minutes, he was snoring away. I had to wake him up to eat, and he ate, and he went to sleep again. And then he had a great smile on him. As soon as it got a little daylight, I woke him up and said, "Colonel, a cup of tea, and we'll be started for home."

The next day was a rest day, and then we pulled out. We were going to climb Mount Bryce. We went up there and the weather started to get bad. So we camped at the ice field and it snowed a foot overnight. Climbing was doomed.

So the Colonel said, "Edward, we can't do anything today. I'd like to have a bath. How can we arrange that?" "Oh," I said, "that's very easy, Colonel. We just make a hole in the ground. I've got a very nice tarpaulin and we put that in the hole. I get the cook to make lots of hot water in the pails and we put it in there, and you just slip out of your tent and jump into your pool and have a little bath right out there in the open, right amongst the snow." "Wonderful," he said. So we fixed it up for him and he had a wonderful bath.

The same evening it started to clear up. I could see that something was bothering him. I said, "Anything wrong, Colonel?" "Well, you know Edward, when we got onto my mountain it bothered me a little . . . this bad weather we had and . . ." "Do you think we weren't on top? Is that bothering you?" He says, "Yes, exactly. I was worried we weren't quite on top." I said, "Well, we'll fix that. It's going to be a nice day tomorrow. Let's climb Mount Saskatchewan. It's right opposite your peak, just across the valley. It isn't a very hard climb. We better just go there, and I'll show you the stoneman. You saw me build the stoneman on top, didn't you?" He said, "Oh, yes."

So we went up Mount Saskatchewan, which is over 11,000 feet, and it was a glorious day. And when we got to the top I said, "Now sit down here. Here is the glass. Look right across. You see your mountain now, Mount Amery, over there." He took the glass and smiled and said, "You're right, Edward. It's right on the very top."

Avis Newhall being dug from an avalanche near Mount Assiniboine in 1928.
Archives of the Canadian Rockies

Spring Skiing
in Assiniboine Park
Avis E. Newhall

*The Marquis degli Albizzi's 1928 ski tour to Mount Assiniboine
established the area as the Canadian Rockies' first ski resort.*

One of the chief troubles with skiing in New England is the shortness
of the season. From Christmas until Washington's Birthday one is
reasonably sure of snow, but with the coming of spring the ardent
skier must journey northward to more snowy regions. Even in
Canada satisfactory spring snow conditions are not easy to find. But
one looking for an ideal spot for prolonging the skiing season need
search no further than Assiniboine Park.

This spring a party of ten, at the invitation of Marquis N. degli
Albizzi, spent a month at his log cabins in this beautiful part of the
Canadian Rockies. The cabins are thirty-two miles south of Banff and
in winter can be reached only on skis or snowshoes, or by dog-sled.

Upon arriving at Banff we learned that the Marquis had gone in
to camp a few days ahead of us, taking with him a Swiss guide,
Charles Coeytaux, and a maid — two luxurious appurtenances for
smoothing out life's details. On March 11th we left Banff to join them,
accompanied by Rex, the cook. A machine took us three miles along
a good auto road to Healy's Creek. Here we put on skis and left all
signs of civilization behind. At the start the snow was about six inches
deep, and with a temperature of about twenty degrees there was no
chance of the skis sticking. We followed a pony trail with gentle up
and down grades through a jack-pine forest. Our chief entertainment
en route was the cook. Before we had gone far we realized that winter
sports were not his hobby. He insisted on "toeing out." That, of
course, caused his skis to cross in the rear, so that he spent most of
the morning either falling down or getting up again. However, we
finally reached Douglas Cabins, a group of tumble-down shacks
patched up just enough for temporary use, situated near the junction
of Brewster and Fatigue Creeks and about eleven and one-half miles
from Banff. Here we spent the night. A dog team had brought our
knapsacks to this point. From then on, however, we each carried our
own. Mine weighed less than nine pounds, and in it was every extra
thing that I anticipated needing during the following month.

After leaving Douglas Cabins the next morning, we followed Brewster Creek some nine miles through a monotonous burned-timber district to Brewster Creek Cabin, where we spent a second night. Brewster Creek Cabin is a rather new building, and very comfortable. There are three rooms, — a large one containing two stoves and a long dining table, and two small bedrooms each containing four bunks.

The third day we started fairly early for a twelve-mile trip over two passes. The first, Brewster Pass, is approximately 9200 feet high. In the summer, when it is comparatively safe, the trail is used by horses, but that one would never suspect at this time of year. Before we had reached Bryant Creek, on the opposite side of the pass, we had gingerly traversed or dodged at least a dozen past, present, or future avalanche areas.

At Bryant Creek, the Spray Lakes and Brewster Pass trails join. It was here that the Marquis met us. He is a tall, well-built man, whose early training in a Russian cadet school makes him stand as straight as an arrow. Several novel bits of his outfit caught my eye. One was a pair of coverings for his ski-boots, to keep him dry shod in wet snow. These were made of canvas, with soles of light-weight leather and leather reinforcements for an inch and a half above the soles to prevent the Haug bindings from tearing them. Another new idea of the Marquis' was a small piece of dark brown crepe-de-chine attached to his smoked glasses and hanging down about two inches, to protect his nose and cheek bones from the burning rays of the sun.

From Bryant Creek we skied along a trail in a southerly direction. Tracks of animals were sometimes noticeable. At one spot we crossed cougar tracks which the Marquis said were less than twelve hours old. We also became quite friendly with the ptarmigans, with their white winter coats and black shoe-button eyes. They looked very picturesque as they walked — not hopped — around on the places where the snow had blown off enough for them to feed on the sparse vegetation. Not far from Bryant Creek we commenced the climb of Assiniboine Pass. . . . Four times by actual count I thought we had reached the top, only to find that the trail went down and then up again to another supposed summit. Needless to say we were all very happy when the highest point of the pass had at last been reached. Here we enjoyed our first view of Mt. Assiniboine, well named the Matterhorn of the Canadian Rockies, about five miles distant. On this side of Mt. Assiniboine and across a diminutive lake (Lake Magog), we could see the little group of log cabins where we were to spend the next three and one-half weeks. Smoke was coming out of the chimneys of the main cabin. We knew that that meant food. Although no one was injured in the rush that followed, the last two miles of our trip down the other side of Assiniboine Pass were made in record time.

The Marquis' camp consists of one large log cabin and about ten small ones. The large cabin serves as the living and dining room, and the kitchen. It is heated by a boiler-shaped stove, which looks like a de-wheeled locomotive and takes a four-foot log. A mountain goat's skin hangs over the front door and on another wall is a large picture of Mt. Assiniboine. Around the inside walls Hudson's Bay blankets have been hung, partly to add distinction but mostly to keep out the cold wind. The small cabins are used as sleeping quarters. Each contains very comfortable twin beds, an airtight stove, and gay-coloured chintz curtains at the windows. As the days passed we became more and more repaid for our struggle to get Rex to camp. With a larder restricted to canned milk, canned meat, cereals, dried fruit, and vegetables, he surely used a great deal of originality. One day he produced some delicious vanilla ice-cream. Of course I was curious, and asked him how he had done it. He replied, "Oh, that was easy, Miss; I just galloped a little flour into some canned milk and added flavoring."

During the time we were at camp the snow was at least six feet deep, and was perfect for skiing as it had a good foundation of crust with soft snow on top. March, with the first part of April, is the only time that skiing is possible in this locality. Prior to that the snow is very soft and fluffy, with insufficient foundation to hold the skis on top, and after the middle of April it becomes uncertain, — the thaws come, and then the mud.

Good skiing could be enjoyed in almost every direction from camp. The valley is wooded enough to be picturesque, but not enough to hinder skiing, and is filled with small knolls and gullies which lend themselves to short runs of all grades of difficulty. The continental divide, forming a horse-shoe on the northern, eastern, and southern sides, provides straight runs perhaps a mile long, while on the ice-field and glaciers there is ample opportunity for some very speedy skiing. One day I was especially impressed by the speed of the slopes. We had decided to climb the ice-field under Magog glacier. Most of us had gone only part way, as the slope became very steep, but the Marquis and Erling Strom had gone to the top. When they came down I was standing part way up the slope and witnessed the fastest skiing I have ever seen, — a gust of wind, a cloud of snow, and then two figures traveling rapidly down the valley below. One of us noted the time as they passed a certain rock in the valley on the way up and on the way down. It took them one hour and ten minutes to go from there to the top, and two minutes to return.

Our trips were very well planned. We did enough skiing so that we had an opportunity to improve day by day, yet at the same time we did not overdo. Each morning, about an hour after breakfast, we would go out and ski until time for luncheon, at one. The sun was high and the skis would stick from then until about three-thirty, when we would go out again until six. In the morning we generally took a little trip somewhere, and in the afternoon we usually played around on a practice hill or jump. Our evenings were spent around the fire listening to the Marquis tell of his thrilling experiences with the skirmishers of the Italian army in the Tyrol during the World War. Sometimes he would play the guitar and teach us Russian and Italian songs. *"Io parto"* seemed to be his favorite, and we all struggled to learn it with the correct Italian accent. But every night, promptly at nine, all the songs and stories stopped, the single kerosene lamp was blown out, and we all departed to our respective cabins for ten hours' sleep.

Weather conditions were on the whole favorable. We were able to go out every day, although on several days there was a very high wind. Snow fell about every other day in small amounts, but not enough to keep us housed.

We all tried hard to improve our straight running, and fully appreciated the fact that it was a liberal education merely to watch the Marquis or Erling Strom make even the simplest straight run. Erling is a Norwegian and has skied ever since he was three years old. For the past two years he has been skiing instructor at the Lake Placid Club. His technique is quite different from that used by the Marquis. Erling goes down the fast runs in a crouch that he has invented. With his right knee bent and that ski slightly advanced, he sits on his left heel, with his weight equally divided between the two skis. The Marquis, on the other hand, runs with both feet together. His feet are flat on his skis and both knees are bent, so that his thighs are almost parallel to the skis. His weight is more or less over his heels.

One day the whole party of ten went to Og Peak, which lay in a northwesterly direction from camp. As we climbed, the mountain became steeper and steeper. Suddenly we heard a loud "Boom!" right under our feet. For a moment we were all startled, the possibility of an impending avalanche flashing through our minds. We were therefore in a very receptive mood when the Marquis, who had had avalanche experience, gave us a few hints as to what to do in case of necessity. "There is a great difference between a 'Boom' and a 'Boo-oom,' " he said. "When you hear a 'Boom' you need not worry; it is only the snow settling. But if you hear a 'Boo-oom,' that is an avalanche, and you had better move quickly out of that neighborhood. Point your skis downhill enough so that you can go fast, yet not so fast that you will fall. Head for the nearest shoulder or knoll. The avalanches follow the gullies."

As the morning progressed, the group of skiers became scattered. I was fourth in the line, the Marquis and two others being ahead of me. The rest of the party were quite a distance behind. I was starting up the last pitch just as the first three came down. The Marquis was in the lead, and was making downhill Telemarks in graceful fashion. One of the other men followed — I don't know what kind of turns he was trying (his subsequent actions indicate that he was "brushing up on his Telemarks"). He fell with a terrific thud less than twenty feet above me. The snow under my feet moved and I looked up to see what had happened. He had started an avalanche right over my head. One of the girls was skiing toward me; I called to warn her, and then tried to remember quickly the advice of the Marquis. The next thing I knew I was buried in snow and was being swept down the slope for what seemed like a long distance. Finally I stopped. I was lying on my back with the snow packed in all about me. It seemed as if there must be at least ten feet of snow above me. My eyes, nose, and mouth were full of snow, and I could scarcely breathe. My hands weren't near my face, and I couldn't quite make out where my feet were. I was panting like a dog and shook my head a little to get more air. At length I located one hand and tried to move it toward my face in order to dig out a breathing space. I wiggled it a little and to my great surprise found that it was free and above the snow. With that hand I scratched a breathing hole, and then waved the hand straight up in the air, knowing that the rest of the party would be interested in my whereabouts. In about a minute I felt a hearty hand-shake — the most welcome incident that could have happened. Soon my head was uncovered and I saw two of the men busily shoveling me out with their skis. It was not long before I was back on my skis and another page was added to my book of experience.

Before we realized, it was April 8th, the day we had set to leave camp and return to civilization. The cook went out with us. He decided that he had had enough skiing and that he would try the trip on snowshoes. We all remained together until we reached the top of Brewster Pass, but on the other side there was a good slope and we skiers left him far behind. An hour and a half after we had arrived at Brewster Cabin, he appeared and declared that he would rather go to the work-house than over that pass again.

As we skied nearer and nearer to Banff we could see and feel spring approaching. The animal tracks became more numerous and the creeks were beginning to break away from their icy covers. Just before we reached town we heard a white-throated sparrow singing. His song exactly expressed our thoughts: "Good times in Canada, Canada, Canada."

The Bridegroom's Ski Tour
Erling Strom

Late in the winter of 1931, Norwegian ski guide Erling Strom and six companions set off from Jasper on a major ski trip to the Columbia Icefield. The party reached the Icefield and returned, but some of the most exciting skiing of the entire journey took place just two days out of Jasper — and it wasn't even performed by a member of the expedition.

Around April 1st we were off. Our first stop was a small cabin on Medicine Lake, sixteen miles out. It was not in good shape but all right for one night. We drew lots for the few bunks and the rest of us slept on the floor. Fourteen or fifteen miles of pleasant skiing brought us to Maligne Lake the next day. We had borrowed the keys to a very fine ranger cabin at the north end of the lake. No ranger was there that winter.

The trail came over a little hill back of the cabin and ended by the back door. Most of us were already inside when we heard a crash followed by considerable swearing in several languages. Our Swiss had run into the wall and broken a ski. Too bad, since we were already about thirty miles out of Jasper. The break was such that it could be strapped with adhesive tape so a skier could manage to get back to Jasper on it, but it would never do for the long trip ahead of us. Naturally, I would have been elected to go back if Joe Weiss had not conceived a better idea. He had a Norwegian friend in Jasper,

234

Frank Burstrom by name, with a reputation as a good skier. Maybe he would come out with a new pair of skis and ski back on the old ones.

Frank was working until 5 o'clock, but since it was Saturday he might be willing to come out that evening and use Sunday for the return trip. Joe got him on the phone a little after five o'clock.

It was a big favor to ask of anybody. Sixty miles of skiing is not to be sneezed at under any circumstances, so we were not surprised when a lot of hemming and hawing took place. From what we could hear at our end, Joe did not have much luck. It struck me that maybe I should talk to him. Thousands of miles from home, one's own language has a peculiar effect. I explained how it would detain us a day or two if I had to go to Jasper and back, while we could continue the next day if he would come out that afternoon. I drew his attention to the fact that he would have full moon that evening and a good trail, not to mention how grateful we all would be.

Finally he agreed to come and ended up by saying that we should not expect him before midnight since he had to find a suitable pair of skis, buy some adhesive tape for the repair job, plus have his dinner before he left. I was much relieved when I hung up the phone, and more so when we heard a knock at the door less than six hours later. He had moved right along without a stop. It had been a good trip, he said. Wet from perspiration, I remember he was standing with his back to the fire while he was having a bite to eat. Soon it was time to go to bed, and we told him where he could sleep.

"Thanks," he said, "but I think I better get back to town."

"What?" said we. "Another thirty miles tonight?"

"Yes," he continued, "the moon is out and the snow is just right. One never knows when the weather might change."

That was that. We could not talk him into staying. Within an hour and a half from the time he came he was off again. During the time he spent with us the man hardly sat down, but stood in front of the fire drying his back.

We knew we had picked on a good man, but what I found out about him when I returned to Jasper fourteen days later made me think him one of the best men I have ever met. I told him we had thought his return to Jasper that night had been pretty far-fetched. The weather had looked steady and the following day was a Sunday. Why, then, ski almost sixty miles in one stretch when it was not necessary?

"But it was necessary," he said, with a twinkle in his eye. "I was getting married that morning at ten o'clock."

235

To the Heart of the Mountains
R. M. Patterson

In the early 1930s, R. M. Patterson travelled on horseback with George Pocaterra, a pioneer rancher in the foothills of southern Alberta, from Pocaterra's Buffalo Head Ranch to the remote Elk Valley in eastern British Columbia.

Always the light sleeper in camp and therefore a nuisance to those who travel with me, I sat up in my eiderdown and considered the frozen darkness surrounding the valley of the South Fork. One could just see the outline of the mountains against the stars — that was all. I reached out of bed and poked the fire with a stick. A few embers still glowed; I raked them together and threw on some dead pine needles and then some twigs. There was a sudden crackle of flame, and Adolf sat up as if impelled by some hidden spring. He blinked at the fire for a minute; then he dressed and disappeared without a word into the darkness to see to the horses. Wriggling around, still in my eiderdown, I drew the logs of last night's fire together; soon there was a blaze and I stood the teapail, which was frozen, in the heat to thaw out a bit. And when these various things were done I rolled out of bed and dressed by the fire.

Soon the tea water was boiling and porridge was made. I got out some eggs and then set to work slicing bacon. Adolf came back and sat by the fire. Between us we upset some plates or something and Pocaterra's voice came from a humped-up sleeping bag, wanting to know what the devil we thought we were doing, getting up in the middle of the night like this. But the smell of coffee simmering and the sizzling of a fryingpan fetched him out, still muttering things about midnight and so forth, but becoming more human every minute.

I offered Pocaterra some porridge — just to see what would happen — but, as usual, he pushed it from him, turning away his head with a gesture of disgust, "No, no, Patterson! You know I *loathe* the beastly stuff!"

I knew, perfectly well; he couldn't bear the sight of it. So now, in the darkness, under Mount Head, Adolf and I cleaned up the porridge while Pocaterra fried the bacon and eggs. Then, breakfast over, we packed up camp, saddled and packed the horses in the first feeble light of day and rode on towards the Grass Pass.

For Pocaterra this trip was, in a sense, a pilgrimage. As a very young man he had hunted with the Stoney Indians in the country to which we were going; and while it might now be known to a few as the West Fork of the Elk, to Pocaterra it was still the hidden valley, the valley of youth. He called it always by its Stoney name, Nyahé-ya-'nibi, the "Go-up-into-the-mountains-country"; and I can see now the name translated, in an article that he wrote for the *Italian Alpine Club Journal*, as "Il paese nel cuor delle montagne" — "The country in the heart of the mountains." No better name could be found for that great, silent meadow, six thousand feet above the sea, ringed around by glaciers and by mountains that rose to 11,000 feet, shut off from the world by passes that were no better than goat trails, by drowning rivers, a wild torrent and a tangle of huge fallen trees. . . .

I had formed a picture in my mind of this valley and I pondered it as we rode, at an easy pace and mostly in silence, up to the Highwood River. The forest ranger station was deserted, which was all to the good as we did not wish to advertize our going, and we rode all that day without meeting a soul. We followed the Highwood until it forked into Storm and Misty Creeks and there we made camp below the first spurs of the Misty Range.

At noon the next day we crossed the Highwood Pass, dropping on to the head of Pocaterra Creek, which was the south fork of the Kananaskis River. There we turned our horses loose to graze and made our noonday fire.

What we planned to do now was to pass unseen through the Kananaskis country by taking an old and almost abandoned Indian trail to the Elk Pass — a trail that was forgotten except by the Stoney Indians, and by Pocaterra who had travelled and hunted with them. This would take us over the Divide into British Columbia; and the first rain would wash out our tracks on this stony ground, leaving no trace of our going.

The others saw to the fire and I went a little distance away to get a picture of the outfit and the valley. In a day or two's time it would be October. Of all seasons in the mountains this was the loveliest: bronze-coloured slopes of short grass and dwarf willow, slashed by the dark green of spruce and fir; larches at timberline spearheading the dark evergreens with points of shining gold. Away in the distance two mountains barred the view: they would be Mount George and Mount Paul, so named after George Pocaterra and his blood brother,

Paul Amos, the Stoney, the old hunter. Between these blue-grey limestone peaks ran a gentler, more rounded ridge of sandstone and coal — the grazing ground of the Bighorn sheep.

In the foreground were the scattered horses and, closer still, the two men busy around the fire from which a blue wisp of smoke was drifting up the valley towards the pass. All seemed peaceful and serene — until I saw the horseman approaching.

Pocaterra had seen him, too, and his very attitude expressed acute annoyance that this man had come blundering into his plans. Now, he was thinking, we should have to ride all the way down to the ranger station on the main trail, and from there double back to the Elk Pass. Catch him showing old Indian trails to any stranger. . . .

The rider proved to be McKenzie, an Australian, recently appointed forest ranger of the Kananaskis country — and he very decidedly got off on the wrong foot with Pocaterra. Instead of dismounting and passing the time of day in the manner of the hills, he sat on his horse and opened fire far too abruptly. "Are you the guide of this party?" he asked.

Pocaterra stared at him with all the anger of an old-timer who is questioned by a newcomer. "Guide?" he said. "I don't know about that, but I am George Pocaterra. Those are my coal claims down there — that ridge between the two mountains — and this creek was named after me by the survey. And this is a private party." And with that, he took a savage bite out of a ham sandwich, thus rendering himself speechless for a while. . . .

Down went lunch in record time, followed by mugs of steaming tea. Then the horses were brought in. Things were slapped together and tied on to the saddles; rifles were replaced in their scabbards, from which they were always removed during a long halt lest the horses should roll on them. At this point McKenzie remarked that he would ride with us as far as the ranger station — whereat Pocaterra in a gust of fury, leapt on his horse and set off at a lope across the open meadows of the pass. The outfit followed him down into the green timber. The trail worsened and we crashed and slid at a fast, racketing trot down the screes and the rockslides, over the debris of avalanches. In this fashion we dropped a thousand feet to the junction with the Elbow River trail; from there on the trail improved but the pace increased. I rarely saw Pocaterra owing to the winding of the trail. After him came two packhorses, then Adolf, then one packhorse, myself and McKenzie.

On a straight stretch of trail through green timber, I saw Adolf hurriedly whipping his lines round the saddle horn. I wondered why — when, suddenly, he leaned out from his saddle and made a terrific swipe at a spruce branch with a willow switch that he held in his right hand. A puff of feathers flew and a fluttering bird appeared. Adolf swung still further out from his saddle, and caught the "fool hen" with his left hand before it could fall to the ground. In one easy, gliding motion he swung back into the saddle, wrung the bird's neck and stuffed it inside his jacket. Then he picked up his lines again and pursued his packhorses. All this was done without the slightest hesitation at this fast, raking trot of Pocaterra's that could keep pace with the average man's lope or canter.

A few feathers floated on the air, I rode through them and turned in my saddle to see if McKenzie had observed anything — but he was only then coming into sight round the last bend. "Does he always travel at this rate?" he shouted.

"Always," I called to him — and I fetched the packhorse ahead of me a crack with the lines. . . .

McKenzie had had enough by the time we reached the Kananaskis Lakes ranger station. A brief farewell — and then we rode away southwards, across the meadows and into the timber, climbing steadily upwards, headed for the Continental Divide. The pace slackened as Pocaterra's equanimity became restored — though still, from time to time, some blistering comment on greenhorn forest rangers would come floating back to us from the head of the pack train. And then, as the sun touched with its dying fire the wall of the Elk Mountains, we crossed the flat meadows of the Elk Pass and came to the brink of a new valley — almost of a new world, for now the water drained to the Pacific.

Pocaterra checked his horse and sat there looking down the blue, shadowy valley of the Elk. It faded away out of sight into the dim haze of the evening, and there was a feeling of mystery to it that cannot be caught and set down in words.

The sight of it moved Pocaterra to speech. "It is beautiful, is it not?" he said. "There is a softness to it that Alberta does not have; it is almost as if one could feel the breath of the Pacific. There is something about this that draws a man — or is it just that I hunted and was happy here when I was young?"

We rode on in silence down into the trees and down the rough, steep trail that led to the Elk Lakes. Halfway down we stopped at a narrow place between great rocks and plugged the gap with fallen timber. This would serve as a drift fence in case the horses strayed back on the homeward trail during the night. Towards the end of the job there was only room for one man to work so I mounted and rode on, leaving Adolf to it.

Pocaterra had already gone on with the packhorses. From far down below his voice floated up to me on the stillness of the evening . . . but this time it was raised in song.

Shoot-out
Dan McCowan

In the long and colourful history of the Canadian Mounted Police many thrilling episodes of heroism and courage have been recorded. Few chapters in the annals of the Force are, however, so surcharged with stark murder and sudden violent requital as that in which the case of the desperate Doukhobors is outlined.

There is no mystery in this strange story, this almost incredible real-life scenario in which a small group of young men, taught from infancy by precept and example to utterly abhor the shedding of blood and to embrace the principles of peace at any price, became involved in a deadly brawl with members of that very Force which was recruited to bring law and order to the mountains and prairies of Western Canada.

While the final act of this stirring drama was staged against an imposing background of towering cliffs in the heart of the Rockies, the opening scene was laid in flat wheatland on the boundary between Manitoba and Saskatchewan. At Benito, near Swan River, three young Doukhobors suspected of minor shop-breaking, were picked up by police at a dance in the early hours of Saturday, October 5, 1935. While being taken to the nearby town of Pelly for further questioning, the suspects, Posnikoff, Voiken and Kalmakoff, disarmed and killed their escort, Constables Shaw and Wainwright, the latter a municipal officer. When last seen alive the two policemen were riding in the front seat of the police car, the others in the rear. Robbing the victims and dumping the bodies in a ditch by the wayside, the murderers drove off in the blood-spattered automobile, visiting acquaintances in various hamlets throughout the district, drinking considerable quantities of potent liquor and boasting openly of their heinous crime.

By nightfall it became evident that something had befallen Shaw and Wainwright and inquiries were set afoot. No trace of them could be obtained on Sunday and it was not until Monday afternoon that their bodies were found. By this time the fugitives had disappeared. A detailed description of them and of the stolen car was immediately broadcast throughout the prairie provinces, service station attendants being particularly requested to check car licence numbers. All roads and railways were closely watched.

First word of the whereabouts of the guilty trio and of their headlong flight from justice came from Exshaw on the eastern fringe of the Rockies. At that point they purchased a few gallons of gasoline and pushed westward along the trans-Canada highway. By this time funds must have been running low. When they reached the National Park gateway ten miles east of Banff, the necessary entrance fee of $2 was apparently beyond their means. So, turning back for a few miles, they halted a car driven by a commercial traveller whom they robbed of ten dollars and a watch.

But Nemesis, if somewhat slow in the take-off, was swiftly overtaking the gang. The garage owner at Exshaw had notified the police at Banff that the missing car together with men answering to the description of the killers was in the neighbourhood. Canmore was also advised and immediately police cars from both centres came roaring over the main highway. Heading into the lights of an oncoming car the Banff officers, Sergeant Wallace and Constables Harrison, Campbell and Combe, swung their automobile square across the road and stepped out into the blinding glare of nearing headlights and into a blast of gunfire from the desperadoes. For several hectic minutes the fusilade continued in the semi-darkness, the police making brisk reply.

The uniformed men fared badly in this encounter, Sergeant Wallace being instantly killed and Harrison fatally wounded. Combe countered by ending the career of Posnikoff, the ringleader and braggart of the group. Voiken and Kalmakoff took to the woods and with that the curtain fell on the second act of this grim tragedy.

Next day at dawn an armed band of angry citizens of Banff set out in the midst of a whirling storm of snow, determined on the capture of the murderers dead or alive. Amongst the man-hunters on this occasion was a Park Warden named Bill Neish, a tall lank Scot then stationed at a remote post twenty-five miles north-west of Lake Louise. His next-door neighbour lived twenty miles away and life at this moment was monotonous. When the radio droned out news of the tragedy at Banff and of the impending hunt for the criminals, Bill's mind was immediately made up. That night, without asking leave of Park headquarters, he left the wild animals to look after themselves and journeyed to the scene of action at Banff.

Walking through the snowy woods next morning, his rifle at the ready, Neish saw two men running across a clearing and called on them to halt. They paid no heed so he bowled one of them over with a single shot: the other man dropped behind a fallen half-rotted fir tree and opened fire on the Warden. Snow was then falling thickly and visibility was poor but Bill sent a bullet smack through the prone trunk of the tree and into the stomach of the last of the felons. Seriously wounded, the bandits both died that night in a local hospital, Kalmakoff with the stolen ring of Constable Shaw still upon his finger.

When the October daily journal of Warden Neish of Mosquito Creek reached National Parks headquarters office in Ottawa it contained one entry which caused some eyebrow-lifting. It read:

. . ."Oct. 8. Killed two bandits." Unfamiliar with the events of the fateful day in Banff Park the authorities at the Capital requested that Neish amplify this somewhat sketchy entry. This he did by adding the simple and terse comment:

"Snowing to beat hell."

Mona's Fire Dress
Sid Marty

The old-time wardens of the mountain parks were a breed apart. Civilization had driven them into the sanctity of the mountains as it had done some years earlier the buffalo, the grizzly bear, the wapiti, and the wolf, and the mountains were the last stronghold of men like Bill Peyto, who once shot a grizzly through the eye with a single bullet from a .22 calibre rifle, men like Frank Wells and Frank Bryant, who had curled up in the snow like wolves all night for the chance to catch poachers and then chased them for twenty miles on snowshoes, finally running them down. They were jealously possessive of their lonely districts and, if they saw more than one person during the course of a winter's travels, they'd complain about "too many goddam people spoilin' the peace and quiet."

Of necessity the women who married these men were as strong-willed and self-reliant as their husbands. In addition to keeping house in the bush, such women were expected to lend a hand on the trail with packing the horses or fixing phone line. In later years, as the number of people travelling in the backcountry gradually increased, the warden's wife acted on his behalf when he was absent, by selling fishing licences, giving information, registering climbers, and manning telephone and radio links to town in cases of emergency. She received official recognition from the parks branch, and no pay. In effect, the government gained two employees for the price of one. A married warden could travel more freely and efficiently in the bush with his wife "minding the store" in a headquarter's cabin. Obviously, such a woman required considerable patience, and most important when dealing with the public, a sense of humour.

We stopped to say goodbye to one of our neighbours at Pocahontas, an old-time mountain woman who took the life of a warden's wife in her stride. Mona Matheson is known to some of the natives around Jasper as "one of the greatest gals who ever laced on boots." She lives in a cabin near the Yellowhead Highway in a clearing of pine and aspen forest with a commanding outlook toward the mountains she has known for most of her life. Though they have dominated her existence for over fifty years, they have never dominated her spirit. Having outlived her husband, Charlie, she stays on in their cabin alone.

Mona met us at the door and invited us in for tea. It would be the last chance we would have to talk with her for several months. She's a slender, grey-haired woman of medium height with a pert, pugnacious nose, and she moves with an ease and lightness that is at odds with her age.

Mona poured cupfuls of tea, the drink that serves as a conversational lubricant in the mountains.

Myrna was full of excitement about our move to the Tonquin Valley, and Mona told her not to listen to my objections because she herself had raised a child in the Warden Service. That had been in the days before helicopters, when the hospital was many days away, and a mother had to be both nurse and doctor to her children in cases of emergency.

I mentioned Charlie and at once her expression changed, her eyes looking inward on a private pain — but only briefly.

"Charlie." She said the name softly, with a depth of feeling that made clear how great the loss was. She had been prepared for his

243

death, though, because she had nursed him through several years of illness.

They had met at Medicine Lake in Jasper Park, where Mona and her sister, Agnes, worked as cooks in a trail-ride camp for Fred Brewster, a Jasper outfitter. The wardens used to drop in for coffee on their patrols to Maligne Lake or the Rocky River. There was a stack of well-worn magazines in the tent for the dudes to read and the men would leaf through these at times, waiting for the coffee to boil, pretending they were reading. Mona noticed that Charlie was the only warden who held his magazine right side up. It seems the others were just using it as a lecher's screen while they ogled the young cooks.

"We didn't like the way they looked at us," she said, and we laughed with her.

Mona soon decided that Charlie would make a good partner, although Charlie, sixteen years her senior, seemed set in his bachelor ways and would be a difficult man to convert. But Mona was determined. She once helped him jingle his ponies at 4:00 in the morning when they pulled out on him at Jacques Lake. She walked and ran nine miles in thin running shoes to help round them up, chasing after the faint tinkle of the lead mare's bell in the timber. Her feet had been slightly frostbitten in the process but Charlie, though sympathetic, was not entirely convinced about matrimony.

While he was making up his mind, Mona and her sister talked Fred Brewster into hiring them as horse guides. They had picked up skills of that trade by watching the cowboys working around camp and practising what they learned on their days off. After a brief confrontation with the Chief Warden and the Park Superintendent, who were alarmed at the idea of women doing what had always been a man's job, Mona and Agnes got their licences and became the first female guides in Jasper Park.

"I wonder why more women didn't apply for those jobs," said Myrna.

Mona thought for a minute. "I don't really know. Maybe they were afraid to try, Nowadays it's different so I'm told."

"In some ways," said Myrna, with a smile, "but in lots of ways it's still the same."

"Well, you see, I've never been afraid of anything. I don't know why, but it's true. Guiding turned out to be a lot of trouble and hard work. But for me, it was worth it. Just to know I could do the job."

The sisters were just supposed to guide dudes on backcountry horse trips and Brewster was to provide them with men to do the packing and horse wrangling. For some reason, these men never showed up. Mona never said why, but knowing a bit about cowboys, I wonder whether there wasn't a bit of male conspiracy there, to test the sisters by seeing if they could do all the work involved, not just the horseback riding. It was a man-size task since each had to do the packing and wrangling as well as guiding for two outfits, totalling thirty-five head of horses. They were up each day before 4:00 A.M. to catch, feed, saddle, and doctor their animals. They had to pack all the food and equipment for the dudes as well, which included everything from thundermugs to outboard engines. They saw each other occasionally in camp that summer, the rest of the time they worked separately, guiding or packing.

Mona, a former cook, slaved away the long hours in her exalted position as head guide, while the new camp cook sat on a log and watched with interest. Holding a heavy pack box in her arms, the diminutive guide had to stand on a stump to reach the back of a tall horse. She was able to lift everything but the outboard engines needed for fishing at Maligne Lake. The motors weighed 200 pounds but Mona's cook, a big strapping man, used to lift them up onto the horse for her with ease.

"Teamwork," said Myrna, giving me a significant glance.

"That's right," said Mona. "As long as he could lift them, I could get them tied on, and as long as it was tied on good, the horse would carry it."

I glanced at Mona in covert admiration. The key to the horse business has always been the skill of the handler, not his or her strength. Still, as a large mesomorph, who once had my hands full just dealing with two horses, I was feeling slightly overwhelmed as Mona modestly described how she packed from ten to fifteen head at a time.

Charlie too had been impressed, so they were finally married.

Mona's skill with the diamond hitch came in handy on many occasions, but none so dramatically as during the dry, hot summer of 1935. That year she and Charlie were stationed at Maligne Lake, thirty-two miles southeast of Jasper townsite.

"We had gone up to the narrows of the lake with our boat one Sunday. About noon, here comes Harry Phillips from the camp at the north end, with two kickers [outboard motors] on his boat, going like blazes. He told us a fire had broken out on the Horseshoe Bend."

Horseshoe Bend is on the Maligne River, between Maligne Lake and the Athabasca River, a good fifteen miles from the narrows, ten by boat and five by horse. They went down the lake as fast as they could. Charlie took some tools and two horses and galloped off down the trail. In an hour he was scouting the fire's perimeter and he saw that he couldn't contain it without help. He had his forestry field-set with him, so he climbed a tree to the phone wire, hooked in his set, and rang up Jasper.

The Administration Building was in an uproar. Sixteen fires had broken out in the park that day and all available men were already committed. The Chief Warden told him to hang on, that he would send him a crew the next day. Charlie fought the fire all day, and late in the afternoon, worn out, he rang up Mona and asked her to bring him his outfit with tents, teepee, blankets, and enough food to last twenty men for three days. Alone, with the fire building up around him, Charlie was lucky to be married to a horsewoman like Mona who could look after this chore without him riding back to help her.

The horses were pastured in the Opal Hills, a high meadowland above Maligne Lake, in the shadow of the 9,000 foot Leah Peak. Mona moved as fast as she could, but it was 7:00 P.M. before they were in the corral and she could start saddling up. It took a while to gather up all the equipment and it was hard work packing the heavy teepee cloth, the bulky crew tents, the boxes of canned goods, wool blankets, and fire-fighting tools. The job had to be done carefully. It's dangerous to have a load slip on the trail, especially in the dark. Mona worked on into the night by lantern light, finally topping off the packs with some empty twenty-five pound lard pails, which would be cooking pots for the big crew.

Late that night she took the string out of the yard, heading down the Maligne River, which led her like a starry carpet through the darkness. She gave the mare its head and kept hers down out of the way of the low branches that swept over the trail. Just before dawn they rode out into a little meadow and, suddenly, there was a rush of heat rising from the ground. A lake of fire stretched out before her, no flames, just the embers scattered like fallen stars along the earth. There was a clink of metal and a shadow drifted across the red coals, little arrows of flame fanned in its wake.

"Looks like hell, don't it?" cracked Charlie, adding, "Thanks, Mona."

They started setting up camp at dawn. The crew came in by boat from the head of Medicine Lake early that morning and Charlie shook his head when he saw them. They were boys, the oldest being about seventeen. Charlie asked Mona if she would stay and cook, since the administration wasn't supplying a camp cook. Mona took on the job.

"Now we had no cook tent," she told us, "and we had no stove either. For a table, we used a pack mantle spread out on the ground. I cooked everything in those twenty-five pound lard pails hung over an open fire. What a job! There were three shifts of fire-fighters to be fed three times a day and only one cook. That fire burned a whole month. It went right over the top of a mountain and down into some blind hole."

As she talked, I pictured the camp, the dirty, exhausted boys lying on the ground, the blackened pots smoking over the fire, and the bulldog flies and mosquitoes clumped in the air, living clouds of torture. I pictured Mona rolling out of her blanket in the teepee before dawn to start the breakfast fire and working late into the evening, the smoke of thirty days' work stinging in her eyes.

"What did they pay you for that, Mona?" I asked.

"Pay!" she exclaimed. "Ha! That's quite a joke. Oh, the firefighters got paid, of course. Charlie got his regular wages, I think $130 a month. No overtime either. They hadn't invented that yet. He had to stay on that fire twenty-four hours a day, until it was dead out."

"Yes, but what about you?" Myrna asked. "Didn't you get paid at all?"

"Well, they didn't quite know what to do with me. I was the warden's wife, you see. I guess they figured it wouldn't look good, putting me on payroll. People would talk. In the end, they decided I should get something, so they gave me a cheque — for five dollars."

"That's terrible," Myrna said, stunned. I sat back in my chair, shaking my head.

"It was about what I'd expected, and anyway, I was doing it for Charlie, not the service. Charlie and I, we shared everything, including the hardships. It was no picnic for him either, at times, but it brought us closer together. I have no regrets, though it was kind of hell at times."

There had been no trace of bitterness in Mona's voice as she told the story, only a kind of ironic amusement at the memory.

"I remember I bought a dress with the five dollars. I called it my fire dress. It was a lovely shade of blue. . . ."

It's a Woman's World
Nello Vernon-Wood

"While I've got nothing personal agin matrimony," says Sawback Smith, "I claim it should be confined to them areas sanctified by precedent and custom, like Niagara Falls, Bermuda, an' such. A huntin' trip's no place for the mele de lune."

"Mile of what?" I ask, mystified.

"That's what the pea soupers down in Quebec call the honeymoon," elucidates Smitty. "Only in this case it means miles of grief. Miles and miles of it."

"Ain't you squealin' afore the loop tightens?" I inquire. "I figger that if Doc is bringin' his bride along she'll probably fit like an old glove. He likes his huntin' trips too much to risk gummin' the works with a female he's only married to. I bet Doc's picked him out a gal what can take it, an' you know good an' well that we've guided many a female that took to huntin' like an Indian takes to lemon extract."

"Yeah," admits Sawback, "which is all the more reason why I'm spooky as a doe with fawns about this trip. Considerin' the law of averages, attraction of opposites, an' the axiom that woman's place is behind a bridge table, I got a forty-calibre hunch that we're in for bushels of trouble."

Well, we'll know all about it P.D.Q. Doc an' his newly acquired Missus'll be in on the Trans Canada tomorrow, an' we are due to drag our tails for the East Kootenay the day after.

I'm down at the deepo with the rest of the hoi polloi next afternoon an' soon's the cars stop, I see Doc eruptin' from a Pullman accompanied by the followin': 1 woman, blonde, 1938 model; 2 rifles, Springfield, .30-06; 3 suitcases, 4 duffel bags, 5 novels, 6 cushions, an' 7 baggage checks to cover the rest of the impedimenta.

Other years, Doc comes boilin' out of the cars, an' grabbin' my hands says, "Tex, you blankety-blank onregenerate son of a blank-blank female coyote, how in blank are you?" an' I reply "Smile when you call me that, you dash-dash unprincipled appendix snatcher! Fine; finer'n frog wool!"

This time we're not so free an' unrestrained in our greetin's. I've got a idee that from now on me an' Doc have got to do our friendly cussin' only at such times as we're removed from the ennoblin' influence of lovely woman.

The two-three days it takes to get into the game country ain't what you'd call eventful, outside of the restraint Mrs. Doc's presence puts on Sawback's pack horse drivin' rhetoric. Them cayuses are used to bein' hollered at in man's language, an' to hear Sawback tryin' to keep them strung out on the trail without enlargin' on their ancestry, personal appearance, an' probable hereafter, struck me as right funny.

We get into camp at the head of the Horse Thief, and from where we've pitched the rag houses we can see a couple of goat sunnin' themselves on a ledge, only about a mile an' a half across, an' mebbe a thousand feet up. I check 'em over through the field glasses, an' decide they're billies, an' trophies.

All we got to do is sneak along the summit grasslands in the stream bed until we get behind an old moraine. From there I figger we can climb above 'em to not more than 150 yards away. It looks like an easy stalk. I'm explainin' this to Doc when his squaw asks do we ride, or go afoot.

"We go afoot, of course," I tell her. "In the first place, it'll take an hour to wrangle an' saddle the ponies, besides which we have to keep out of sight while crossin' this open country. After that, there ain't a cayuse in Canada could climb in that broken rock."

"I don't think I have the inclination to go scrambling about in all that horrible rock," she decides. "Haven't you got any goat somewhere down where it's all grass, and I can chase them on my pony?"

I let Doc explain the habits, disposition, an' method of huntin' billy goats to her, but I can see that she thinks it's all mostly hooey, an' that there must be better ways of bustin' a goat than to go side hill gougin' after 'em on your own feet.

"How far will this gun of mine shoot?" is her next question.

"It would kill a man at 2000 yards, I suppose," replies Doc.

"Well, why don't we walk along until we are below them? It can't be more than half a mile from the grass to where they are. If this gun shoots 2000 yards, I'm sure it should get one of those things at 880."

"Which it undoubtedly should," I chips in, "but it's got to have a heap of co-operation from the butt end."

Her only reply is a look that reminds me of the time I got caught by a blizzard while crossin' the Columbia ice field.

However, we get her started, an' injun along the crick bed until we get to where the goat can't see us, an' stop for a couple of minutes at the foot of a mess of glacial deritus an' slide rock. I point out a big old boulder just under a cliff, an' opine that if we climb to it, we'll be high enough to start a traverse that will bring us over our quarry, at the same time givin' us the wind on 'em.

Mrs. Doc takes one look, an' right there decides that she ain't lost any goat on that mountain.

"You men go ahead," she says, "and I'll stay here until you come back, or I get bored." I can see Doc waverin', an' before he can pull a bridegroom act, an' decide to stay an' keep her company, I start climbin' an' tell Doc to get goin'.

It's steep, an' broken all the way to the big rock, an' we're blowin' hard by the time we reach it. Stoppin' to catch our wind, I notice that the bride ain't where we left her, but I don't say anything to Doc, figgerin' she's probably settin' behind a scrub balsam or somethin'.

The traverse ain't so awful bad. Once across the moraine, there's grass ledges an' shale slopes, so we make good time to where I figger we should begin to start down. We sneak along, right circumspect, expectin' to spot them billies any old time now. After a while I whisper to Doc that I'd swear we're on the same ledge that we saw 'em on, so let's drift up wind a mite. That brings no luck, so we continue to descend, checkin' over every foot of the visible terrain.

Fifteen or so minutes later, we both stop with a jerk, as a shot rings out, an' echoes all over hell's half acre. Then another, an' whammy-bang-bingo; it begins to sound like a busy day in Madrid.

There's no sense stayin' where we are after all that ruckus, so we hightail down as fast as the broken country will let us. Doc is quite some trepidated, as he thinks mebbe the little woman has tangled with a grizzly, or seen a mouse or somethin'.

We found her settin' on a knoll about five hundred yards from where we left her, an' as Doc dashes up to see if she is still all in one bundle, she says, "You'll find your goat just over there, by the creek. I knew all the time it was just silly to go scrambling after them all over that mountain. I just waited until they came down to eat, and shot the biggest."

She had him, all right, but whoinhell would have expected them ornery critters to come down? An' the worst of it is, Doc goes all mushy, an' tells her that she's the best little hunter in five Provinces, includin' Rupert's Land an' the Arctic, 'stead of explainin' that she's lucky enough to fall into a garbage scow an' come out with a diamond ring.

Next mornin' Doc an' me take a pack pony over to the kill, and skin out the head, also savin' the meat for eatin' purposes. The little woman is left in camp, not being interested in the bloody details of side hill surgery. When we get back to camp, she's missin' and Doc has another spell of inquietude until she comes strollin' in.

"Oh, you're all here," she says. "Tex, do you suppose there is anyone else camped near here?"

"I don't reckon so, why?"

"Those are our horses up there on the slide, aren't they?"

"Sure, they're all there, except these three me an' Doc just got in with."

"Well, then," she says, "it's all right. That must have been a bear I shot down there on that grassy slope. I didn't go right up to it, after it fell down, because I didn't have any more ammunition, but I'm sure you will find it dead. I aimed right where its heart ought to be."

Doc an' I rode down to the grass slope, an' sure enough, there's a darn good black bear stretched out dead as Dan'l Boone. An' if you'd a' heard Doc gush all over Mrs. Doc that night, your stummick would have turned almost inside out.

After we've got the hides fleshed an' salted, we move camp down the valley a ways to harry the old wapiti. The elk are about, and every so often we hear the buglin' of some pugnacious bull, answered by another from across the valley. It's mighty sweet music, an' I figger on the Doc stoppin' a royal head before many days, an' as he's never accumulated an elk, we're both right up on the front end of our feet.

For three days steady we hunt the slides, with all the pediculous luck in the world. Any bulls we see are spikes, or measly little four-pointers at most. Or if we do see a real head, he's surrounded by a flock of jittery cows that spook for no good reason at all, takin' their lord an' master with 'em.

An' every evenin' when we drag our creakin' bones into camp, the little woman tells us about some "perfectly enormous" bull she's seen through the glasses right above camp, or some place where we ain't been. She's spendin' the days trying to get Sawback to try her recipes for crapes susies, an' marshmeller fudge, 'stead of good goat mulligan an' beans, but up to now, thank God, that old misogynist is stubborn, so we continue to get man's grub.

As we're leavin' camp on the fourth mornin' I tell Doc that if we see a ten-pointer, he'd best accumulate it. I've just about given up hope of gettin' a Royal, an' he agrees.

We eat our cold liver an' bannock that noon, 'way up on a hogback that separates two slides, an' there are eight elk in plain sight — four cows, two yearlin's, a spike buck, an' a scrub four-pointer. Across from the other side, another is buglin' and tellin' the world that he's the toughest guy of the whole Rockies, an' who'd like to make something of it? If we only had a trophy stretched out, it would have been the middle of a perfect day.

"Did you hear a shot?" asks Doc.

"Nope, not me," I reply. As a matter of fack, I've been half asleep. "Just a rock fallin', I expect. Come on, let's cross the valley an' see if mebbe that feller that's doin' all the blowin' is as good as he thinks he is."

It's a long way down, an' twice as long up on the other side, an' by the time we're out of the timber, that elk has quit advertisin' himself, so we still hunt until it's too dark to see our front sights.

Sawback has a big ole campfire goin', and settin' in its light is busy takin' the scalp offen a twelve pointer, with a beam durn near as thick as my leg.

"Perigrinatin' porcupines! where'd you get it?" I ejaculate.

"Didn't," says he, "Mrs. Doc blasted him this afternoon. She went down to get a pail of water, an' this bird was standin' in her way, so she got her bang stick, an' banged."

"You know, dear," she says to Doc, as we're surroundin' a mess of stew, "I think you shouldn't go tearing all over the country like you do. It's all right for the guides; I think they actually like it, but I'm sure my way of huntin' is nicer. Besides, look at the game I've got."

Her goat head is hangin' in a spruce, an' her bear robe is stretched on a frame by the tent. The elk is takin' up all the room in camp. I look, an' says to Sawback, "Hell, you just can't win."

He wags his head real doleful. "Tex," he says, "it's a woman's world."

Which now I figger it is.

Companions of the Bath
Dan McCowan

On a sunny afternoon in September, the while enjoying a bath in the outdoor hot-water pool at Radium in British Columbia, I watched a chipmunk busily employed gathering food for use in spring. In northern latitudes the nimble chipmunks hibernate the whole winter through and consequently require no food during the season of frost and snow. Awakening in April they then have recourse to the emergency rations so prudently laid away in the fall of the year. The scientific name of *Tamias*, a steward, one who has charge of supplies of food, is singularly appropriate to the chipmunk tribe whose autumnal hoarding is notable.

In this instance the seeds of grasses and of various kinds of alpine plants were eagerly harvested by the active little animal, the fodder being stowed in a secret granary amongst the limestone rocks above the pool. There was of course nothing unusual in the behaviour of this four-footed harvester until, halting momentarily in its gleaning, the creature ventured down the cliff side to the water's edge and drank what one might term a copious draught of the bubbling steaming liquid. Never before had I seen one of these animals quenching thirst from stream or lake and I wondered if by any chance this sagacious squirrel had found virtue in the hot springs at Radium and was actually "taking the waters."

Certainly he had found ideal living-quarters in the grottos by the thermal spring, alongside rushing Sinclair Creek. Abundance of berries and seeds in the neighbouring woods gave assurance of food and to spare. A steam-heated apartment with hot and cold running water available at all hours must surely have made this a most desirable country residence, but I was led to speculate as to whether or not such a lodging might attract other prospective tenants. Bats are not likely to seek sleeping accommodation in such a humid atmosphere but snakes would gladly huddle in the grateful warmth during the chill months of winter. There are no poisonous reptiles in the Canadian Rockies but considerable numbers of garter snakes habitually find refuge from frigid winter weather in natural-heated caves near the hot sulphur springs at Banff.

Some years ago I had the pleasure of meeting and photographing a Cinnamon bear who had spent the previous winter in one of these caves in the sulphur rock. A Cinnamon bear, be it understood, is not a distinct species but is simply a red-haired member of the Black bear tribe. When this particular animal denned up in late autumn his coat was rich chestnut in colour. Exposure for several months to sulphur fumes in his bedroom worked amazing transformation. He emerged in early April as a pronounced platinum blonde and so thorough was the bleach that I doubt if even his own mother would have recognized him.

At Vermillion Lake near Banff a spring of warm sulphur water forms a large pool which remains open throughout the winter. For some years, successive generations of a muskrat family built houses in and around this pond, doubtless finding life very pleasant where outdoors swimming could be enjoyed all the year long. Green feed there sprouted early in spring and during the summer a thick growth of tall reeds afforded shade from the hot sun and covert from keen-eyed hawks. In autumn the withered stalks yielded goodly supply of material for the building of houses. The well-developed roots of underwater plants provided ample food to the hungry rodents. Unfortunately for the rats, a mink discovered the settlement and wrought havoc amongst the inhabitants. The same warm spring water which otherwise was entirely beneficial, rendered the winter quarters vulnerable to this murderous water weasel and the luckless muskrats were undone.

Over this same area of warm water a number of bats flitted about in the twilight. To these flying animals the tepid pool was a natural incubator from which abundance of toothsome insect food emerged for months on end. Here also a pair of kingfishers was gratified in finding the open season for trout greatly extended. Once in Christmas week, when almost all other streams and lakes in the Rockies were padlocked by frost, I saw a small flock of Mallards swimming and feeding in this steaming pool whilst air temperatures were far below zero. I waited to see what would happen when one stepped out of the water on to the ice at the edge of the pond, thinking that it would immediately be frozen there. But nothing happened for — as I learned later — their feet are coated with some natural oily substance which prevents any such mishap.

Grizzly Country
Andy Russell

In 1961, guide and naturalist Andy Russell set out to make a movie on a subject that had been near and dear to him most of his life — grizzly bears. After an unsuccessful trip to the interior ranges of British Columbia, he decided to go looking for the animals in his backyard, the Rocky Mountain valleys just west of his southern Alberta foothills ranch. Travelling on horseback with wife, family, and a few friends, he found the grizzly and much more.

Upon arrival at the ranch immediate preparations for an extensive pack train trip went into action. Horses were rounded up, packs made up, and everything moved over the summit of the Divide at Akamina Pass, twenty miles to the southwest, to our old Sage Brush Camp — the jumping off point for many previous hunts with guests. The cook tent was pitched with one end of the ridgepole tied to a big pine — a grizzly's rubbing tree. From this primitive backscratcher there was a set of big tracks pressed into the grass and pine needles which led right through the tent.

My good friend Clarence Tillenius, one of the world's foremost wildlife artists, joined us at this camp. He was working on a commission to paint the dioramas for the big-game groups being set up in a new wing of the National Museum in Ottawa. Among these he was planning the background for a grizzly group and was most anxious to obtain a suitable setting close to the Alberta–British Columbia border in these colorful mountains.

Kay was with us as official cook, a most welcome addition to the crew. Naturally daughter Anne was with us, too, vibrating with the excitement of joining in our grizzly hunt. Our third son, John, joined us to guide two fourteen-year-old boys, Tom Rankin and Del Marting, from Cleveland, Ohio. I planned to use this active trio for scouts to cover the high country and also to provide fresh trout for our camp.

Almost immediately more grizzly sign was found. About a mile downvalley from camp there was a mineral spring at the site of the old oil prospect hole drilled in 1908. The strong-smelling sulphur water is a great attractor of all kinds of big game — so desirable that I have seen moose wade Akamina Creek to drink from it. Our horses were attracted to it, too, and the morning following our arrival Dick found them near this spring. On the way back to camp he spotted the place where a grizzly had ambushed sheep and goats. . . .

Traveling high country by pack train successfully requires some important features of terrain. Each camp location must above all have plenty of feed for the horses plus shelter, wood, and water for the tents. Because the timberline country was just emerging from the winter snow, our initial reconnaissance was concerned with finding these in good bear country.

My journal for July 7, 1961, reads:

Clarence, Dick, Charlie, and I rode up Grizzly Gulch this morning toward Starvation Pass. The trail through the heavy timber of the lower valley was wet and boggy. Although fallen trees had to be chopped out of the way in several places, we managed to get

255

through to the foot of the pass without undue difficulty. Fresh grizzly tracks were seen in several places along the trail. The open face of the pass was still deep in snow in many places, but the drifts were hard enough to carry our horses. We topped out on the summit about noon to find the basin on the southern exposure almost free of snow with a good cover of new grass on the meadows. The alpine parks were a vivid green and just coming into bloom. There were the tracks of a big bull moose crossing the pass. While we ate lunch, we located seven goats feeding on the shelves below the glacier on the face of Sawtooth. The Starvation Lakes were free of ice. Investigation of my old hunting campsite revealed our tent poles in good shape where they had been stacked on end under the big trees. Arrived back in camp at 8:30 p.m. to sit down to a wonderful dinner: soup, baked ham, boiled potatoes, carrots and peas, canned peaches and cream, along with plenty of hot tea. Although at home on the ranch this would be ordinary, here in the mountains it was a delicious feast.

We moved camp the following day. From the tents we could look out on the north face of Sawtooth Peak, dropping an almost sheer four thousand feet to the emerald-blue jewels that were the Starvation Lakes far below. Our hanging basin was surrounded by jagged peaks. A clear stream ran merrily past the cook tent. Grassy, terraced benches afforded plenty of feed for the horses, and by throwing a couple of logs across a narrow place in the trail on the pass, we had them effectively fenced into the basin.

Next morning we shouldered camera packs and tripods to set out toward the razorback ridge rimming the basin to the south. We went along a broad shelf among feathery larches, past pocketed meadows unfolding to some of the most rugged mountain country in the world.

These mountains are very colorful, shades from brilliant yellow and ochre to rich, deep rose. Some of this color comes from rock lichen painting the stones brilliant Indian yellow and orange in curious, maplike formations. The softer shades are in the rock itself — sedimentary rock laid down as silt in the bottom of a great ocean when the world was young. After these waters receded, the crust of the earth buckled in a great upheaval of overthrusts, anticlines, synclines, and faults, and thus the mountain ranges were born. Resulting pressures and great heat brought about metamorphic changes shown in great variation of color. As proof of its origin, we often found the stone matrix of ripple marks made by the lapping wavelets of silty beaches. Collectively it was a color photographers' dream come true.

At every step our boots crushed brilliant alpine blooms. Glacier lilies, spring beauty, Indian paintbrush, alpine gentian, saxifrage, heliotrope, rosewort, and forget-me-nots blended with a host of others into natural rock gardens through which fountains of clear water played. Our trail led us up over rocky ledges, past a roaring waterfall, into a high basin just beginning to clear of winter snow. Here we nearly stepped on a mother rock ptarmigan almost invisible against her background in summer plumage. She was sitting on two fluffy, newly hatched chicks. We promptly named this place Ptarmigan Valley.

The face under the rim back of this basin was a semicircular wall fifteen hundred feet high broken only by a narrow ledge like a slightly winding staircase without a hand rail. A heavy goat trail led us up onto the foot of this. The ledge was littered with goat sign, and in one spot we found the week-old track of a grizzly. This was a regular thoroughfare used by these high climbers to cross the ridge. At the top of the rim we squeezed through a narrow crack in the rock and came out on another broad ledge overlooking a vast sweep of country beyond.

Not wishing to clutter this place with our scent, we sat down with our glasses to watch. Below us in the middle of the valley stood the Nunnatuk, a spectacular monument of rock standing like a giant tombstone a thousand feet high where it was carved by a passing glacier long ago. Across from us loomed the great square bulk of the Ball Park. At our level near its flat top, we could see the natural amphitheater lined with short alpine herbage looking like a well-kept lawn. This natural bowl, from which the mountain got its name, is big enough to seat thousands of spectators overlooking the flat bottom, where a ball game could be played. At our feet and a bit to the right we looked out through the great open gate of an unnamed pass at the majestic Kintla and Kinnerly Peaks of northern Glacier National Park across the International Border in Montana.

All of this wild and beautiful country full of big game in the high alplands at this time of year. Almost immediately we saw seven large mule deer bucks lying placidly chewing their cuds among gardens trapped between lingering snowdrifts directly below. Farther down the valley by the Nunnatuk five bull elk loafed on a green meadow under the spreading limbs of alpine larches. Looking over my shoulder, I found myself gazing into the whiskery features of a mountain billy goat. He was sprawled indolently on a narrow ledge under an overhang to one side of the notch in which we sat, and he was not

257

sufficiently alarmed by the sight of us to bother getting to his feet. If we were to find grizzlies in the Rockies of southeast British Columbia, this was the place. While Clarence sketched, the boys and I combed the country with our glasses looking for bear, but none appeared.

Toward evening the giant stage of the mountains to the west was obscured by a lowering curtain of black clouds, which was our cue to come down off the rim in a hurry as thunder growled along the ridges. We made the shelter of camp barely in time to escape a downpour of rain and sleet accompanied by terrific explosions of thunder with lightning leaping and crackling overhead. John, Tom, and Del had come up from the lakes just minutes ahead of us with a fine catch of trout. We sat down to a feed fit for kings while rain drummed and roared on the cook tent roof.

All night long the thunderheads marched across the mountains. Sometimes the tents were lit for minutes on end by flickering blue-white lightning flashes in a crazy dance among the peaks. Kay and I watched the pyrotechnical display of nature gone wild through the open flaps of our tent. It was like trying to sleep during an intensive artillery barrage. It was a mountain show to put a man in his proper perspective. Sometimes the concussion of giant explosions shook the solid rock beneath camp. There would be a simultaneous flash and a sharp snap followed instantly by an earsplitting explosion, and then the long, heavy, rolling echoes cannonading through cliffs and canyons — a mad symphony of fire and giant drums. It was the beginning of a long stretch of such weather that was to harass us for the entire trip.

But next morning the sun broke through the clouds, bright and clear, to light up a bejewelled world glistening with dripping water. Across the canyon below the glacier twenty-one goats fed placidly on the hanging meadows among the cliffs. The stream draining the glacier ice was swollen, and after a short precipitous gambol down over the ledges it plunged over the lip of a cliff. There it played gracefully, a natural veil of crystal drops lifting and blowing in the wind, undulating, sometimes almost disappearing and then steadying to form a shining curtain falling into the depths far below. It was hard even to imagine the conditions those goats had endured during the night on that exposed face, but these phlegmatic animals showed no effect other than being washed snow white.

While John and his friends scouted the mountain ridges, we went back repeatedly to our lookout point above the alplands by the Nunnatuk to watch for a grizzly. Sometimes we froze on our lofty perch in chilly winds. More than once thunderstorms drove us half-drowned for cover. We luxuriated in the sunny spells when the mountains slept peacefully under sailing clouds.

We used every opportunity to film various sidelights to the story, for the grizzly has many associates. There were tiny, fast-moving pikas busily scurrying among the rocks, busily putting up hay for the winter months. We caught the beautifully marked, golden mantled ground squirrels in our lenses and recorded the rock ptarmigan. For a full day and a half we were in the midst of a great migrating river of monarch butterflies — millions upon uncounted millions of these handsome insects all flying in a southwesterly direction along the face of the mountain. We could not help wondering how far they had come and where they were going.

Day after day went by with our watching unrewarded by the sight of a grizzly. Clarence sketched continuously. We envied him a bit, for he could capture the changing moods of the mountains on his canvas, and when a scene particularly appealed to him, he could quickly create a burly grizzly standing in spectacular pose. Our films would not respond to things we had seen in the past.

Then one morning our luck began to change. Upon climbing up onto our ledge, we immediately spotted a buck deer lying dead on the edge of a snowdrift below. Two well-fed coyotes moved around the carcass. We guessed that they had either made the kill or had hijacked it from a cougar. If the smell of venison rapidly getting high in the warm sun caught the nose of a grizzly, we were due to see our jinx broken.

Two more full days went by, and still no grizzly appeared. We were beginning to feel a bit edgy, for time was running out. Almost two months had passed since we had started our hunt, and as yet we still had to shoot a single picture of a grizzly. Our supplies were running low.

The third morning following our discovery of the kill dawned clear as crystal. The air was sharp and cool, heralding an ideal day in the high country. As we checked the camera packs after an early breakfast, I had a strong hunch that something was about to break for us, and I led out along our trail feeling lighthearted.

My premonition was a good one, for when we looked down off the rim, the buck carcass was gone. Our binoculars revealed big dirty grizzly tracks crisscrossing the snowdrifts. Then I spotted a velvet-covered antler sticking up out of a familiar-looking pile of fresh-dug rubble.

Dick hissed softly through his teeth and pointed just as a fine, big, dark-colored silvertip grizzly appeared directly below coming out from under an intervening bulge of the mountain. He stood at the top of a drift swinging his big snout into the wind, and then he sat down on his broad rump and slid happily down the steep-pitched snow. Our cameras fairly leaped from the packs onto the big tripods.

The bear went down almost to the jagged rocks at the foot of the drift, then he stood up and set his claws and turned in a shower of slush. By the time I got my lens on him, he was climbing back up the coarse talus slope. The sun was slightly in front of us, and its reflections off the snow patches made for tricky exposures. The wind was eddying, so we dared not try to get closer.

While the grizzly veered across a strip of talus, I followed him with my telephoto lens out onto another snowdrift. We kept both cameras trained on him, hoping for another slide, but instead he climbed up to a hole just under the cliffs where the snow had melted away from the rock and began to roll in it. The heat was bothering him, for he subsided into this cool niche on his back with all four feet sticking up. He presented a ludicrous contrast to the usual picture of a grizzly, and apart from his paws and nose we saw little to record.

Meanwhile the sun climbed higher to beat directly against the face of the mountain until it was like a reflector oven. Then the two coyotes showed up, coming across the pass at a business-like trot toward their hijacked booty. When they came under the grizzly's cache in a patch of shintangle brush, they set up a terrific yapping and yowling that sounded more like six coyotes than two. The grizzly jerked himself into a sitting position with his ears cocked. Perhaps this noisy addition to discomfort from the heat was a bit too much to stand, for he suddenly erupted from his snow bath and tore diagonally down the patchwork of snowdrifts at a long angle toward the Nunnatuk. Taking jumps yards long, with the snow leaping in showers over his back every time his feet came down, he covered at least a mile in short minutes and finally disappeared into the heavy timber far down the valley. Even though the buck carcass was buried beyond their reach, the coyotes were apparently delighted at this precipitous exodus of the robber baron, for they proceeded to celebrate his departure by gamboling like pups, chasing their tails and each other, rolling and romping in the snow.

Although we waited until sundown, the bear failed to reappear. The remains of the deer could not last long under this combined attention, so I planned to come back very early the following morning. Our camp grub supplies were almost gone, and it was necessary to move out next day.

Before dawn I was back on the mountain, climbing fast, and I reached the rim just as the sun was tinting a few high puffs of cloud over the peaks a pale pink. There was no sign of the grizzly, but as usual the magic of this moment was irresistible, and I stood entranced. Like the soft playing of distant strings the sky lit to a pale blue and the clouds to pink and rose. Then the tempo picked up as the waking light softly fingered the tops of the tallest mountains, turning them to deep rose and gold. One by one the lesser peaks joined in, until the sun leaped over the horizon in a great crashing climax. I stood, very small, in the royal box overlooking the great stage. The hush was broken by the long howl of a coyote from somewhere away down the far side of the pass. Then from the black shadow in the lee of an old moraine stepped the grizzly.

Quickly screwing the camera down solid on the head of the tripod, I shouldered it and began climbing down an inclining ledge toward the bear. Meanwhile the grizzly climbed up and began digging out his cache. The morning thermals were blowing up and with a minimum of luck would allow me within easy range. Then my ledge began giving trouble by dividing into a series of shallow, rubble-strewn steps, and it was only with the utmost care not to dislodge loose stuff that I was able to reach a buttress at the foot of the cliffs directly above the bear. A look through the long lens showed him feeding hungrily.

The camera had just begun to hum softly when the coyotes came drifting like gray ghosts through the rocks. The instant they came upwind, the grizzly picked up their scent and was alert. When one of the pair came over a rise of ground about twenty-five yards in front of him, the grizzly left off feeding and stalked toward the coyote at a slow walk. The coyote edged away, keeping just out of rushing range and leading the grizzly into a patch of tangled scrub firs. While the bear was thus being tolled from his cache, the other coyote slipped around behind him to steal a feed. It was a fine example of intelligent teamwork.

But this grizzly was far from stupid and seemed to realize that he was being outsmarted. He swung away from the decoy and circled back against the wind toward the kill. The feeding coyote took no chances and drifted away to join its mate. The bear was using his nose and not his eyes, for he apparently thought the coyote was still

261

at the kill. Pussyfooting up to within twenty yards, he suddenly charged in a flash of movement to pounce on it, ready to annihilate the cheeky thief. For a few moments he stood on top of his plunder like a carving in stone, while the coyotes edged closer and closer, trying to toll him away again. But the bear was now wise to their trick and would not be moved. He went back to his feeding finally, as though coyotes no longer existed on the face of the earth.

Finishing his breakfast while the coyotes sat forlornly on a nearby drift like two disconsolate dogs, the grizzly proceeded to rebury the carcass. This was a drawn-out and very thorough process that entailed heaping hundreds of pounds of earth and rock over the remains of the deer. Using his front paws like shovels, the bear built a mound over it until the whole cache was surrounded by a sort of moat.

Then as though satisfied with a job well done, the grizzly walked out on a snowdrift to lay down and roll, scrub his face and head in the snow with obvious enjoyment. While doing this, he suddenly began to slide and went several yards on his back before rolling back up on his feet. Without another glance at the pestering coyotes, he strode off downvalley in the grand manner — proud and very dignified — toward the cool timber.

As he left, the last of four hundred feet of film ran through the camera. Knowing a charged and prolonged excitement like nothing ever experienced while hunting with the rifle, I shouldered the tripod and camera to start the long climb back to camp and breakfast. Elation made my feet light, for the first episode of grizzly life was "in the can."

Too Hot to Sleep
Sid Marty

He was sleeping when bear
came down from the mountain
by the water trap
after cleaning the screen
of branches and gravel

He fell asleep, a hot june morning

above Wapta Lake, the Kicking Horse Pass
When Muskwa came down without a sound
and snuffed at his jeans

Who's this asleep on my mountain?

It's my friend Birnie asleep I said
(in my head)
I didn't hear you coming bear
I was dozing, I looked up
and there you were

You never know said Bear
just where the wind will lead me
when I'll be around
or what beat I'm hunting on

and sniffed at Birnie's collar
at his ear, which he licked tentatively
causing Birnie to moan softly

Nothing doing here he said, nothing doing

"We were just going bear," I said quietly
edging backwards

Don't move too quickly will you, said Bear
when you move, or better still
don't move at all

Are you here often, are you coming again?
he asked, flipping over a stone
licking delicately the underside
"No," I said. good he said, that's good.

I just came down from the pass
the wind blowing up my nose
to see who was sleeping on my mountain
he said, and sniffed at Birnie's armpit
Whoosh   whoosh he snorted

and turned away, clattered down the creek

popping his teeth, his hackles up
Went out of sight
around the shoulder of Mount Hector

as Birnie woke up rubbing his eyes
"Too hot to sleep he said." Yeah.

Paradise Lost?
Valerius Geist

We were progressing on our hands and knees. I had planned to approach the sheep from above in order to obtain some photos. After all, this strategy had worked with Stone's sheep, and it should work with bighorns. Karli, my brother-in-law, was sweating from the strenuous exercise, and so was I. A moment earlier we had reached a little rock platform, and I had peered across only to discover the ewes and two big rams peering back at us. The sheep were about 150 yards away. I slowly sank back behind the rock and paused, wondering what to do. We had been discovered. Maybe the sheep would run; maybe they would stay. I decided to creep on. We had barely begun to advance when a rumble erupted above us. Before I could lift my head, the rumble had changed to a drumbeat of hooves, swirling dust, and clanking stones, and seconds later we were engulfed in a band of bighorn sheep. We crouched on our hands and knees looking up; they stood, taller than we, looking down. We appeared — pardon the expression — sheepish, to say the least, not knowing whether we were dreaming or hallucinating. As the dust began to settle, another roll of hoof beats sounded, and two big rams burst through the females into sight before us. There we were, face to face with the legendary creature of the wild and towering Canadian Rockies — the bighorn ram. But this "legend" was flesh and blood and was breathing into our faces, since our noses were only a foot apart.

When I raised my hand the "legend" licked it, while another "legend" pulled my parka with its mouth. We stood in their midst as they gazed at us and pressed closer. I tried to think of a parallel to this occurrence, or for some clue to an appropriate action, but there simply was no precedent. Nothing I had learned previously equipped me for this surprise. Mountain sheep were not supposed to act like this. I had stumbled onto another "accident."

Much of my research has been a progression of accidents. To someone blessed with the asset of an orderly mind, it would be intolerable to have his plans dissolve in a string of calamities. But then, for research in the field in Canada's western mountains where unpredictable weather patterns, sparse animal populations, and highly seasonal events are customary, an orderly mind and polished research plans are, at best, a doubtful asset. One must learn to take advantage of the unexpected and let plans go down the drain without shedding too many tears. The best course is to make every calamity an asset.

The puzzle of the tame sheep had a perfectly rational explanation — as we discovered later. For fourteen years prior to my arrival at Banff National Park, a park warden, Ernie Stenton, had tamed and tagged a group of sheep at Lake Minnewanka. In early summer, shortly after lambing, the animals crave salt, and they had learned that this treat could be had close to Warden Stenton's station. Soon they were licking salt out of his hand and — while they were licking — he clipped small metal tags onto their ears. Stenton was mainly interested in learning if his sheep went beyond the park boundary where they might fall victim to hunters. Over the years a few rams were shot, but there were so few that Stenton concluded, correctly, that his sheep were confined mainly to the park. Some hikers or exploration parties brought back word of tagged sheep approaching them, but a systematic search for the animals had not been undertaken up to the time of my arrival, and I had no warning that the Palliser sheep were the very ones tagged by Stenton.

In earlier years, Stenton stood in rivalry with another warden, Green, who pre-empted the right to tag sheep above the Vermillion Lakes where the Trans-Canada Highway now runs. Since Green used green ear tags and Stenton used red ones, it soon became evident that they were tagging different groups of sheep. A third group at Aylmer Pass was kept under close watch by another old gentleman, Norman Tithrington, who for seventeen years occupied the Aylmer lookout tower each summer. When Tithrington was not watching sheep (for which he provided a salt block at the foot of the tower) he was spotting for boats putting out illegal set lines on the lake below, or for parties making an illegal campfire in a hidden bay during the preseason, or for couples making legal love on the beaches. Nothing escaped his eyes and telescope. Tithrington reported his observations vividly to his friend Ernie over the wireless — to the mirth of other operators on the same frequency and to the dismay of Department of Transport supervisors of radio.

Tithrington had fallen in love with the sheep and kept daily counts on them. He also observed cougars each summer and is the only individual I know who saw a cougar stalk and kill a young bighorn ram. The Aylmer sheep were a group quite separate from the Palliser group, even though they lived on different sides of the same mountain, and they were not quite as tame as those tagged by Stenton. They tolerated humans well, though. Tithrington had tried his hand at tagging, but a ewe had clipped him across the hand with her horns, and the old fellow declined any closer contact thereafter. Thus, when I arrived in Banff National Park after my Stone's sheep study, a group of enthusiastic amateurs had long known something professional zoologists were not quite conscious of: namely, that wild, unhunted animals can get along with man in a fashion reminiscent of the Biblical paradise.

In retrospect it is hard to understand why such insight had not come to me earlier, although I was not alone in my mental blindness. I had spent hours close to Stone's sheep, dressed in white coveralls and pretending to be a mountain goat; I had tamed whisky jacks and a weasel at my cabin; I had seen tourists with tamed mountain sheep along the Trans-Canada Highway in Banff. Yet we did not get the message the animals were shouting at us. It was this group of bighorn sheep — far away from tourists and out of contact with the wardens, galloping up to us and surrounding us — that made me see the obvious for the first time. In the years following I got to know them well and with their help I tamed others — in the process gaining a deeper insight into the habits of this beautiful animal.

Have you ever sat on a mountainside and observed a ram graze below you, watched the ram finish feeding, then look up and come to you, paw a bed that sends the dust and pebbles striking your legs, and then lie down beside you? There you sit, the cunning hunter and the cunning prey, while the wind plays gently with your hair, and his heavy eyes blink, ready for a little nap. The clouds move past overhead and their shadows play in the valley, the grasses rustle in the breeze, and the eagle soars past along the slope below both of you. The creature resting beside you is as free and wild as the mountains that nourish it. It can choose to leave you, but it does not. For the moment, it prefers your company.

I well remember the day when Number 48 returned after a long winter of absence. Number 48 was a five-year-old ram and a particularly trusting type. He disappeared prior to the rut, and I wondered what had happened to him. In the previous spring he had limped a little, and I speculated that perhaps his leg ailment had returned and finished him. So I often wondered if I would see him again in spring.

One evening in May I saw him. There was no doubt: it *was* 48, and at a distance he appeared to be quite well. Since dusk had fallen, I postponed climbing to him till the following morning. Early the next day I began the ascent, although I could not see him anywhere. "He must be *somewhere*, though," I thought, and I searched all morning in vain. Then I climbed across the range to its precipitous opposite side and continued my search. Suddenly I spied a lone sheep far away across many gorges and snowfields, but so far away I could identify the figure only as a ram in my field glasses. The sheep was feeding. I waited until it raised its head, then I began waving my arms to attract its attention. The sheep paused, only momentarily, and then it came — dashing at a full run across scree slopes and gorges, across cliffs and snowfields. The dust flew, the stones rolled, and the snow splattered as it ran. Ever larger grew its image until, frolicking and bouncing, the young ram descended the slope and slid to a halt in front of me amid a cloud of dust and rolling stones. His breathing was heavy, his nostrils flared, and those big eyes glistened. It was, indeed, little 48.

I gave him what he wanted most, a bit of salt. But, even after I had signaled that no more was forthcoming, he made no move to leave me. Together we climbed through the cliffs to the southern side of the range, where I eventually left him with a group of other sheep. His leg had healed well — and yet it was the last spring I saw little 48. He vanished during summer with the other sheep and never appeared again. I could not know whether a coyote had killed him, or a hunter at the distant boundary, or a poacher inside the park.

These sheep that trusted man gave me opportunity to study at close range much that I had previously seen at long distance, and they allowed me to gain insights that only work with free-living, yet tame, animals allows. Some of my concerns were rather mundane, such as checking if chronological age, as determined from dates of tagging, did coincide with the age rings on the horns. It did. I could demonstrate to my satisfaction that the sheep were exceedingly loyal to their seasonal home ranges and reappeared at the same seasons each year in the very same places. I could show that females tagged in the Palliser female group stayed in the Palliser female group, while rams moved between the female groups. Thus, the female sheep in a group were largely related by maternal descent.

The scientific discoveries pale, however, beside the recollection of the individuals I came to know for a few years of their short lives. Some were shy individuals who waited a long time before they decided to come to me. Such a one was ram 616, who took about a year to make up his mind. He was one of the few sheep whose body was found after death. His floating body was picked up in Lake Minnewanka where it must have been deposited by the swift waters of the Cascade River which 616 crossed in the spring on his return to the Palliser Range. Apparently he was drowned while attempting to cross the swollen, rapid river.

Others, in particular the females, became exceedingly tame, and stuck their noses into everything — my pockets, my rucksack, my camera lenses, and even my cameras if I had to change film. Soon I learned to change film while sitting in a tree since, up there, the eager crowd could not reach me. One young ram pulled a camera from my rucksack and dropped it down the mountainside. I recovered the camera's remains 300 yards below. The sheep allowed me to pluck ticks from their withers, and they went out of their way to stay with me. This gave me my first opportunity to observe how sheep search. I had anticipated that, if I ran off, they would seek for me where I had been last. This, however, they did not do. Instead, they searched on the basis of a priori expectations, or hypothesis. They always sought first where I *should* have been, had I continued in a *straight line*. Failing to find me, they searched against the wind. If this also failed, they reverted sometimes to tracking me.

It was soon after my initial surprise over their search methods that their significance became clear. Of course, it would be highly adaptive to track something mentally; usually this object would be a wolf or coyote. On such occasions it is pertinent indeed for a sheep to anticipate the movement of the predator. If the predator *fails* to appear where expected and cannot be found, it is obviously time to flee. The predator may be stalking by this time. As long as he is in sight, all is well, and young rams in particular may follow wolves on the uphill side for some distance. As long as sheep are on the uphill side of wolves, many will stand and observe the predator, even if it is only a dozen paces away.

My next surprise came when I discovered that, if I climbed a tree out of sight of sheep, they would fail to discover me even though I sat close enough above ground to touch them. It appeared that once I was in a tree, I became somehow unrecognizable. However, if I climbed a tree in their sight they clustered around the base for a while, looked at me, and then returned to grazing. I wonder to this day if a mountain lion maintains an advantage over sheep simply by sitting in a tree.

After a couple of years the females performed another maneuver which surprised me. My usual manner of breaking contact with the sheep was to turn suddenly from the group and run downhill into the timber. The animals generally stood watching me, and, by the time they had decided to follow, I was usually at the timber's edge and soon out of their sight. Then one day a female sprinted after me, overtook me, and then pressed her body against mine, pushing me off course, away from the timber. This is identical to the behaviour used by lambs to stop their mothers in order to suckle. Here an adult, even old, female was using this method apparently in an attempt to hold me back — a rational act, since I did carry salt, which the animals craved.

The craving for salt, particularly in spring, is quite understandable. During winter the skeleton of wild sheep probably grows thin, light, and porous, just as did those of domestic sheep or reindeer where this subject was investigated. During winter, the mineral content of the forage is apparently quite insufficient, and the animal attacks its own skeleton to satisfy its metabolic needs, as well as to grow the skeleton of the lamb inside the uterus. Shortly after the lamb's birth, the female must provide many minerals in the milk, and again she attacks her skeleton. Only after lactation do females rebuild their skeletons in readiness for the next winter. Hence, the highest demand for minerals comes in the spring and early summer, and sheep then flock to salt licks. So do other big-game animals, in particular mountain goats.

While the craving for salt is great, it is not so great as to cause sheep to commit acts dangerous to themselves. They would not, for instance, cross deep, loose snow in a gorge in order to reach me. They would come at once, however, if I plowed a trail for them. Then they would navigate the deepest snow — just so long as I went first. If an avalanche descended and left hard-packed snow in its path, the sheep used the avalanche paths like a highway for their travels. If the snow grew soft, one could see at close distance how they placed their feet — namely, in a fashion so that both the hooves and the dewclaws were almost flat on the snow surface. Simultaneously they spread their legs. In very deep, loose snow the animals preferred to jump, which is, of course, a difficult and wasteful way to move.

On the whole the sheep regarded me as a two-legged salt-lick, as a curiosity, but not as one of their own. This was fortunate. In sheep society, subordinates have the prerogative to be aggressive, and had I belonged to their pecking order, I would have been butted to a pulp. There is no way that a human body could accept the crushing blows delivered by bighorn rams. Hence, it was fortunate for me that I was excluded from their social hierarchies. Yet, attacks did occur.

The first ram to attack me was one I had known for two years, and it came as a surprise. During a cold day in late November I ascended a steep slope, well covered with fresh tracks of rutting sheep. No animals were in sight, and I expected to find them somewhere on the other side of the mountain. On the top of the slope was a tiny plateau, and when I reached it I was confronted by about 40 sheep, including a half-dozen large, rutting rams. They came to me at once.

The purpose of my climb was to check on the tags of ewes, checking out those that had been on the range as well as searching for new animals. I was quickly surrounded by the animals, and my task, reading small metal tags partially covered by hair on sheep's ears, became very difficult. The big rams, each one of which I knew anyway, pressed around, making it difficult for me to get at the females. The big boys wanted their bit of salt and grew noticeably impatient. My efforts were in vain. I could scarcely remain upright as forty sheep pushed, forcing me downhill. The animals were rather cheeky, which they always are in big bunches. In small groups, or in pairs, sheep are quite careful, even cautious. But give them a mob, and they grow bold. These were rutting sheep, and they were terribly brave. There was nothing to gain by staying further, so I turned and in long jumps hurled myself down the steep slope. Suddenly, about four jumps from the sheep, something solid hit my pack-board. Glancing over my shoulder, I saw one of the large rams, Crooked Horn, with his head lowered to the ground. He had rushed me and hit a glancing blow at the parka trailing behind me, thereby hitting my pack-board. I stopped, and at once Crooked Horn was confronting me — face to face. Taking a little piece of salt from my pocket, I let him lick — a grave mistake as I soon realized. I had rewarded him for charging and butting me. The reason I was undamaged, thus far, was due to a sheep's habit of aiming a *downward* blow at a *specific* part of its opponent. The specific part is usually that closest to the sheep — in my case the pack-board.

Again I turned and ran off, and again Crooked Horn charged and hit my flying parka and pack-board. This was not funny! I had still a quarter mile to go to the timber, and with a big, rutting ram blasting me all the way I could expect not to make it. The moment the ram aimed poorly he would probably wrap me around his horns, or he could cut me deeply with one of his broken horn tips. At that point I realized that my piece of salt was just large enough to place it into the ram's mouth sideways, meaning he would be unable to spit it out for a few minutes. It worked. Crooked Horn stood still, completely absorbed in sucking on his "candy." I departed — in haste.

In later years, Crooked Horn showed that he had learned his lesson well. A number of times he rose against me, but I had also learned a trick or two. First, a ram cannot clash uphill effectively. Hence, I stayed uphill from him. Second, I faced him in a firm nononsense fashion — even though, inwardly, I was not full of confidence. If I walked toward him he would noticeably lose assurance and hesitate, then turn, glance back at me, and begin feeding. If he rose against me, I stood and looked down on him, and he dropped down on his legs.

How well these rams noted if someone were afraid of them I saw when a friend of mine first visited them. He was clearly ambivalent as the big rams came closer. Within minutes one ram lurched forward and butted him. A year later he confronted Crooked Horn who proceeded to crash into him, knocking him flat on the ground. Clearly these big animals can be dangerous, though minimally so to someone unafraid of them.

Crooked Horn did me a number of favors, however. Twice I acquainted colleagues with my work by taking them on the sheep ranges. Each of these colleagues was a passionate hunter. Keeping this point well in mind, I informed them of the terribly dangerous ram that roamed the mountains who took out his vengeance on people on sight. Each time Crooked Horn did me the favor of appearing, and each time, as soon as he spotted us, he came at a run from about two hundred yards away. A big ram approaching at full blast is a sight that causes anxious moments in the hearts of even brave men. When Crooked Horn was about 150 yards away, I yelled "It's him! It's him!" What splendid results! My pals took to their heels, lickety-split, down the mountain. What a sight it was to see a dedicated hunter running as hard as possible from a fine bighorn ram.

One of the dangers in the mountains in late winter is the possibility of a fall on a steep snowpack on a mountainside. At that season the snow melts a little each day and freezes hard at night, forming an impenetrable snowpack that may have not only an ice crust on

271

top but an ice crust on the bottom as well. I had not realized how dangerous a fall on a steep slope could be till I found a ram just after he had suffered the mishap. The ram had slipped on the hard crust and rolled downhill, as the trail revealed. While I did not witness his fall, I arrived shortly after and could see his trail.

I followed this track with my binoculars and saw the sheep lying in the avalanche gorge below. Believing him to be dead, I took the camera and commenced the hour-long climb to the fallen animal. It had rolled down a good four hundred yards before hitting the avalanche gorge.

When I arrived beside the big ram and began to set up the camera tripod, he suddenly flailed weakly with his front legs. At once I glanced at his head. The ram's eyes were open and alert; his tongue darted weakly in and out of his mouth. Far from death, the poor animal was alive but badly paralyzed. In fact, both his neck and back were broken, as the autopsy shortly revealed. To judge from the tracks, he must have rolled over and over again coming downhill, gathering speed with each foot of descent. It was a wonder and a tribute to the tough bodies of bighorns that he was not killed at once. I plunged a knife into his heart and cut short his suffering. Other rams were less fortunate.

One ram apparently walked on a snowdrift beneath a telephone line that ran to a distant fire lookout. The animal caught its horn in the wire; next spring the wardens removed its lifeless body hanging several feet above ground from the wire.

Old Tithrington saw a young ram walk out on a snow cornice. Suddenly the cornice caved in, and the young ram sank into his white grave. I saw several rams and ewes return with broken legs. How these legs were broken I shall never know. Some healed, to give the sheep a clubfoot and a limp; but other sheep disappeared after their mishaps, never to be seen again.

In one case a young, lamb-leading female broke her hind leg. For days she lay in one spot while her lamb tried in vain to get her up so he could suckle. The little fellow stole short suckles from other ewes while they fed their own lambs and was frequently punished for it with severe butts, for a ewe rejects all but her own offspring. Yet the lamb only rose to try again. The female did finally rise and feed, but I soon lost sight of her. Several weeks later I saw her again with her poorly grown bedraggled lamb. She had become little more than skin and bones and limped pitifully, but her leg was well along in healing. I saw her for a few more days, and never again thereafter. Nor do I know what happened to her lamb.

Another female had a clubfoot and was blind in one eye. She was butted around pitifully by other females, but she hung on to life. For the last two years of her difficult life I made periodic contact with her. She had no lambs of her own but was a favorite "aunty" for lambs to cluster around. In spring, when the other females were off lambing, she was followed closely by a group of yearlings wherever she went. I still don't know why this ewe (or other old girls) attracted lambs, causing them to gather around. In spring these old ladies perform a very real service to sheep society by acting as focal points for the motherless youngsters to group around, while the adult females lambed in hiding. One of these old girls even licked lambs — a most unusual behavior; I saw her bounce and frolic through the cliffs followed by a stream of frolicking youngsters, and I saw her turn and call after departing yearlings. Could it be that, barren as they are, these old females somehow begin to "mother" the youngsters that have just broken contact with their dams? The period when old barren females act as a focal point for the yearling sheep is very short, however — a couple of weeks more or less. Then the first females with the newborn young return, and the yearlings begin following them, deserting the old ladies. Oh, how fascinating the new little lambs were to the old ladies and the yearlings alike.

During my daily association with the bighorns it began to dawn on me slowly, ever so slowly, that maybe paradise had not been lost after all but only mislaid.

When I Joined the Outfit
Sid Marty

When I joined the outfit
they issued me
a 30-30 lever action rifle
20 rusty bullets, binoculars
a saddle and a bridle

With two old
but foolkilling horses

Death of a Warden

And a log house
in which I found
a package of noodle soup
three Hudson's Bay blankets
and no maps
to tell me where to begin

The house was where
the roads stopped and
when I joined the outfit
they gave me

400 square miles
of rivers, lakes
glaciers, mountains

The key to all the gates
They said Lock them all
behind you, I

Had time to travel in
peace of mind

Death of a Warden
Dale Zieroth

In the mountains, blue on blue and
full of blackflies, a young warden
is killed by his horse
kicked hard as iron on flesh — just once, and then the horse
spooks away

he is down
and slowly the world goes by
like his thoughts on their way . . .

but the pain! and the goddam

horse and the eye-jumping
taste after taste coming up but
no sound in my mouth
these fingers gone straight stiff like this and blood
pumping, pumping
I can't ride this, I can't ride this
it's eating out my head, all this pain
like blue light inside my veins, I am busted
open like a thing stepped on in rain
I am puking myself up
it hooks me all the way out
it's passing and it's
passing

I've got to stand, look
up to the valley where the world begins and so
this is how it looks when it ends — that peak
caught in the sky, a curl of cloud, all earth
sloping to the river and I am
no longer young but like
the river as it goes past
as all things that are young and green
go past
The sun in the west, already?
It keeps piercing its way through,
winter into spring,
one, two, twenty-five years through and into
the season of the catkin
the time of the mating of the wild duck
when the sun returns to heat the stones and flow over
onto the green ground and the dusty boots
of wandering men
when peace come up through our feet
knowledge of the paths
leads us to the smell of a lake

but the pain and the damn
horse and all the careful how-to moves
failing me now
in clear sky day and everyone else has
the ordinary and I roll in the dirt

275

and why?
and why now lord is nothing like the ways
we die, horse and chrome and
murder and war and plutonium death
the wary wrong is here
under this spruce, looking out, and my blood
bubbles inside me like a call of crow
for even at the edge of the mountain
we are not safe: whatever it is that kills us
kills us here
Call it names but
ungraspable death is here to stay, call it
horse, it's just another word for the death that
makes the words break down and I can't find
the solid life in me
We are all crippled anyway
information like cancer out of control, men and women leaving
men and women, children out of control
those whom we pledge our lives to
enter the work force
change
        limp into bed
and who we are raised to be
is no longer required and all the same
I am down

but still it is true
the tree has a similar complaint
the fish and the thrush, each green moment
dissolves into dust and I remember
we are born of the sun, we are
the earth and the sun mixed and the
sun stopped by the rock
and the rock that rose up in the clear air to think

if only I could be that quiet
would it be that hard to reach out here
open the door into death
see the power that
adds and subtracts from us all
I would not be afraid to touch it here

(this blood on my mouth
the smell of the dirt so near)
like these stones in the sun
I would stroke it on the cheek, I would guess
here is common ground

*

He turns into the fetal pain,
the home of blood and flies, the hole
as he waits for the other wardens
to pull in
the riderless horse, he is down and the jays come
dropping down beside him with a fluff
his poncho like a caul across the ground . . .

o mum and dad and lord I know
this is a better place to die
I am open to the ancient breeze, here
on the guilt-free mountain,
the song of the thrush has reached deep inside
it has cut out the snake tongues of worry
and I am ready to receive
this thing slow-turning my way
the green bough bends down to meet me
here is my equal
catkin pollen is sugar in my eye

look the jays throw themselves
up to the air and I remember
to pray is to concentrate

my back against this tree, we are breathing together
my lungs full up to the edge with the pain
and then the air
is out in the world again, the tree takes it in and
I will not close my eyes
My hands are not hearing what I say
Mixture of earth and sun
place me

accept and prepare and this
spinning blood take as you would from any animal . . .

*

And the older wardens say
it could have happened to anyone and they tell
the story of Ed Carleton
kicked in the brisket and kicked in the head
and still red-faced today

they roll their smokes more thinly now
as they lean toward each other
but there is no version that doesn't end in death
and when it comes to one of their own this way
they go soft for a while
and they hide in their paperwork
or drive the grey highway all day . . .

The Rescue
Andrew Jones

One August afternoon a group of hikers reported to the Lake Louise warden office that they had heard faint cries for help in the peaks above Consolation Lakes. Wally McPhee, in charge of the Lake Louise District at the time, guessed immediately what the problem was. It would be two climbers who had set out the day before to scale the as-yet-unconquered east face of Mount Babel, one of the most difficult ascents in the Canadian Rockies. They were Brian Greenwood and Charles Locke, a couple of Calgary men, both expert mountaineers. Wally dispatched his assistant, Jay Morton, to see if he could spot them with binoculars. Then he called the Banff office and alerted it for a possible emergency.

Morton came back ashen-faced. "They're on a ledge maybe 400 feet from the top," he said. "The whole bloody mountain slopes *in* where they are!"

McPhee called Banff again, was told that Walter Perren and others were on the way; then he drove to the lake where Morton pointed out the spot — a little sliver along the side of a sheer face, a chink in a pinnacle of rock culminating in a towering dome that loomed above like a monstrous, brooding cloud. In the chink were two tiny figures, smaller than ants. Their perch was so narrow they had had to tie themselves to the mountain with their climbing ropes. One of them appeared to be hurt. Their cries were faint, barely audible. Wally gasped at the impossibility of their predicament. "How are we going to get 'em?" he wondered under his breath. "It can't be done!"

The Banff contingent arrived and Perren stood for long minutes looking up at the men on the ledge. Then he began making decisions, chattering like a machine gun. The rescue could not be effected by helicopter because of an overhanging ridge of rock above them. It would have to be done by lowering someone from the top. It would take a lot of manpower — he wanted ten men up there at daybreak tomorrow. Jim Davies would fly them.

He sent Morton off to Moraine Lake with the astonishing instructions that he was to bring back as many rolls of toilet paper as he could lay hands on. Then he began listing the equipment they would need — 600 feet of wire cable, an assortment of pulleys and clamps, the usual hardware and body harnesses. They would need a tripod pulley, a grooved wheel at the end of a three-legged bracket that would be placed at the edge of a precipice to hold the cable out clear of the rock. They didn't have one in their equipment inventory, but Perren dismissed this with a wave of the hand. "Vee vill make one tonight," he said in his heavily accented English.

Jay Morton returned with the toilet paper and in fading daylight they spelled out a message on the valley floor:

WAIT
HELP
COMING TOP
A M

Then Perren, his eyes serious, scanned the faces of his men. "A difficult operation, chentlemen," he said. He looked at Bill Vroom. "To go down on the cable — Billy, vill you do it?"

Bill nodded.

Back in town, Perren made a sketch of a tripod pulley, and Stan

Peyto, supervisor of the government garage, set to work with steel pipe and welding apparatus. Calls went out to men in district cabins all over the Park. The men he had assembled by early morning had worked together before in mountaineering emergencies. Watching them sorting their equipment in the darkness and loading it aboard the helicopter, he knew the two people on Mount Babel would be in as good hands as could be found anywhere on the continent.

First, Jim Davies flew Perren and Bill up for a close look at the ledge — the climbers waved, appeared to be in good shape and high spirits — then he landed them in a saddle near the top of the mountain and went down for the others. The plan called for Bill to make one exploratory descent, then two more, each time bringing up a man piggyback style in a canvass diaper-like harness called a Gramminger Seat.

From where Perren and Bill stood in the saddle the precipice dropped straight down to a shelf of overhanging rock which obstructed a view of the ledge the men were on; it would be like dangling a wire down a 400-foot well and trying to guess where the end was. Once Bill was below the overhang they would have to depend on their radios for all raising and lowering instructions, all exchanges of information.

Half an hour later the pulley system and cable drums were anchored in position and Bill, with his harness clipped to the cable end, was easing himself over the edge of the cliff. The support crew lowered him to the overhang. He pushed out from it and signaled to be lowered again. Suddenly, as he was descending below it and out of sight of the crew on the summit he began to spin dangerously. It was all he could do to get the radio to his lips.

"Spinning badly!" he shouted. "Speed up descent." His only thought was to get lower down where he would come in contact with the mountain face again and be able to stop these crazy gyrations. He felt himself dropping faster. As he held his arms around his head for protection, his boots struck rock and he was able to stabilize himself against the side of the mountain. When the dizziness wore off he found he was 50 feet below and a little to the side of the climbers. He called for tension on the cable. When he was at their level one of the two climbers threw a rope out to him and pulled him over onto the ledge.

The pair were dehydrated and hungry and Locke had a dislocated wrist. They told their story. They had bivouacked on this ledge two nights before and Locke had started up to the overhang yesterday morning, hammering in pitons and hoisting himself by his rope.

Three of the pitons had pulled out and he had fallen 20 feet to the ledge, landing on his wrist. As this entire section of mountain face had to be negotiated by ropes and hardware, a type of ascent which requires two physically sound climbers, they could go neither up nor down. The only thing they could do was shout for help and hope someone would hear.

Bill radioed for ascent tension and swung out from below the overhang and was lifted to the summit. Perren questioned him down to the smallest detail. Then he nodded and said they would proceed as planned.

With the Gramminger Seat on his back, and some candy bars and a canteen of water in his pack, Bill went down to bring up Locke. The two were lifted to the summit shortly before noon. But even with most of the work being done by the cable, the job of carrying more than his own weight on his back had taken a lot out of Bill, and Perren ordered him to rest half an hour before going down for Greenwood. They discussed letting someone else go down this time, but decided against it. "I know the way now," Bill said. "It gets easier every time."

He brought Greenwood up on his back two hours later. Then he sat on a rock to catch his breath. He was nauseated from the effort and from the dizziness of the morning. It had taken 11 men and a lot of risk to save the lives of two, and the two were at a loss to express their gratitude. For the moment, Bill didn't want gratitude. He stood up and, suddenly depleted mentally and physically, began to walk away. Perren materialized at his side, put his arm around his shoulder and said all that needed to be said because it came from the right man. "A good chob, Billy. A fine chob."

Floe Lake
Dale Zieroth

for Ian

1.

We climbed through summer towards the lake
as if the lake were all
the promises we needed, climbing hard
through the larkspur and the
elderberry, friends ahead and friends
behind, the world in order
coming with us to the lake.

At the switchbacks we met
the first of the strange new flowers coming
through the snow as if this were
the very beginning of life.
Under each tree, where the snow had gone,
we watched the spreading circle of spring
and looked into the meadows and into
the trees where each man heard inside himself
words he had never heard
before. Until the lake
which put an end to words.

2.

The mountain stands up
on the broken feet of its glacier,
tosses rock, then ice down into the lake where the water
moves like the breaking of mirrors,
or birds jumping into flight, ptarmigans
catching on the edge of the glacial wind
that sucks me out of the scrawny trees, the broken
dwarfs of treeline

and only the lake is
approachable, at the shore where the harmonicas
and fires are already warming up,

the noises of tent and pack as the mountain booms again,
fills the camp with
silence as white and endless as the
cornice that dives for the lake

this is the place to sleep
where the lake hugs the Rock Wall and is
content to be small and green and ice
nine months of the year, our dreams will
scale the face of the mountain all night long
this is how we will connect and disappear
not falling but
flying, hooked together in
hand to hand combat with the rocks up above
the ice floes that sail like swans
across the lake and past the dreamers who are
stirring in the yellow dawn, tasting the stars in their coffee

3.

Coming back, we begin by forgetting,
where we are going now there is no room
for perfection. Once there was
a bird to remember, the way it flew, the call
it made, another time
the colour of a tree. Or the young men
standing all along the shore
feeling as strong and as wild in their minds as
the water itself. These things
are making room for the highway that is
a dark line on the mountain.
We are half-way back and the loss
comes down like rain. I have found
another place to leave behind like a home
and only these friends will bind me to it, this
smell of rock on their hands, these men
in the same rain all around me
like the shy sound of wind across water.

Beyond Here
Jim Green

Beyond here,
up a thousand feet,
on the third bench
above the valley
floor   there is an elk
carcass with grass
eight inches high
between the ribs,
and beside it a bear
skull with short
worn teeth and
no bottom jaws.

At night coyote
calls out from shadows
and dogs answer
back   talking tough,
bellowing to each other
how they'll rip
right out there,
raise hell
with a coyote or two
but   they never stray
beyond the fire light.

The Woman at Banff
William Stafford

While she was talking a bear happened along, violating
every garbage can. Shaking its loose, Churchillian,
V for victory suit, it ripped up and ate
a greasy "Bears Are Dangerous!" sign.

While she was talking the trees above signalled —
"Few," and the rock back of them — "Cold."
And while she was talking a moose — huge, black —
swam that river and faded off winterward,

Up toward the Saskatchewan.

Epilogue

There is always so much that is worth
seeing in the wilderness; but if that
wilderness has witnessed the passage
of men of one's own race — raiders,
traders or explorers — then something
is added to the scene and it comes
alive through a human association, a
past which we can share and
understand
> R.M. Patterson, *Findlay's River*

The End of the Trail
J. Monroe Thorington

And so we come to the End of the Trail. What, after all, has it amounted to — this riding in the wilderness, this mad scrambling on inaccessible crags? If you ask us, "Of what use?" perhaps we shall only smile and remain silent, answering not at all. If your curiosity be aroused, perhaps you will go and see for yourself — and find the answer we might have given. That for a little moment we have transcended ourselves; and, upon a mountain top, looking off across the vastness of a glorious earth, have felt ourselves apart from the sham and pettiness of daily life, and have come a little nearer to the Unfathomable Presence.

It seems to me as if the *Striving for a Goal* were the outstanding virtue of mountaineering. Life, and Youth in particular, are uncertain in their offerings of success. Most of us have ideals, of course, but the opportunity for attaining them is often remote, and the desired ends float away into the realm of impossibility. How different it is with the climber! He has a peak to scale, and with it the enjoyment of all the splendour of the mountain world — and in a day, usually in less time, he sets foot on the desired height with all the joy that comes from the completion of a self-appointed task.

One should visit the Canadian Northland with eye and mind alert to the beauty of Nature's handicraft: the artistry in all of it; from the broad sculpturing of crag and chasm to the delicate perfection of a tiny flower.

288

The things we treasure — the memories of peak and sunlit ice-field; of forgotten trails; of haunting melodies of the homeland, piped on a harmonica, in the glow of northern campfires — where indeed can one discover these in the musty pages of a Geography? No map of a river valley can visualize a Canadian forest, with laden horses swinging along in line; no plaster relief can ever make one understand the moods of mountains, half-hidden in cloud or towering in the many-hued glory of early morning. What Atlas can picture Singing Youth, on horseback, crossing a sparkling ford to flower-decked meadows, with distant mountain spires dim blue in the noon haze? These trails are not for everyone, but for those who go there will result such memories "as dreams are made on," and the reward is great enough.

Pack-trains of yesterday: "Slim," the horse that always had to be packed twice; "Fanny," who carried the dishpan and the ice-axes; "Gunboat," who carried me; "Beauty," the white, belled steed that Conrad rode and who bucked on occasion; "Hammerhead," "Briden," and all the rest — I wonder if they remember the boys who rode them so gaily, cinched them so tightly after a night's feeding of green grass, and drove them with such strange language? I think it unlikely; their minds — and with all their eccentricities, I still believe these cayuses have minds — are doubtless more attuned to the present and the future than to any thoughts of the past. Their dreams, quite likely, are of lush-pastures where the grass is never bitter, and of shady paths where flies and the diamond-hitch are things unknown. We, remembering, are ourselves forgotten.

Back-trails of tomorrow — God willing, there will be some who come after us, finding in the light of new campfires, built on hearth-stones that were once ours, that Peace we know. We who have travelled the long, lone trails of the Northland, know that Peace-of-the-hills is an Angel whose blessing is only obtained by wrestling.

"What if I live no more those kingly days?
    their night sleeps with me still.
I dream my feet upon the starry ways;
    my heart rests in the hill.
I may not grudge the little left undone;
I hold the heights, I keep the dreams I won."

Notes on Contributors

Pierre Berton (born 1920). A journalist and broadcaster who was born in Whitehorse, Yukon, and educated at the University of British Columbia, he is one of Canada's most popular writers of history and social criticism. His description of the early CPR surveys through the Rockies appeared in *The National Dream: The Great Railway 1871-1881* (1970), the first volume of his best-selling two-volume history of the CPR.

Cora Johnstone Best (?-1930). Born in Minnesota, she was educated in the United States and Europe and worked as a physician for a number of years before giving up her practice to pursue interests in conservation, mountaineering, and adventure travel, writing many magazine articles on nature and travel. She spent many summers in the Canadian Rockies and completed more than fifty difficult climbs in the range.

J. Burgon Bickersteth (1888–1979) was a British-born missionary sent to western Canada in the spring of 1912 by the Church of England to minister along the new transcontinental line being constructed through Yellowhead Pass. Stationed at a small camp 140 miles west of Edmonton, he traveled all or part of the line through the Rockies to Tête Jaune Cache on a number of occasions.

Earle Birney (born 1904) is one of Canada's best-known poets with more than fourteen volumes of poetry and two Governor General's awards to his credit. He was born in Calgary, Alberta, but spent much of his early boyhood in Banff. His first volume of poetry, published in 1942, was *David and Other Poems*. He has also written two novels.

Chief Brings-down-the-Sun. Chief of the Piegan tribe at Brocket, Alberta, shortly after the turn of the century. The American ethnologist Walter McClintock visited his camp, recording many of the tribal legends that the chief related and publishing them in his book *The Old North Trail* (1910).

Rupert Brooke (1887–1915). A gifted young English poet, he died while serving in the Royal Navy during World War I. He traveled through Canada and the U.S. in 1913–14, and his impressions from that journey were published posthumously as *Letters from America* (1916).

Gordon Burles (born 1949) is a native of Banff whose poetry has been published in a number of anthologies and periodicals including *Storm Warning II*, Al Purdy's second collection of new Canadian poetry. While his poetry covers a broad spectrum, he has displayed a special fascination for Bill Peyto, having written two poems and a biographical essay on this colourful pioneer outfitter and park warden.

William Francis Butler (1838–1910). An Irish-born career officer in the British Army, he saw service in Canada and traveled extensively throughout the country between 1867 and 1873. He made two trips to the far west, traveling to the foothills of the Rockies in 1871 and then through the range via the Peace River in 1872. These two expeditions were described in his books *The Great Lone Land* (1872) and *The Wild North Land* (1873).

Robert E. Campbell (1871–1965). Educated in Ontario as a teacher, he came to Banff in 1896 to work in the town's small school. The following summer he was hired by outfitter Tom Wilson as a guide and packer, and in 1901 he quit teaching to become a partner in Wilson's business. His reminiscences of his life as a guide were published in 1959 under the title of *I Would Do it Again*.

Walter Butler Cheadle (1835–1910) and **Viscount Milton** (1839–1877). Dr. W. B. Cheadle was a British physician who accompanied William Fitzwilliam, Viscount Milton, on a journey across the northwest from Fort Garry to the Pacific in 1862–63. In July of 1863, they crossed the Canadian Rockies via Yellowhead Pass, an adventure graphically described in *The North-West Passage by Land* (1865). Though published under both their names, the book was subsequently discovered to be the work of Dr. Cheadle alone.

Walter J. Clutterbuck. See James Arthur Lees.

Arthur Philemon Coleman (1852–1939) was a Canadian geologist who traveled extensively in the Rockies from 1884 onwards. Much of his early exploration in the range centred upon a search for two mythical 16,000-foot peaks that supposedly stood above Athabasca Pass, and later he made several attempts to climb the true monarch of the Canadian Rockies, Mount Robson.

J. Norman Collie. See Hugh E.M. Stutfield.

Ralph Connor. The pen-name of Charles William Gordon (1860–1937). An ordained Presbyterian minister, he lived in Banff in the early 1890s and served a number of communities and work camps in the upper Bow Valley. Under his pseudonym he wrote some twenty-five novels about pioneer life in western Canada including such titles as *The Sky Pilot* (1899) and *The Man from Glengarry* (1901). His piece recounting an early climb of Cascade Mountain was published in the first *Canadian Alpine Journal* in 1907.

Ross Cox (1793–1853). Born in Ireland, he joined the American-based Pacific Fur Company in 1811 and was employed at the company's Astoria post at the mouth of the Columbia River until it was taken over by the North West Company during the War of 1812. He worked for the latter company on the Columbia until returning east in 1816, when he crossed the Rockies by way of Athabasca Pass.

James Oliver Curwood (1878–1927) was an American novelist who specialized in adventure stories set in the Canadian wilderness. Educated at the University of Michigan, he worked as a newspaperman in Detroit until he was thirty, when he began writing fiction full-time. He made numerous pack trips into the wilderness of Jasper Park between 1915 and 1925 and utilized his Rocky Mountain experiences for several of his twenty-six novels, including *The Grizzly King* (1928).

Pierre Jean De Smet (1801–1873). A Jesuit missionary from Belgium, he spent most of his life from 1840 onwards ministering to the Indians of the American and Canadian West. He traveled up the Columbia Valley and crossed the Rockies via White Man Pass during the summer of 1845, a journey described in his published letters, *Oregon Missions and Travels Over the Rocky Mountains in 1845–46* (1847).

David Douglas (1799–1834). This Scots-born botanist made a number of expeditions through North America, from 1823 until his death, collecting and recording the flora for the Royal Horticultural Society of London. He was responsible for the naming of many species, including the tree which bears his name — the Douglas fir. In the spring of 1827, he crossed the Rockies from west to east with the Hudson's Bay Company brigade and climbed a mountain above Athabasca Pass.

Thomas Drummond (1780?–1835). A Scots-born botanist, he was assigned to John Franklin's second land expedition (1825–27) as assistant naturalist. He left the main party on the lower Saskatchewan River and traveled with the fur trade brigades to the Rocky Mountains, where he spent a year collecting botanical specimens in the Jasper House vicinity.

Peter Erasmus (1833–1931) was a Métis interpreter and guide who traveled with Dr. James Hector of the Palliser Expedition during his 1858 exploration of the Rocky Mountains and discovery of Kicking Horse Pass. Erasmus's reminiscences were recorded by an Edmonton newspaperman in 1920 and published under the title *Buffalo Days and Nights* by the Glenbow-Alberta Institute in 1976.

Charles Ernest Fay (1846–1931). Dean of the Graduate School at Tufts College, Massachusetts, and a founding member of the Appalachian Mountain Club and the American Alpine Club, he was one of the earliest American alpinists to visit the Canadian Rockies. In the decade following his first visit in 1894, he brought numerous parties from the eastern U.S. in pursuit of unclimbed peaks. He wrote many articles promoting the sport of mountaineering.

Edward Feuz, Jr.(1884–1981) was the son of one of the first Swiss guides brought to Canada by the CPR to lead tourists up the mountains of the Selkirks and Rockies. Edward Jr. came to Canada in 1903 to apprentice under his father and later moved to the Canadian West permanently, working as a guide for the CPR until 1949. He is credited with more first ascents in the Rockies than is any other climber. His reminiscences were recorded by Imbert Orchard in 1964 and published by the Provincial Archives of British Columbia in 1980.

Valerius Geist, Professor of Environmental Science in the Faculty of Environmental Design at the University of Calgary, has written numerous articles, books, and papers on wildlife and conservation. Born in Russia in 1938, he studied at the University of British Columbia where he received his Ph.D. He has been studying mountain sheep in western Canada since 1959, and his book *Mountain Sheep: A Study in Behavior and Evolution* (1971) won the 1972 Book of the Year Award from The Wildlife Society in the U.S.

Jim Green (born 1941) is an Alberta-born poet who has been published widely in Canadian poetry magazines, literary journals, and anthologies. Following graduation from Utah State University, he lived and worked in the Canadian Rockies and the Northwest Territories, and experiences in these regions have supplied much of the inspiration for his poetry. His first book of poetry, *North Book* (1975), received the Canadian Authors Association Award for poetry in 1975 and the Province of Alberta's Award of Excellence. He lives with his wife and children in Fort Smith, NWT.

William Spotswood Green (1847–1918). An Irish cleric who was one of the first mountaineers to visit western Canada following the completion of the CPR. During the summer of 1888, he climbed in the Selkirk Range and made a number of side excursions in the Rockies, including a difficult hike to Lake Louise. These adventures appeared in *Among the Selkirk Glaciers* (1890), a book that introduced alpinists around the world to a new sporting ground.

James Hector (1834–1907). Scottish-born, this physician and geologist was appointed to the Palliser Expedition (1857-60) investigating the British possessions in western North America. Under the command of Captain John Palliser, he made a number of explorations into the Rocky Mountains, including the most thorough survey to that date of the area encompassed by today's Banff, Kootenay, and Yoho National Parks. His description of this trip, which included the discovery of Kicking Horse Pass, appeared in the journals and reports of the expedition published in 1863.

William Temple Hornaday (1854–1937) was a renowned zoologist and wildlife conservationist. Born and educated in the American midwest, his long and distinguished career included the positions of chief taxidermist and curator of the Department of Living Animals at the National Museum in Washington, D.C., and director of the New York Zoological Park. As a conservationist he was a leading force in saving the North American bison from extinction. He was the author of numerous books on wildlife and travel.

Alice Huntington. A writer for the *Calgary Weekly Herald*, her byline appeared under the column heading of "The Cozy Corner." Her column described the Calgary district scene in 1897.

Andrew Jones, born in 1921 in South Orange, New Jersey, is an American journalist who has worked for many years as a roving editor for *Reader's Digest* magazine. Following service in the U.S. Marine Corps as a fighter pilot in World War II, he completed his education at Princeton and Yale universities. He was an associate editor for *Field & Stream* magazine until 1954, when he joined *Reader's Digest*

Conrad Kain (1883–1934). An Austrian alpine guide of considerable reputation, he was brought to Canada in 1909 by the Alpine Club of Canada to lead climbs at the club's Lake O'Hara camp. In 1913 he led the first ascent of Mount Robson, the highest peak in the Canadian Rockies. He is credited with over fifty first ascents in western Canada. His accounts of his early climbs with the alpine club as well as later adventures in Canada and abroad were published in his autobiography, *Where the Clouds Can Go* (1935).

Paul Kane (1810–1871). Born in Ireland, as a boy he came with his family to Ontario, where he was educated and studied portrait painting. In 1846, after studying and practising his art in Europe for some four years, he made a trip across North America to the Pacific Coast, traveling with the assistance of the Hudson's Bay Company. He painted numerous portraits of the Indians he encountered as well as many landscapes. His published journal of this expedition, *Wanderings of an Artist* (1859), has become a classic of Canadiana.

George Kinney (1872–1961), Methodist minister who was a charter member of the Alpine Club of Canada. He made a number of attempts to climb Mount Robson, starting in 1907; in 1909, climbing with a young guide named Donald Phillips, he succeeded in reaching a point on the mountain just a few feet short of the summit. Though he claimed victory, his success was later refuted, and the first official ascent of the mountain was made by a party led by Conrad Kain in 1913.

James Arthur Lees and **Walter J. Clutterbuck** were two travel writers from Britain who collaborated on the book *B.C. 1887* (1892), one of a number of perceptive and humorous volumes which they wrote together or singly. It is one of the earliest descriptions of the Canadian West following the completion of the CPR.

John Keast Lord (?–1872) was a British naturalist assigned to the British Boundary Commission surveying the U.S.–British Columbia boundary from 1858 to 1862. Lord was noted for his writings on natural history and travel which frequently appeared in both book and journal form. His works include *A Naturalist in British Columbia* (1866) and *At Home in the Wilderness* (1876).

Dan McCowan (1882–1956). One of the most prolific writers to live in the Canadian Rockies, he was born in Scotland, came to Canada for a visit in 1907 and decided to stay, settling in Banff. He was an avid naturalist and an accomplished amateur photographer. Following World War I the CPR sponsored his slide-lecture tours through Canada and Europe for many years. He eventually wrote six books on the natural and human history of western Canada, including *Hill-Top Tales* (1950) and *Tidewater to Timberline* (1951).

Susan Agnes Macdonald (1836–1920) became the second wife of Prime Minister Sir John A. Macdonald in 1867 and traveled across Canada with him in 1886, following the completion of the CPR. She often wrote articles for periodicals such as *Ladies' Home Journal, Pall Mall Magazine*, and the Montreal *Star*, and the description of her trans-Canadian journey appeared in *Murray's Magazine* in 1887. A cottage was built for her beside the Banff Springs Hotel, and she returned for a number of years to holiday in the Rockies.

Alexander Mackenzie (1764-1820). A Scottish-born fur trader, he made two epic explorations for the North West Company, traveling the length of the Mackenzie River to the Arctic Ocean in 1789 and traversing the Rocky Mountains to reach the Pacific in 1793. Mackenzie's journals of these trips, along with a history of the fur trade, were published in London in 1801 and have been reprinted in numerous editions down through the years.

George McLean (1871–1967), also known as Chief Walking Buffalo of the Stoney tribe. As a chief of the Bear's Paw band, he played a major role as tribal leader and traveled around the world as a spokesman for the Moral Rearmament movement. In 1926, he was a major resource for the ethnologist Marius Barbeau, who was recording the Stoney tribal legends.

Sid Marty (born 1944). Raised in Alberta, he attended university in Montreal. He worked as a park warden in Yoho, Jasper, and Banff National Parks from 1966 to 1978. His experiences as a warden have served as major themes in his writing, including his best-selling memoirs, *Men for the Mountains* (1978), and two volumes of poetry, *Headwaters* (1973) and *Nobody Danced with Miss Rodeo* (1981). He lives with his wife and children on a small foothills ranch in southern Alberta.

Viscount Milton. See Walter Butler Cheadle.

Henry John Moberly (1835–1931). Born and educated in the Ontario region, he was the brother of British Columbia surveyor Walter Moberly. He joined the Hudson's Bay Company in 1854 and served in the Saskatchewan district for six years, including a period when he was in charge of Jasper's House in the Athabasca Valley. His offspring by his Indian wife later became the first settlers in the valley.

Avis E. Newhall (born 1896), later Mrs. E. Gerald Adams, was an active climber and skier from the New England region of the U.S. A member of the American Alpine Club and Appalachian Mountain Club, she climbed extensively in the U.S. and Europe, ascending many major peaks in the Alps. In 1928, she was a member of the first ski party hosted by the Marquis degli Albizzi and Erling Strom at their fledgling ski resort at Mount Assiniboine. Today she lives in Marblehead, Massachusetts.

Howard O'Hagan (1902–1982). Born in Lethbridge, Alberta, he grew up in the Yellowhead Pass region of the Rockies. After completing his formal education (B.A. and LL.B.) at McGill University in 1925, he worked as a guide and packer for Jasper outfitter Fred Brewster before becoming involved in journalism and writing. He is one of the most respected authors of fiction set in the Canadian Rockies, his major works being the novels *Tay John* (1939) and *The School-Marm Tree* (1977) and a volume of short stories, *The Woman Who Got on at Jasper Station and Other Stories* (1963).

Elizabeth Parker (1856–1944) was a writer and literary critic for the Winnipeg *Free Press*. She first visited the Rockies with her children in the 1890s (when she participated in an informal climb up Cascade Mountain — see Ralph Connor's "How We Climbed Cascade"). She played an important role in the formation of the Alpine Club of Canada in 1906 and later served as club secretary, writing a number of articles for the *Canadian Alpine Journal*.

R.M. Patterson was born in England in 1898 and emigrated to Canada following service in World War I. In 1929, after working in British Columbia for a few years, he married and settled on a cattle ranch in the foothills of southern Alberta. The ranch served as a base for numerous pack trips into the Rocky Mountains, adventures documented in his book *The Buffalo Head* (1961). He moved to Vancouver Island after World War II and wrote a number of books on the northern rivers of B.C.

Morley Roberts (1857–1942). A British adventurer and travel writer, he worked his way through the western United States and Canada in 1884. He spent a brief period as a labourer constructing the CPR through Kicking Horse Pass — an experience recounted in the book *The Western Avernus* (1887). *On the Old Trail* (1927) describes a return visit to the Rockies in 1926.

Edward Roper was a nineteenth-century British travel writer who is reputed to have fictionalized many of his experiences. His style is notable for its condescension towards "colonials" wherever he traveled.

Robert Terrill Rundle (1811–1896) was a Methodist missionary from England who served on the western Canadian prairies from 1840 to 1848. He made a couple of brief visits to the mountains in the Bow River area, attempting to climb one peak in the front range and holding a service for Stoney Indians at Lake Minnewanka. His *Journals* were published by the Glenbow-Alberta Institute in 1977.

Andy Russell (born 1915). A native of southern Alberta, he has worked in the region as a trapper, mountain guide, photographer, and writer. He was awarded the Order of Canada in 1977 for his work as a conservationist. He has written a number of popular books, including the best-seller *Grizzly Country* (1967). He lives on a ranch at the edge of Waterton National Park.

Mary T.S. Schäffer (1861–1939) was born into a Quaker family from the Philadelphia area and first visited the Canadian West in 1889. She met her first husband, Dr. Charles Schäffer, on that trip and worked with him during annual botanical trips to the Rockies until his death in 1903. In 1906 she joined with Mary "Mollie" Adams, a geology teacher from Boston, and hired an outfit to go exploring north of the CPR line at Lake Louise. In 1908 they reached Maligne Lake in today's Jasper Park and completed the first exploration of that major body of water. She later married her guide, William Warren, and settled in Banff.

George Simpson (1787?–1860). Born in Scotland, he came to Canada in 1820 in the employ of the Hudson's Bay Company. In 1826 he was appointed governor of the company's territories, with the official title of Governor-in-Chief from 1839 until his death. In his administrative position, he traveled extensively throughout the Canadian Northwest and crossed the Rocky Mountains on several occasions, including trips through Athabasca Pass in 1824 and Simpson Pass in 1841. These journeys were documented in his journals, which were later published (in the case of the 1824 expedition, much later) under the respective titles *Fur Trade and Empire* (1931) and *Narrative of a Journey Round the World during the Years 1841 and 1842* (1847).

James Sinclair (1806?–1856) was a free trader at Red River who was appointed by the Hudson's Bay Company to lead a party of emigrants to the Oregon Territory to help establish British claims in that region. His first expedition, with twenty-three families, crossed the Rockies via White Man Pass during the summer of 1841. In 1854 he led a similar party consisting of some one hundred emigrants — men, women, and children — and their livestock through North Kanan-askis Pass, making the passage in October with three feet of snow on the ground.

John Snow (born 1933) is chief of the Wesley band of the Stoney tribe. He was born and raised on the tribal reserve at Morley, Alberta, and is an ordained minister of the United Church. His book, *The Mountains Are Our Sacred Places* (1977), relates the history and traditions of the Stoney people.

Earl of Southesk (1827–1905). James Carnegie, Earl of Southesk, was a Scottish nobleman and sportsman who undertook a personal expedition to the western prairies and Rocky Mountains in 1859–60. In September of 1859, he traveled and hunted his way through the front ranges from the Medicine-tent River to the Bow River. The account of this journey was later published in *Saskatchewan and the Rocky Mountains* (1875).

William Stafford (born 1914). One of the United States' most respected poets, he was born in Hutchinson, Kansas, received his doctorate from the University of Iowa, and has taught in universities throughout the United States. His book *Traveling Through the Dark* (1962) won the National Book Award for Poetry.

Samuel Benfield Steele (1851–1919) served as an officer in the North West Mounted Police from 1873 until 1901. His career in the NWMP spanned the most colourful period in the history of the Canadian West, and he was directly involved in the march to the western prairies in 1874, the Northwest Rebellion of 1885, and the Klondike gold rush of 1898–99. During the building of the CPR through the Rockies in 1883–84, he was in charge of detachments at Laggan (Lake Louise) and Golden.

Erling Strom was born in Norway in 1897, came to North America following World War I and, in 1927, was hired as one of the early ski instructors at Lake Placid, New York. He first came to the Canadian Rockies in 1928 and returned for subsequent winters through the thirties to operate a ski camp at Mount Assiniboine. He was involved in a number of major ski expeditions, including a trip to the Columbia Icefield in 1931 and an ascent of Alaska's Mount McKinley in 1932. Following World War II, he ran Assiniboine Lodge as a summer-only operation until his retirement and return to Oslo in 1977. *Pioneers on*

Skis (1977) recounts his skiing experiences in Norway and North America.

Hugh E.M. Stutfield (1858–1929) and **J. Norman Collie** (1859–1942) were British mountaineers who visited the Canadian Rockies together in 1898, 1900, and 1902. They participated in a number of important first ascents; their 1898 expedition mapped much of the Great Divide north of Lake Louise and discovered the Columbia Icefield. The pair later collaborated on the book *Climbs and Explorations in the Canadian Rockies* (1903).

Frederick Arthur Ambrose Talbot, a British travel writer, born in 1880. He wrote a number of books on the Canadian frontier at the time of the Grand Trunk Pacific Railway construction. He was particularly interested in the potential for settlement.

David Thompson (1770–1857). English-born and -educated, he was brought to North America in the employ of the Hudson's Bay Company at fourteen years of age. In 1807, working for the North West Company, he crossed the Rockies via Howse Pass to establish the first fur trade post in the Columbia Valley. When the Piegans turned him back from Howse Pass in the autumn of 1810, he detoured north and made a mid-winter crossing of Athabasca Pass, eventually reaching the mouth of the Columbia River the following summer. Trained as a land surveyor, he mapped much of the country through which he traveled.

J. Monroe Thorington, born 1894, a prominent Philadelphia physician, climbed extensively in the Canadian Rockies from the early 1920s onwards and completed many first ascents and new routes up major peaks. He has written scores of articles on the history of exploration and mountaineering in the range, most published in the American and Canadian alpine journals. He compiled and edited the autobiography of guide Conrad Kain, *Where the Clouds Can Go* (1935), and was the co-author of the first definitive climber's guide to the Canadian Rockies.

Mary M. Vaux (1860–1940) was a member of a prominent Quaker family from Philadelphia. Her first, brief visit to the Canadian West in 1887 was with her father and two brothers, but she returned with the family in 1894 and spent nearly every summer for the next forty years in the region. She was an avid climber and an accomplished amateur photographer, and her skilfully rendered wildflower paintings were used to illustrate the Smithsonian Institution's *North Amer-*

ican Wildflowers (1925). In 1914 she married Dr. Charles D. Walcott, secretary of the Smithsonian Institution and a geologist renowned for his studies of Cambrian fossils near Field, B.C.

Nello "Tex" Vernon-Wood (1882–1978). Born in England, he came to Banff in 1906 to "take the waters" at the local hot spring. He ended up settling in the Rockies and hired on as a packer with Brewster Brothers. In 1915 he was hired as one of the early wardens in Rocky Mountains (Banff) Park. He later went into the outfitting business on his own. Noted as a colourful storyteller, he wrote numerous articles for American sporting magazines, relating his adventures and misadventures in the guiding business.

Henry James Warre (1819–1898), as a staff officer in the British Army, made a transcontinental journey to the Oregon Territory in 1845–46 with fellow officer Mervin Vavasour to determine Britain's ability to defend the region in the event of war with the United States. His route west crossed the Rockies via White Man Pass and his return east utilized Athabasca Pass. He made the first landscape paintings of the Canadian Rockies, many of which were reproduced in *Sketches in North America and the Oregon Territory* (1848). His journals covering the trip are held in the manuscript collections of the Public Archives of Canada.

Arthur Oliver Wheeler (1860–1945) played a prominent role in the founding of the Alpine Club of Canada in 1906. He was a professional land surveyor, born in Ireland, who worked extensively in the Canadian mountain west from the turn of the century onwards. From 1913 to 1925 he was responsible for the surveying of the Alberta–British Columbia boundary along the crest of the Great Divide. Throughout these years, he organized the summer camps of the Alpine Club of Canada, directed the club's activities, and edited its annual journal.

Jon Whyte (born 1941). A native of Banff and a descendant of one of the town's early pioneer families, he works as a museum curator in Banff and is the author of a number of histories of the region. His poems have been published in numerous collections and individual volumes; in 1983 he won the first Stephan Stephansson Award from the Writers' Guild of Alberta for his book-length poem *Homage, Henry Kelsey*. "Winter Journey," which appears for the first time in this book, is for him "a shorter poem."

Walter Dwight Wilcox (1869–1949) was an American mountaineer and photographer who spent many summers in the Canadian Rockies, starting in 1893. In the early years he traveled with fellow graduates of Yale University and made several first ascents while exploring near Lake Louise. He later made a number of extended trips by horseback to Mount Assiniboine and the Columbia Icefield region. His book *Camping in the Canadian Rockies* (1896) and its revised editions described many of his early adventures and served as an early guidebook for visitors to the Rockies.

Charles William Wilson (1836–1905). Born in Liverpool, he was a lieutenant in the Royal Engineers when he came to western Canada in 1858 to serve as secretary to the British Boundary Commission, which was surveying the international boundary between British Columbia and the United States. In the summer of 1861 the surveyors reached the Rocky Mountains and placed the last boundary marker on the crest of the Great Divide.

Thomas Edmonds Wilson (1859–1933). Born and raised in Ontario, he came to the Rockies in 1881 and worked as an assistant to Major A. B. Rogers, surveyor in charge of locating the CPR route through the mountains. During the survey, Wilson was credited with the discovery of Lake Louise. He settled in Banff following the railway construction, became the town's first outfitter, and led some of the first parties into the backcountry adjacent to the CPR. His memories of the early days in the Rockies were recorded by Banff writer W. E. Round in 1929 and published by the Glenbow-Alberta Institute as *Trail Blazer of the Canadian Rockies* (1972).

Dale Zieroth was born in 1946 in Manitoba but now resides in Vancouver. His work has appeared in numerous literary journals and anthologies, and he has produced two collections of poetry, *Clearing: Poems from a Journey* (1973) and *Mid-River* (1981). He draws much of his inspiration and subject matter for his poems from his years working for the parks service in the Canadian Rockies and his life in the small village of Invermere, B.C., during the 1970s.